Esperanto and Its Rivals

HANEY FOUNDATION SERIES

A volume in the Haney Foundation Series, established in
1961 with the generous support of Dr. John Louis Haney

ESPERANTO AND ITS RIVALS

The Struggle for an International Language

Roberto Garvía

PENN

UNIVERSITY OF PENNSYLVANIA PRESS

PHILADELPHIA

Published by
University of Pennsylvania Press
Philadelphia, Pennsylvania 19104-4112
www.upenn.edu/pennpress

Printed in the United States of America on acid-free paper
1   3   5   7   9   10   8   6   4   2

Library of Congress Cataloging-in-Publication Data
Garvía Soto, Roberto, author.
   Esperanto and its rivals : the struggle for an international
language / Roberto Garvia.
      pages cm — (Haney foundation series)
   Includes bibliographical references and index.
   ISBN 978-0-8122-4710-7
   1. Language, Universal—History—19th century.   2. Language,
Universal—History—20th century.   3. Languages, Artificial—
History—19th century.   4. Languages, Artificial—History—
20th century.   5. Esperanto—History.   6. Volapük—History.
7. Ido—History.   I. Title.   II. Series: Haney foundation series.
PM8008.G37 2015
499'.99—dc23
                                                      2014040819

Der Weg der neuern Bildung geht
Von Humanität
Durch Nationalität
Zur Bestialität
                    —Franz Grillparzer (1849)

I cannot take very seriously the arguments of those who
assert that an international auxiliary language might
be suitable for business affairs and perhaps for natural
science, but could not possibly serve as an adequate
means of communication in personal affairs, for
discussions in the social sciences and the humanities,
let alone for fiction or drama. I have found that most
of those who make these assertions have no practical
experience with such a language.
                    —Rudolf Carnap (1963)

CONTENTS

Introduction

In 1928, the young Eric Blair, later known as George Orwell, moved to Paris to begin his career as a writer and to improve his French. He first set up quarters at the home of his bohemian aunt Nellie Limouzin and her lover, Eugène Adam. Better known in revolutionary circles as *Lanti*, the man who is against everything, Adam was a radical Esperantist. He was the founder of Sennacieca Asocio Tutmonda, an international—or, more accurately, a non-national—working-class organization that combined class struggle with the advancement of Esperanto as the language of the coming proletarian revolution. Adam refused to speak French at home. Since Esperanto was the home language, Orwell soon had to find different lodgings in order to refine his French.[1]

This was not Orwell's last exposure to Esperanto. During the Spanish Civil War, when he volunteered to fight against General Franco's pro-fascist forces, Esperanto was widely used in newspapers and on radio stations and even by the Catalan government to inform International Brigades about the war.[2] Nor was Esperanto Orwell's last encounter with international language projects. From 1942 to 1944, while working for the Eastern Service of the BBC, Orwell broadcast news commentaries in Basic English, an artificial language fashioned by the linguist and philosopher C. K. Odgen.

Given his long acquaintance with artificial languages, it is not surprising to find in Orwell's fiction the most notorious, effective, and popular use of an invented language. In *Nineteen Eighty-Four* (published in 1949), Orwell introduced us to Newspeak. Deliberately designed for totalitarian dominance, Newspeak "was not only to provide a medium of expression for the world-view and mental habits proper to the devotees of Ingsoc [English socialism], but to make all other modes of thought impossible."[3]

Orwell's portrayal of an artificial language as a potent tool of political submission was certainly not the kind of speculation that many Esperantists and Basic English adherents might have expected from a former supporter

of artificial languages. In any case, by the time Orwell published his dys-
topic novel, Basic English and Esperanto were not the only artificial languages
on the market. Ido, created in 1907 by the philosopher Louis Couturat, still
had some supporters, as well as Occidental and Novial, devised in 1922 and
1928 by Edgar de Wahl and the linguist Otto Jespersen, respectively. Volapük,
an artificial language created in 1879, still lingered in the memory of many
Europeans, too. And shortly after *Nineteen Eighty-Four* went to press, yet
more artificial languages appeared. Interlingua was sponsored by the International Auxiliary Language Association and supported by the philanthropist
Alice Vanderbilt Morris.

Although today it is barely remembered, a spirited, intense "battle of
artificial languages," as contemporaries called it, figured prominently in the
intellectual landscape from the late 1800s to the outbreak of World War II.
The American Philosophical Society, the International Association of Academies, the International Peace Bureau, the League of Nations, and even the
Comintern participated in this battle. The problem posed by emerging
nationalisms and linguistic chauvinisms, and the increasing international-
ization of scientific research, persuaded many that an increasingly interconnected world plainly required a lingua franca. There is currently a debate
on the problem of international communication, linguistic rights, and the
impact of globalization on less commonly used languages.[4] But, truly speaking, this debate began more than one hundred years ago, when the first wave
of globalization took place and artificial language supporters raised their
hands to make it clear to whoever was willing to listen that they had found
the solution to all those problems.

This book is about the battle of artificial languages and of the social
movements that supported them. It focuses on the three most prominent languages that contended for supremacy: Volapük, invented by the German
Catholic priest Johann Martin Schleyer; Esperanto, created by a Russian
Jew, Ludwig Zamenhof; and Ido, a reformed Esperanto created by Couturat,
a French philosopher. Volapük, Esperanto, and Ido, however, did not stand
alone. Other minor contestants, such as Reform Neutral, Latino sine flexione, Occidental, Novial, and Basic English also made their mark.

If, strictly speaking, rationality recommends learning the language of your
neighbor, or, perhaps better, an international language, what drove Volapükists,
Esperantists, and Idists to invest so much time and energy to learn and promote their languages, when many others deemed it preposterous, when not
anti-patriotic? Were they sharing the same dream, or were artificial languages

going to serve different purposes and interests? Why were there so many artificial languages, and how was it that the Esperantists managed to crowd out their rivals? Was it because Esperanto was a better language, or because the Esperantists proved to have the best strategy?

As detailed in this book, the battle of artificial languages was fought neither by marginal people nor in an institutional vacuum. Rather, the battle of artificial languages was entwined with the intellectual dilemmas of the time, reflecting the anxieties that traversed the European mindset amid the drastic economic, social, and political transformations taking place in every corner of the continent. Whether these anxieties were based on the effects of science on human relations, the fate of spirituality and religion in a more secularized world, the importance of ethnicity and national identity, the so-called "Jewish problem," the prospects for peace, or the place of nature in a more mechanized world, artificial languages supporters liked to think that they had the cure.

Among all the artificial languages created between the last decades of the nineteenth century and the outbreak of World War II, only Esperanto is still thriving; its former rivals are only ghosts on the Internet.[5] And after more than 100 years of face-to-face interactions and an impressive literary corpus, Esperanto has been transformed into a full-fledged language, with its own irregularities, ambiguities, exceptions, and conventions.[6]

Although Esperanto won the battle of artificial languages, it did not become a global language. Today, English holds that position. But at the time the battle of artificial languages began, nobody could tell which, if any, of the three main national languages, English, German, and French, would become the global language. In fact, it was the fierce competition between English, German, and French, and the national rivalries between their speakers that opened a window of opportunity for the cause of an artificial language. A non-ethnic lingua franca would not only assuage national rivalries but also put everybody on equal footing. Since a lingua franca is a collective good, we might then wonder why a neutral language such as Esperanto did not prevail. If linguistic fairness recommends a neutral language, then Esperanto or any of its rivals would seem like a better choice for an international language. This book explores how Esperanto won the battle for supremacy among competing artificial languages, but lost the war to become a lingua franca.

Confident that the balance of power among leading nations and international rivalries would prevent a national language from becoming the lingua franca, Volapükists, Esperantists, and Idists worked hard to make their case. They set up journals, collected membership fees, organized language courses, issued language certificates, created their respective language academies, organized at the local, national, and international level, convened international congresses, participated in special interest organizations, lobbied international bodies, forged links with other social movements, and fought bitterly against each other.

In this fight and the fight for universal acclaim, Volapükists, Esperantists, and Idists pushed forward different strategies. It is around the role of the movement leaders in the imprinting and implementation of these different strategies that the narrative of the book unfolds. This focus on strategy and leaders helps to explain the strength and weaknesses of each of the movements, their inception, reception, and eventual failure. In one respect, the battle for supremacy among Volapükists, Esperantists, and Idists resembled other "standardization" battles. Readers may well remember the long battle between VHS and Betamax to become the standard videotape recording system. Similar standardization battles have taken place in the past, including the QWERTY versus the Dvorak keyboard, the light water design for power reactors versus other choices, or the alternating versus direct current for electrical supply systems.[7]

Economic historians have tried to explain the mechanisms of these standardization battles. In their words, the adoption of one standard over another is "path dependent." Path-dependent processes occur where positive feedback mechanisms operate; in other words, where one person's decision to adopt one technology instead of another increases the probability that the next person will follow suit. People follow the path that others have opened for them—in a sense, the path of least resistance. At a certain point, the process tips over and one technology takes a clear lead over its alternatives, making it practically impossible for losing options to dislodge the probable winner.

Interestingly, however, the winning technology is not necessarily the best or the most efficient. Its victory is largely the result of decisions made at the beginning of the process, under conditions of relative uncertainty as to both the qualities and the real potential of competitors, and the eventual result of the contest. This means that first movers have an advantage, but nothing makes it inevitable that they will emerge as the final winners. As the economic historian Brian Arthur put it, the final outcome of a path-dependent process is not "guaranteed to be efficient." Nor is it "easily altered" or "predictable in advance."[8]

Since languages are technologies of communication, we can interpret the battle of artificial languages as another example of a path-dependent process.

This battle, however, differs from other standardization battles in three important respects. First, whereas a typewriter, for example, is a single-purpose technology—it only serves to create a document—an artificial language might serve two or many purposes. Very much like natural languages, artificial languages are instruments of communication, but might also serve non-communicative purposes and become identity markers.[9] In this sense, an artificial language can be marketed as a purely neutral instrument of communication, or be symbolically attached to a social or political agenda, such as universalism, pacifism, the advancement of science, the promotion of minority languages and nations, ecumenism, socialism, and so on. Unlike typewriters, artificial languages can have multiple purposes.

Second, in addition to being single-purpose instruments, typewriters and video recorders are end products. They do not change after use. Artificial language speakers, on the contrary, do not "buy" an end product. Using the language they have chosen to learn, they can try to change it regardless of the opinions or priorities of the language's inventor or other speakers. All languages are conventional, but the conventional nature of languages is most visible in the case of artificial ones. Some may be happy to say "et" to mean "and," others might prefer the Greek "kai," and the same goes for grammar or any other component of the language. Not being an end product, an artificial language can mutate in a thousand directions. Whereas changes in the design of end products are in the hands of the producers, changes in an artificial language are in the hands of the users, who, for the survival of their language should be willing to reach a collective agreement as to its basic characteristics.

Third, whereas it is difficult to imagine VHS or Betamax adopters in the pre-blog and social media age launching periodicals and setting up local organizations or sites dedicated to promoting and extolling their chosen product, this is indeed what happened among international language supporters. Artificial language users committed their time and effort in varying degrees to their language's success. In the case of artificial languages, unlike other standardization battles, we find collective action rather than individual adoptions.

These three qualifications suggest that in the case of languages, path dependence intersects with social movements. Social movement literature and scholarship is important for understanding the fate of artificial languages because, ultimately, it is not purely technologies or formal qualities that compete, but the social movements that embrace those languages.

A common ground between path dependence and social movements literature are the topics of leadership and strategy.[10] Artificial language users may agree or disagree on this or that word or grammatical rule, and they also might have different understandings about the nature of the language, as a pure instrument of communication or as a tool that might serve other purposes or identities. How they resolve these potential disagreements depends a great deal on leadership and the decision-making process, which may or may not facilitate agreement, evolution, and growth.

An important characteristic of the language movements covered in this book is the crucial role of their inventors. Whereas in other social movements it is possible to separate leadership and issues, grievances and demands, in the Volapük, Esperanto, and Ido movements the language and the organizational template imprinted by their leaders were two sides of the same coin. In this sense, artificial language movements resemble social movements of a messianic character, where the message converges with the strategy to popularize the chosen language. It is for this reason, and also because research on path-dependent processes focus on the early stage of the process, that I concentrate on the organizational templates and strategies that leaders imprinted on their movements.

Leaders mobilize and inspire followers, set up an agenda for action, frame a discourse that helps them identify the challenges and legitimize their actions vis-à-vis the external world, collect resources, outline an organizational strategy, and decide on decision-making processes. To understand the organizational and decision-making repertoires that artificial language inventors imprinted on their language movements, I explore the social and political contexts that shaped their thinking.[11] As we will see, their conceptions of how language works and the organizational strategies they advanced largely determined their followers' responses, and, ultimately, the fate of their languages. But before turning to Johann Martin Schleyer, the first mover and the inventor of Volapük, it is important to understand how Europeans ceased to think of languages as artifacts, or as mere instruments of communication, in order to transform them into markers of identity.

CHAPTER 1

===

The Emergence of Linguistic Conscience

Social scientists use the term "critical junctures" to describe those historical periods when the power of standing institutions weakens and societies are forced to choose among new institutional trajectories.[1] In the recent history of the European linguistic regime it is possible to identify two such critical junctures. The first took place in the late seventeenth century, when Latin was abandoned as the lingua franca and replaced by a competing, unstable array of vernacular languages. The second was in the late nineteenth century, when English, French, and German competed to become the first global language. Meanwhile, the rediscovery and reinvention of an array of new languages stirred by the nationalist élan of the time produced a new Babelization of Europe.[2]

Interest in and research on artificial languages was particularly intense at these two critical junctures, when the need for an international lingua franca was so evident. This interest did not emerge in an intellectual vacuum. It co-evolved with ideas about how languages work, how they relate to the people who speak them, and how states should think about or handle their populations' linguistic repertoires.

*   *   *

The decline of Latin in the first critical juncture is easy enough to track. In 1687, Newton published his *Principia Mathematica* in Latin. Some years later he sent his *Opticks* to press in English. He followed the example of Galileo, who decided to publish his *Dialogue Concerning the Two Chief World Systems* in Italian, when he had previously written his *Siderius nuncius* (The sidereal messenger) in Latin. Descartes wrote his *Rules for the Direction of the Mind* in Latin, only to later publish his *Discourse on the Method* in French.

Beyond philosophical and scientific circles, Latin eroded in other spheres of life. Inspired by the emergence of the modern state, a new literary genre emerged, devoted to the questioning of Latin, particularly in Protestant countries, and the exaltation of the national languages.

This literary genre initiated a new epoch of linguistic conscience. Language had scarcely been a political issue in antiquity and the Middle Ages.[3] France, striving to become a world power, most colorfully illustrates this linguistic conscience. In 1549, Joachim Du Bellay published his *La défense et illustration de la langue française*, in which he claimed that the language of the French royal court could more than satisfactorily compare not only with Greek and Latin, but also with Tuscan. Rabelais, Montaigne, and others also paid homage to the mother language, but those with closer court contacts, or looking for social recognition, did so most energetically. This was true with François Malherbe, or Le Labourer, who, in his *Avantages de la langue française* (1667), claimed:

> Our language is so beautiful when one knows how to use it! If you are careful with it, Sir, it derives more from the spirit and depends less on the organs of the body than any other language. . . . One must not speak from the throat or open the mouth too wide or strike with the tongue between the teeth or make signs and gestures as it seems to me most Foreigners do when they speak the language of their countries. . . . Beyond that, the various terminations of our words give our language an amenity, a variety, and a grace that other languages lack, and that is what makes [French] Poetry so beautiful, for its lines, sometimes masculine, sometimes feminine, create through their mingling and commerce a harmony that exists nowhere else. . . . And if you consider the way in which we construct words, you will find that they stand in relation to one another in the order that nature lays down.[4]

And for just one example of the salesmanship of an Englishman promoting his language, William Bullokar insisted that "in all Europe, I dare well say, (for true orthography) no nation hath so plaine a way, to write their speech truly." This is a curious assessment, to say the least, for a language whose native speakers find spelling so challenging they would later make spelling bees part of their popular culture. But in this international contest for the pre-eminence of one's own vernacular, the limits were never very clear. The Portuguese João de Barros, for example, claimed that "the Spaniards weep, the Italians howl and the French sing," indicating than only the Portuguese talk. To which French Jesuit Dominique Bouhours replied, "The Chinese, and almost all the peoples of Asia, sing; the Germans rattle; the Spaniards declaim; the Italians sigh; the English whistle. To be exact, only the French speak."[5]

Linguistic pride heralded the ethno-linguistic nationalism of the nineteenth century and had a political rationale. Modern states needed to standardize, codify, and purify whatever language variation had been chosen to become the official language, and, to this end, they founded language academies. The first language academy, that for Italian, was established in 1582 in Florence, followed by academies for French (1635), Spanish (1713), Danish (1742), Portuguese (1779), Russian (1783), and Swedish (1786). In any case, by the end of the seventeenth century, the erosion of Latin seemed irreversible. Around 1650, 67 percent of the books for sale at the Frankfurt Book Fair were published in Latin; in 1700, only 38 percent were.[6]

Scientists and philosophers worried about the abandonment of the lingua franca and the corresponding Babelization of science in the seventeenth century, but they were mostly responsible for their own predicament. When Latin was still widely used in law, religion, and diplomacy, natural philosophers came to believe that the language was unfit to keep pace with advances in science and technology. A dead language, Latin was cumbersome, ridden with irregularities, ambiguities, redundancies, and syntactical complexities. It also lacked the necessary richness, logicality, and precision that natural philosophers demanded. For these reasons, vernaculars took the lead in the scientific world. And with the vernaculars came the Babelization of science.[7]

To cope with Babelization, some proposed to give Latin a last chance and translate the main scientific works into this language. Thus, Descartes' benefactor, the friar and mathematician Mersenne, conceived of an academy in every country entrusted with this task, somewhat akin to the Toledo School of Translators in the twelfth and thirteenth centuries.[8] But these academies never came to be. Instead, scientific journals emerged. They tried to keep readers abreast of scientific progress by translating and publishing articles and book reviews from one vernacular into another. The French *Journal de Sçavans*, established in 1665 under the sponsorship of Jean-Baptiste Colbert, was the first of its kind, and set a good example for other countries.[9]

Or, scholars could become multilingual, but this was deemed impractical. It would have required a reform of higher education, which still concentrated on instruction in classical languages. Also, languages were conceived in the seventeenth century as mere instruments for communication, rather than repositories of cultures or worldviews. Learning another language was considered tantamount to tedious memorization of new words and grammatical rules. Progress in the study of nature required a concentration on nature itself, rather than on the many ways different people arbitrarily referred to the same natural phenomena. Time and effort could be most efficiently invested in the improvement of the description or explanation of nature, not on its linguistic replication. Romanticism was still distant, and rather than view language diversity as a token of the endurance and creativity of the human race, scholars and the literati considered it a curse.

A third solution, championed by some of the most powerful minds of the era, was to invent a new language, more rational and suitable for communication than Latin or existing vernaculars. That such a language could come to exist was already suggested in the utopian literature of the sixteenth and seventeenth centuries. In his *Utopia*, originally published in 1516 in Latin, Thomas More had inhabitants speak a language that was rich, precise, perfect, and pleasant to the ear. Jonathan Swift's Lilliputians in *Gulliver's Travels* used a language that was so well constructed and easy to learn that Gulliver could converse with the natives in three months.

Renewed interest in Chinese script reinforced the feasibility of a new language. Contemporaries knew that, although Chinese people spoke different languages, they could communicate in writing. It would be useful to have a similar script for Europeans. This was Francis Bacon's (1561–1626) proposal: a language based on a system of "real characters," which conveyed the real essence of things and concepts, would solve the problem of international communication. A system of real characters would help solve another problem. Once we discovered, enumerated, and arranged all the basic, irreducible concepts that convey the essence of physical and non-physical phenomena, we could achieve an unequivocal transmission of meaning. A language of real characters would be the antithesis of natural languages, which were redundant, deliberately ambiguous, and full of inconsistencies and meaningless terms. By helping to distinguish between real and imaginary concepts— invented for the purpose of extending and elaborating futile theological or philosophical disputes—a language of real characters would accelerate knowledge.

There were others, however, who thought that a language based on real characters was out of the question. Such a language, argued Descartes, would require a previous and complete knowledge of the components of the world, a necessary prerequisite to differentiating between real and unreal characters. In the absence of that knowledge, and without criteria to distinguish between the irreducible or real and the not so real things, the whole project was inconceivable.

Despite Descartes' warning, more enthusiastic people got down to work and crafted artificial languages based on real characters. The most influential of them came from members and friends of the Royal Society, such as George Dalgarno (1626–1687) and John Wilkins (1614–1672). Isaac Newton also outlined an international language, but, as with much of his writing, he did not publish his ideas.[10] Dalgarno's proposal came first, with his *Ars Signorum* (1661). He divided physical experience into seventeen irreducible categories, each denoted by a letter. Second and third letters conveyed further subdivisions of those categories. For example, the natural world was subdivided between animate and inanimate things. The former included plants or animals. Animals fell into the categories of aquatic, aerial, or terrestrial. Dalgarno placed human beings in a different category and then differentiated between terrestrial creatures with a cloven hoof and a single hoof, like a horse or "nηkv," in Dalgarno's vocabulary. Word order rules denoted when a word was a noun, an adjective, or an adverb, and special suffixes indicated verb tenses.

Wilkins's proposal resembled that of Dalgarno, his erstwhile collaborator. The Royal Society, which he helped to establish, had commissioned his work. In his *Essay Towards a Real Character and a Philosophical Language* (1668), Wilkins enlarged the number of irreducible categories to forty and increased the number of subdivisions. Wilkins also paid more attention to grammar, which he made a little more complex. Like Dalgarno's, Wilkins's language could be spoken. He published an alphabetical dictionary that first distinguished various meanings of English words to later refer to them by their exact location on the tables of real characters.

Significantly, this endeavor provided the basic infrastructure for a thesaurus; namely, a list of words, arranged by categories, distinguished by their meaning. In fact, Peter Roget's *Thesaurus*, first published in 1852, is a spinoff of these artificial language projects.

Leibniz surpassed Dalgarno and Wilkins, ambitious though they were, in his dreams about the content and goal of an artificial language. Leibniz

aspired to curb the number of words and give them the precise and unequivocal meaning that scholarly exchange and international communication
demanded, but he had more ambitious ideas about the ultimate goal of an
artificial language. In his youth, Leibniz had tried to create a set of real characters, but he gave up, since there was no way to be certain that things or concepts deconstructed could not be fractured yet further. This was a quite natural
concern for the discoverer of infinitesimal calculus. Rather than a language
based on real characters, intended to univocally represent meaning, he imagined one whose characters, or "primitives," represented basic reasoning op-
erations. Combined in an algebraic fashion, this language of primitives,
advanced for ease of calculations, would directly adjudicate between truth
and falsity. Leibniz envisioned the construction of a logical language, an al-
gebra of thought processes that could augment our reasoning capacities. (A
similar research program emerged in the early twentieth century under the
name of symbolic logic, which engaged Bertrand Russell, Couturat, and Peano,
among others. We meet them later.)[11]

These first artificial language projects rested on the idea that words stand
by themselves, that there is an unequivocal relationship between the word
and its referent, as the myth of the Adamic language suggests, where words
directly convey the essence of things. The book of Genesis tells us that God
created the heavens and the earth, light and darkness, just by naming them.
In the Adamic myth the things and their names are one and the same. Like-
wise the artificial language projects of the seventeenth century were based
on a narrow conception of language. Their goal was to create a perfect language: a language that conveyed the true essence of things and concepts
straightforwardly, as if naming something were tantamount to giving it a distinctive identity.

A different conception of language in the eighteenth century put an end
to these projects. A basic tenet of this new conception, advanced by the Idéologues, among others, is that there is no fixed, one-to-one relation between
a word and its meaning. Such a relationship can be posited for mathematical
terms (the concept "angle," for example, has a fixed and unambiguous meaning), but not in other realms. To quote Destutt de Tracy, who anticipated
twentieth-century semantic theory, "it is impossible that the same sign has
exactly the same value for everybody who uses it, or even for every one of
them every time he uses it."[12] Even if it were possible to agree on an international word for "honor," for example, this word would still elicit different
meanings to different people and contain ambiguity. Moreover, it is precisely

language's context-specific nature that makes it such an efficient tool for everyday communication.

Rather than looking for an impossible perfect language, the Idéologues asserted that a more feasible and helpful task would be to use a common language with as much precision as the context required, or to reform it as necessary by producing, for example, unambiguous scientific symbols or nomenclatures.[13]

This was a turning point in the history of linguistics.[14] The abandonment of the search for a perfect language encouraged those interested in the study of language to concentrate on fluidity and context-specific meaning. The idea emerged that languages, rather than mechanically reflecting a fixed reality, change and evolve in conjunction with the people who speak them, and in ways that satisfy their communication needs. This idea heralded a more distinctive organicist, or Romantic, view of language. According to this vision, the spiritual or cultural progress of a people—its genius, soul, national character, or *Volksgeist*, as it was later called—could be captured in the language spoken by that people. This is one of Johann Gottfried Herder's basic tenets (1744–1803). He argued that "each nation speaks in accordance with its thought and thinks in accordance with its speech."[15] Wilhelm von Humboldt (1767–1853) expressed it more plainly: "The *mental individuality* of a people and the *shape of its language* are so intimately fused with one another, that if one were given, the other would have to be completely derivable from it. . . . Language is, as it were, the outer appearance of the spirit of a people; their language is their spirit, and their spirit is their language; we can never think of them sufficiently as identical."[16]

Franz Bopp (1791–1867) was the father of comparative linguistics and a scholar of the genealogy of language families. He further reinforced the organicist view of language. The discovery of the Indo-European language, comparative studies by Bopp and his contemporaries, and the ethnicization of language as proposed by Herder and Humboldt opened the way to a racialist understanding of human societies. Comparative linguists originally coined the terms "Aryan" and "Semite" to refer to the peoples who spoke a language in the Indo-European or Semitic family. But by the mid-nineteenth century these terms conveyed a distinctly racial meaning, which invited comparisons of the moral qualities of the two races, the Aryan and the Semitic, and claims about the supremacy of the former over the latter.[17]

Although Bopp led the way in referring to languages as "organisms," the Darwinian influence in the second half of the nineteenth century closed the circle. Biology and linguistics were linked in a way that necessarily had political valence. In his *Die darwinsche Theorie und die Sprachwissenschaft* (The Darwinian Theory and the Science of Language [1863]), the German linguist August Schleicher placed languages on par with living organisms. Languages are born, and they die. While some strive and produce more offspring, others disappear or languish in isolation. The fate of a language ultimately reflects that of its speakers, involved as they are in a constant struggle for life.[18]

This naturalization and ethnicization of language moved vastly beyond the traditional understanding of language as a purely communicative tool. It put language at the forefront of politics and imbued it with other meanings. If language and ethnicity are overlaid, then an ethnic group could be identified if it had its own language. Even more significantly, as Fichte put it, language legitimated claims to national self-determination. "Whether a particular language is found," he said, "there exists also a particular nation which has the right to run its own affairs."[19]

The abandonment of the artificial language solution heralded a new and politically charged conception of language. Languages were invoked to prove or certify claims to national identity, to make an argument for the strength of one nation vis-à-vis other nations, as well as to delineate the proper or "natural" geographical boundaries between them. By the era of nationalism in the late nineteenth century, languages were already first-rate political weapons.

*   *   *

It is precisely when languages were most politically instrumentalized that we reach the second juncture in the European linguistic regime. Economic historians refer to this period as the first wave of globalization, from 1870 to 1913.[20] New transportation and communication technologies (railways, steamships, the telegraph, and telephones) abolished the tyranny of distance, reduced freight costs, and fostered international trade. European international trade, at current values, increased by 294 percent.[21] The state of relative peace between the main European powers and the adoption of the gold standard also contributed to this unprecedented expansion of international trade. International migration was equally paramount. From 1850 to 1880 an average of 300,000 Europeans a year emigrated to other continents. At the turn of the century the number exceeded 1,000,000. [22]

A more interconnected world demanded broader cooperation and new international bodies. The International Telegraph Union was established in

1865 and, nine years later, the Universal Postal Union. The International Meridian Conference agreed to establish standard coordinates and time zones in 1884. But cooperation at the international level was neither confined to the field of communications or trade agreements, nor exclusively championed by public actors. The International Committee for Relief to the Wounded was founded in 1863 in Geneva, which paved the way for the first Geneva Convention a year later and the founding of the Red Cross in 1876. Meanwhile, the trade unions had already established their First International, also in Geneva (1866). World fairs were held regularly after the success of the Parisian World Fair in 1867. They gave participating countries a chance to show off their scientific and technical acumen. The modern Olympic Games, first staged in 1896, and the Nobel Prizes, established in 1901, created new arenas for international competition.

To facilitate scientific research and the transfer of knowledge, the International Bureau of Weights and Measures was established in 1875. The fields of pharmaceuticals, bibliographical systems, cartography, and technical drawing also established standardizing bodies.[23] More than 300 international organizations flourished in this period, and the number of international conferences escalated from a mere 20 in the 1850s to 1,062 in the first decade of the twentieth century.[24]

Talking about the current wave of globalization of the late 1990s, and in a bid to explain the ultimate success of English as the international language, David Crystal claims that "there [has] never been a time when so many nations were needing to talk to each other so much. There has never been a time when so many people wished to travel to so many places. There has never been such a strain placed on the conventional resources of translating and interpreting."[25]

But a quite similar scenario took place 100 years earlier during the second linguistic juncture, although with an important difference. Whereas nowadays there is a common understanding that English is the language of international communication, at the turn of the twentieth century the linguistic competition was still open. Although in the last third of the nineteenth century French was already losing ground to English, especially in trade and commerce, it had managed to retain its prestige as the language of diplomacy. In science, too, the linguistic balance was shifting and unstable. In the eighteenth century the Royal Academies of Berlin, Saint Petersburg, and Turin had adopted French as their official language, but by the late nineteenth century, German was poised to surpass it. In fact, by 1910, German was already

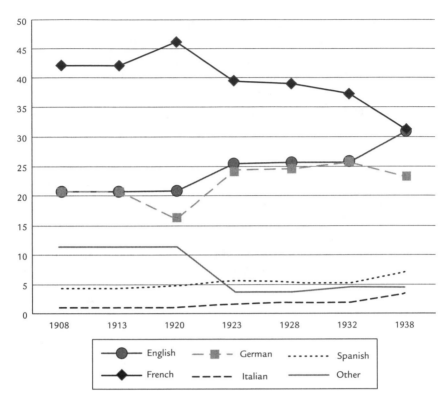

Figure 1. Hours of instruction in a foreign language as a percentage of all foreign language instruction in European secondary schools, 1908–1938. Source: Ulrich Ammon, "The European Union (EU—formerly European Community): Status Change of English During the Last Fifty Years," in *Post-Imperial English: Status Change in Former British and American Colonies, 1940–1990*, ed. Joshua Fishman, Andrew W. Conrad, and Alma Rubal-Lopez (Berlin: Mouton de Gruyter, 1996), 250.

the leading language in the natural sciences, a position that it retained for the next ten years.[26] The international scenario from late nineteenth to the first decades of the twentieth century was diglossic—or, more accurately, triglossic, with French still holding a privileged position in diplomacy and international politics, English becoming ever more important in commerce, and German prevailing in science. Figure 1, which shows the percentages of foreign language instructional hours in European secondary schools in the first decades of the twentieth century, illustrates the shifting fortunes of the main European languages.

This was an unstable international linguistic scene, and many believed that national rivalries would derail any international agreement to grant a national language the status of lingua franca.

This skepticism led some to think that a non-ethnic, artificial language could be the solution. As Herbert Spencer said, "It is quite possible . . . that the time will come when all existing languages will be recognized as so imperfect, that an artificial language to be universally used will be agreed upon." Or, to quote from Nietzsche's *Human, All Too Human*: "In some far-off future time everyone will know a new language, a language of commerce at first, then a language of intellectual intercourse generally, and this as surely as there will one day be aerial navigation."[27]

But by this time languages had become something more important than pure communication tools. With language envisioned as a carrier of national identity, neither old nor aspiring nations could afford indifference to their "national" languages. Nationalist movements on the periphery of Western Europe, especially in the multinational Austro-Hungarian and Russian empires, drove linguists, literati, and political agitators to cooperate in language matters. Big nations strove to disseminate their national languages to strengthen their privileged position in the international arena, and reawakening nations such as the Basque, Occitan, Catalan, Czech, Rusyn, Lithuanian, and Magyar endeavored to rediscover and reinvent their languages.[28]

Against this backdrop of tension between the more pressing need for a lingua franca boosted by globalization and the politicization of language, artificial language movements found their footing, in both linguistic and political terms. Either led by Johann Martin Schleyer, the inventor of Volapük, or Ludwig Zamenhof, the creator of Esperanto, or Louis Couturat, the initiator of Ido, artificial language supporters were in no doubt that they had the key to the problem of international communication. But it was only Schleyer, a German Catholic priest, who hinted that his particular solution was inspired by none other than God.

PART I

Volapük

CHAPTER 2

A Language in Search of a Problem

On the night Johann Martin Schleyer was born in 1831, and as he later claimed as an omen to his remarkable life, a new volcanic island, Ferdinandea, emerged from the Mediterranean Sea. Strategically located between Sicily, Malta, and Tunisia, the island soon became the source of a political dispute, when the Kingdom of the Two Sicilies, France, Spain, and the United Kingdom claimed their sovereignty over it. Fortunately, in January of the next year, and before the dispute could turn into armed conflict, the forces of nature let the island sink. But this was not the only eventful night in Johann Martin Schleyer's life. Forty-eight years later, Schleyer, now a Catholic priest in the small town of Litzelstetten in southern Germany, had another extraordinary experience:

> In a somehow mysterious and mystical way, in a dark night in the
> rectory of Litzelstetten, near Constance, in the corner room of the
> second floor overlooking the yard, while I was vividly reflecting on
> the follies, grievances, afflictions and woes of our time, the whole
> edifice of my international language suddenly appeared before my
> spiritual eyes in all its splendor. To pay tribute to the truth, and let
> her bear witness, I must say that on that night of March 1879, I was
> very tired; thus, I can only proclaim with all gratitude and humility
> that I owe to my good genius the whole system of the international
> language Volapük. In March 31, 1879, I set up to compile and write
> down for the first time the principles of my grammar.[1]

The fourth of five children, Schleyer, the inventor of Voläpuk, was born in Oberlauda, in northern Grand Duchy of Baden. His father was a school-teacher, as had been his grandfather and great-grandfather. Along with teaching, the priesthood was a vocational tradition on both sides of his family, and Schleyer took holy orders when he was twenty-five, apparently against his father's wishes, after spending three years at the University of Freiburg. At Freiburg, in addition to theology and classical languages, Schleyer pursued his interest in poetry and modern languages. Schleyer served as a vicar and in other subordinate positions in different locations for eleven years. He befriended the writer Alexander Kaufmann and his wife, Mathilde (aka Amara George), a Catholic poet. He corresponded with Countess Ida von Hahn-Hahn, also a relatively popular writer who had converted to Catholicism in middle age. In 1862 he was sent to Krumbach bei Messkirch, in southern Baden, where he published Catholic and patriotic verse, and built a reputation in literary circles. Shortly before the unification of Germany, he was given his own parish, and in 1875 he was sent to Litzelstetten, at that time a small village of 250 souls, and today a section of the city of Konstanz. In Litzelstetten, he published *Sionsharfe*, a periodical devoted to Catholic poetry. Four years after his arrival, Schleyer had that mysterious and somewhat mystical experience in which he first conceived of the Volapük language.[2]

His international language project did not proceed straightforwardly. First he developed an international phonetic alphabet that allowed words in every language to be phonetically transliterated and understood by both native and non-native speakers. This alphabet would prevent German people from writing "Eiauä," as it would look if it were a German word, when they wanted to send a letter to Iowa. If they could not spell "Iowa" in English, they could use the new international alphabet and write "Aioua" instead. He was hopeful that the Universal Postal Union would adopt his "world alphabet," and to this end submitted his manuscript to the German postal administration. In 1878, the Universal Postal Union kindly published his proposal in its official journal, but that was the end of the story.

His idea of a world alphabet probably derived from the different spelling reform projects afloat in Germany at the time. Recently unified, the new country needed a unified spelling, and different proposals were discussed. A compromise was reached in 1876, but it did not satisfy many, including Schleyer, who favored a more phonetic German spelling. Schleyer liked to use his homemade German spelling system in his publications.

But Schleyer's international phonetic alphabet went a step further: it was not intended to be applied to German or any other national language, but focused instead on how the same sounds could be represented in all languages.[3] What he had, then, was a new alphabet, but not a unique language upon which this alphabet could be tested, so it was only logical for him to create such a language. This was the idea that seized his mind on that memorable and sleepless night of March 31, 1879, when the entire scaffolding of Volapük took shape.[4]

Apparently, Schleyer began to construct his Volapük with the grammar. Like German, Volapük had four cases: nominative, accusative, dative, and genitive, which were denoted by the vowels at the end of words. Vowels could also be used to form compound words, such as *Volapük* (*vol* from "world," *a* for the genitive case, and *pük* from "speak"), meaning "the language of the world." Regarding verbal forms, there was only one conjugation. Specific particles at the end or beginning of the infinitive indicated tense, person, and voice. If *löf* meant "love," for example, *löfob*, *älöfob*, *elöfob*, *ilöfob*, *olöfob*, and *ulöfob* meant "I love," "I loved," "I have loved," "I had loved," "I will love," and "I will have loved," respectively. Since prefixes and suffixes were used to denote grammatical functions, root words had to be easily identified in the final shape of constructed words. To allow for this, Schleyer decided that root words should begin and finish with a consonant, so that prefixes ended and suffixes began with a vowel. Given that root words had to begin and end with a consonant, and that the alphabet had only nineteen consonants and eight vowels (a, ä, e, i, o, ö, u, ü), coining a word often posed a combinatorial challenge, which became more constraining with two additional rules: that words had to be short, and preferably derived from English. Thus *pük* (from "speak") was chosen because there was already a *pik* word. *Beatik binoms, kels klödoms,* for example, means "Blessed are those who believe."[5]

Schleyer did not create an international language in order to solve communication problems; he just came around to such a language almost through revelation, as a complement to his queries in phonetic spelling. To Schleyer, Volapük was not a solution to a problem; it was a solution in search of a problem.

More a man of *belles lettres* than science and philosophy, Schleyer knew nothing about the artificial languages of the seventeenth century when he created his language. Nor did he care much about them, or feel compelled to examine them when told about their existence. More concerned with remaining original, he was convinced he had done better than Wilkins, Dalgarno, and company.[6]

He had good reasons to feel this way. Escaping the oblivion to which its dozens of predecessors had been consigned, Volapük was the first artificial language to obtain wide recognition from an interested public, gather a community of committed speakers, and have its own international social movement.

And all of this was accomplished rather quickly. Only nine years after publication of the first scheme of the language in *Sionsharfe*, there were 15 Volapük journals and 257 clubs around the world, from Europe to America, and from China to Australia. These clubs offered language courses, organized official exams and, more important, promoted the language locally. In some European countries, the language was also taught in public schools, business schools, and universities, and a new profession, *Volapükatidel*, or teacher of Volapük, was created. Schleyer, the priest of a tiny village in southern Germany, became an international celebrity.[7]

Schleyer had not focused energetically on potential uses or users, but once he invented the language, the users found Volapük, and him.

CHAPTER 3

Who Were the Volapükists?

The first Volapükists were the readers and collaborators of his Catholic poetry journal *Sionsharfe*, where Schleyer published a first draft of his language, mostly southern German Catholics interested in poetry.[1] In his first separate brochure on Volapük, Schleyer explained its grammar and vocabulary and established the organizational imprint of the Volapükist movement. This brochure included an invitation to send a short text in the new language to obtain a certificate or diploma that automatically granted membership in the movement. The bylaws of the movement, included in the official diploma, clearly indicated that it was not his intention to govern the movement in accordance with democratic principles. Article 7 stated that its "supreme leader" was himself, and Articles 16 and 17 provided that decisions reached by majority vote required that the supreme leader also voted with the majority.[2]

In its first years, and much to Schleyer's surprise, the movement gained strength quite rapidly. By 1883, Schleyer's textbook, already in its fourth edition, had been translated into ten languages. Volapükist clubs sprang up in Germany, the Netherlands, Sweden, and Austria, and in addition to the official *Weltsprache-Volapükabled* journal, founded by Schleyer in 1880, two other Volapükist periodicals emerged in Breslau and Rotterdam. Volapük enthusiasts in Germany and abroad organized public conferences in educational and professional settings, and by May 1884, seven general assemblies, mostly gathering German adherents, had taken place.

The Volapükist press usually included names and addresses of people who supported the movement and wanted to correspond with other Volapükists to practice the language. A combined file with the names, addresses, and occasionally the occupation of a total of 1,709 Volapükists, included in the French 1887 Volapük yearbook, the Volapük almanac of 1888, and the pages of the Vienna-based journal *Rund um die Welt* (1889–1892), gives us an approximate picture of the movement membership.

To begin with, Volapük was a male-dominated movement. Women were only 10 to 15 percent of Volapükists, a rather low percentage compared with that of the Esperantists, as we will see in later chapters. Most of these women were either related to a male Volapükist or trained as teachers.

One-third of Volapükists were German, mostly concentrated in the Catholic regions of southern Germany and western Prussia. Austrian Volapükists were the second-largest group, with 12 percent of total membership, followed by the Dutch (9.5 percent), the French (9 percent), and the Belgians, mostly in the Flanders region (7 percent). Although information about the professional and social status of members is very limited (only a third of them said something about their profession), Ph.D.s were overrepresented when compared with the average population. Around one-tenth of the Volapükists who reported their occupation had a doctorate. Middle-class professionals, such as public employees, teachers, bookkeepers, and typographers, also abounded. The combined file includes nineteen priests and a similar number of merchants and manufacturers. The average Volapükist was male, Catholic, German-speaking, and an upper-middle-class professional. It seems that the brief history of the movement did not allow for a diversification of its membership, which corresponds very closely to the original characteristics of the first-comers: Catholics and German speakers. For example, the small Volapük club of Saint Petersburg was mainly composed of German immigrants,[3] and among the American Volapükists, German names were not uncommon—in fact, one of them, the librarian Klaus A. Linderfelt, was the author of the first Volapük handbook published in the United States.

The relatively well educated was Schleyer's target group. As he indicated in the subtitle of his first handbook, Volapük was not invented for the common people, but for the *Gebildete* (the educated). Like Latin in the Republic of Letters of the seventeenth and eighteenth centuries, Volapük was meant to be a written language catering to the needs of "scholars, travelers, and merchants" (*Studierenden, Reisenden und Kaufleuten*).[4] Schleyer had these people in mind when he revealed his invention to the world, but it is not possible to say anything definitive about the intentions and visions of rank-and-file Volapükists. Still, the biographies of some of the movement's characters give us clues.

Among the most important Volapükists in Germany was Alfred Kirchhoff. Although born in the predominately Lutheran city of Erfurt, Kirchhoff was a raised as a Catholic. (His mother was French and Catholic.) A member of the German Academy of Sciences, and a scientist with international reputation, Kirchhoff was probably the most learned Volapükist. Initially interested in philology and history, he began his scholarly career by publishing manuscripts on the ancient history of his hometown. But Kirchhoff really excelled and obtained an international reputation in the field of geography, and the discipline of *Landes- und Volkskunde* (cultural and ethnic studies). His popular *Mensch und Erde* (Man and Land) was published in multiple editions in Germany and was translated into English. From 1887 to 1904, he was editor of *Forschungen zur deutschen Landes- und Volkskunde*, the most influential journal of his discipline, which at that time was striving for academic recognition as a separate scientific field. Toward this end, Kirchhoff and his disciples introduced the basic tenets of evolutionary theory into their discipline by studying the interaction between humans and nature. Whereas linguists were trying to establish the connection between national language and national *Geist*, Kirchhoff and his disciples studied the mechanisms by which the adaptation of men to their natural surroundings produced different national characters. For example, inhabitants of the more fertile northern Spain were, according to Kirchoff, hardworking (*arbeitsam*) and serviceable (*dienstwillig*), whereas people living in the poor soil of Castille were proud (*stolz*) and direct (*freimütig*), although less industrious. Laziness (*Faulheit*) and dirtiness (*Schmutz*) were more common in Extremadura, a little farther south.[5]

Initially skeptical about Volapük, Kirchhoff became its most committed propagandist in central Germany (Halle, Erfurt, Magdeburg, Weimar, and Kassel) after 1886, when he was captivated by the language's simplicity.[6] He was a regular contributor to the *Rund um die Welt*, the most popular Volapük journal, and his handbook *Volapük. Hilfsbuch zum schnellen und leichten Erlernen der Anfangsgründe dieser Weltsprache* was translated into English. As a scientist and university professor, Kirchhoff took the leading role in Volapük's defense against its detractors. He also persuaded other scientists to join the movement and learn the language. Among them was the small network of Volapükist mathematicians led by the renowned Rudolf Menke in Darmstadt, and including Friedrich Pietzker in Nordhausen, Hermann Schubert and Rudolf Böger in Hamburg, and Ritter von Rylski in Vienna.[7]

As his former student and biographer recounts, Kirchhoff could not endure criticism. A vehement character, he was often too quick to draw wrong conclusions about people and ideas. This inclination was the source of his life's two bitterest disappointments: his marriage and Volapük. But while he was quick to realize the collapse of his marriage, he could not anticipate the failure of Volapük.[8]

The growth of scientific research demanded that a common, scientific language be used, and Kirchhoff thought that Volapük could satisfy this demand. Knowledge of the three main scientific languages, German, French, and English, was insufficient. The scientific reports he received from the geographical society of Budapest, for example, were published in Hungarian, and those from Bucharest were written in Romanian. He had tried to learn Russian, but because of his many other commitments, he had to interrupt his studies on different occasions and never succeeded. Kirchhoff thought that the already bad confusion of languages in science was only going to get worse: "How can one learn all these languages [when] in the next centuries many other nations will, quite understandably, come forward and use their national languages for scientific purposes?"[9]

Other Volapükists believed that the language was suited for other purposes aside from scientific communication. Given its extraordinary capacity to host all nuances of human language—the German stenographer and first certified Volapük teacher, Karl Lenze, had calculated that there were 505,440 ways of using the language's verbal modes—some were convinced that it was not only useful to translate literary works, but also to create its own literary body. This was the position of Theddäus Devidé, a journalist and relatively successful Austrian writer, and Siegfried Lederer (1861–1911), the editor of *Rund um die Welt*. Born in Prague, Lederer studied classical languages at the German university there, the Karl Ferdinand Universität, obtained a Ph.D., and worked as a language teacher in different gymnasiums in Prague, Vienna, and Radautz (Bukovina, currently in Romania). To prove the literary precision of Volapük, and, at the same time, to bait an important public figure, Lederer translated *Eine Orientereise* by Koprinz Rudolf, the only son of the Austrian kaiser.[10]

Still other Volapükists thought that Schleyer's international language could be valuable for the promotion of international peace. They noticed that in the introduction to his first handbook, Schleyer had referenced the cosmopolitan spirit inspired by new technological inventions. Volapük could work like the linguistic equivalent of the railroad, steamboat, telegram, or telephone to bring people of all corners of the world closer together. The Swiss Konrad Meisterhans and the Dutch Simon Buisman suggested that Volapük could serve international peace. As the former saw it, pacifists were "the natural allies of the Volapükists," and since international peace organizations were already receptive to the idea of an international language, Volapük could fulfill this task easily enough once it was brought "to flawless perfection and completion." Buisman conceded that Volapük was useful to merchants, scientists, and men of letters, but thought that its "most elevated function" lay in the promotion of "mutual understanding and the unity of nations."[11]

Other Volapükists, such as the Austrians Ludwig Zamponi and Sigmund Spielmann, editor of the 1888 Volapükist almanac and author of a book on bank and business correspondence; Joseph Bernhaupt, a postal employee stationed in Beirut; the Catholic teacher Carl Zetter; and the Danish L. P. Jensen, claimed that the language was of greatest value to the *Nicht-Gelehrten* (the non-learned).[12] Since the learned (*Gelehrten*) had a tendency to unnecessarily complicate the language for aesthetic reasons, Volapük would be best used by practical people, the merchants and businesspeople. An artificial language could save in translation costs and help standardize business communication, making it more transparent and less liable to costly misinterpretations.

In the United States, the retired Colonel Charles E. Sprague (1840–1912), whom a former student described as "a gentleman of the old school, courtly, sensitive, tactful; a man of wide culture with a genuine love for beauty in art and literature,"[13] was also very much convinced that "the most obvious application of Volapük is for international correspondence, especially commercial correspondence, which is numerically the most important. . . . If firmly established for this purpose, the extension of its usefulness into the fields of science, diplomacy and literature may safely be left to the future to determine, as well as whether it will ever be used by travelers."[14]

Like his friend Melville Dewey (1851–1931) (or Melvil, as he preferred to spell it), who invented the Dewey Decimal cataloguing system, Sprague was very active in the American spelling reform movement.[15] Both men were born standardizers. Dewey obtained public recognition in library and information sciences, and Sprague succeeded in accounting. Beginning as a clerk, he became president of the Dime Savings Bank of New York City. In his capacity as a prominent banker and the first university professor of accounting, Sprague played a leading role in the professionalization of accounting in the United States and the standardization of accounting methods, critical for the transmission of reliable information in economic transactions.[16]

Second in the official hierarchy of the North American Society for the Propagation of Volapük was the Bostonian Charles C. Beale (1864–1909), the publisher of *Volapük: A Monthly Journal of the World Language* (1888–1890).

Like Sprague, Beale was interested in Volapük as a standard medium of communication for commerce and economic transactions. He was a member of
the Boston Shorthand Bureau, and owner of the Boston School of Phonogra-
phy, which offered instruction in shorthand methods, typewriting, and business correspondence. He was also editor of the journal *Stenography*, which
discussed the pros and cons of different shorthand methods and advocated
for a shorthand standard for the English language.

But the most critical character in the history of Volapük, after Schleyer,
was the Frenchman Auguste Kerckhoffs (1835–1903). Kerckhoffs was born
in the Netherlands, in the eastern part of the Catholic province of Limburg,
a region assigned to the Dutch after the secession of Belgium. He studied philosophy and natural sciences at the universities of Liège and Louvain. In 1860
he moved to France, where he worked as a private instructor in mathematics,
history, Latin, German, and English. For the next ten years, he taught in the
lycée of the small town of Melun, close to Paris. During the Franco-Prussian
War (1870–1871), he served in the French National Guard and became a
French citizen. He later moved to Germany and studied at the Universities
of Bonn and Tübingen. In 1876 he returned to France with a Ph.D. in German literature. For the next four years he worked as a private instructor, and
in 1880 he became professor of German language at the École des hautes études
commerciales of Paris.[17]

By the time Kerckhoffs learned Volapük, he had already demonstrated that
he was a very learned person with a variety of interests. On top of his dissertation on German drama, he had published books on Flemish literature,
English grammar, and a research piece on art history. In 1887 Kerckhoffs set
up the Association française pour la propagation du Volapük, imitating the
Association nationale pour la propagation de la langue française (or the Alliance Française, as it was later named). In 1887, he launched the monthly *Le
Volapük* and published a *Grammaire abrégée de Volapük*, a *Dictionnaire
Volapük-Français et Français-Volapuk*, and the *Premiers éléments de Volapük*.
But it was his *Langue commerciale internationale: Cours complet de Volapük*
that secured him a leading position in the movement. His *Cours* was the most
successful Volapük handbook. It was translated into German (1880), English
(1887), Italian (1887), Portuguese (1888), Russian (1886), Dutch (1886), and
Spanish (1885). His success made Kerckhoffs the most prominent rival to
Schleyer's leadership.[18]

Kerckhoffs's first encounter with artificial languages was not with Volapük.
Nor has he entered the annals of history as a Volapükist. Rather, Kerckhoffs

is remembered historically as a cryptographer. His book *La cryptographie militaire* (1883) was a brilliant analysis of military encoding systems from antiquity to his own time, and his research on cryptography is still recognized and now known as "Kerckhoffs's principle." The principle broadly stipulates that more important than hiding secret information is the protection of the key code. His research in cryptography acquainted him with artificial languages, more specifically, with Solresol, a bizarre language code invented in the 1830s and occasionally used by the military for encryption.[19] A person with a strong character, Kerckhoffs was not a conformist. He was not inclined to remain silent when he thought something was wrong, as his fellow Volapükists would very soon learn. His criticism of the way the French Ministry of Education administered state exams cost him his job at the École des hautes études commerciales and forced him to become an itinerant teacher.

Like Sprague, Kerckhoffs thought that the language should mostly serve commercial purposes, as the title of his successful handbook, *Langue commerciale internationale*, clearly indicated. This was also Adolphe Nicolas's position. Nicolas was a maritime physician and vice-president of the Association française pour la propagation du Volapük. As he put it, Volapük is "a commercial, telephonic and telegraphic language, a language of commercial relations par excellence."[20] A common language, according to Kerckhoffs and the official French Volapükist movement, could boost economic growth not only because of the savings in translation costs, but, more important, because it would eliminate the information noise associated with translating back and forth from different languages. A shared and transparent communication system, they argued, could promote trust among economic agents, and thus contribute to a more efficient allocation of economic resources. But since appeals to general interests are usually less attractive than appeals to private ones, the French Volapükists polished their argument accordingly. An artificial, commercial language, they claimed, would level the international playing field and let France demonstrate her real economic power by trimming the undeserved advantage of English and German.[21] As Kerckhoffs saw it, Volapük did not jeopardize the "patriotic" mission of the Alliance Française. On the contrary, it would undergird French's status as the international language of diplomacy. He simply envisioned a diglossic regime, with French dominating in international relations and Volapük in commerce and perhaps in science.[22] To quote from the English edition of his *Cours*: "In the same manner that diplomats have a universal or common language for their international dealings, scholars, agents and merchants would also find a great advantage in possessing a simple and practical means of communication."[23]

Kerckhoffs's patriotic reassurances proved somewhat successful: he was able to persuade the board of the École des hautes études commerciales to hold courses in Volapük. By 1889, the school was offering fourteen weekly courses, and one of them was specially tailored for employees of the Grand Magasin de Printemps, an elegant department store. In fact, among the 470 French Volapükists who reported their profession for the 1889 edition of the French Volapükist yearbook, 160 of them were active in the commercial sector (mostly bookkeepers, employees, agents, merchants, and traders).[24]

Volapük enticed people with different tastes. We find people interested in standardizing communication and information technology, such as stenographers and librarians. There were also Volapükists concerned about the utility of a standard means of communication for commercial and scientific purposes, as well as people who saw Volapük as an instrument for world peace.

This constellation of interests shows that Volapük had a strong potential for growth in different directions and the chance to become the international language it claimed to be. But in order to realize this possibility, it was necessary to organize accordingly and draw more attention from the public, something which ultimately depended on Schleyer's leadership skills.

The first official congress of Volapük took place in 1884 in the public hall of Friedrichshafen am Bodensee, a small town on the banks of Lake Constance. It was a three-day congress, attended by only about thirty Volapükists from Bavaria, Württemberg, Switzerland, Austria, Alsace, and Lorraine. The French and American Volapükists were not yet represented. Since all of them spoke German, Volapük was barely used. This first congress launched the movement and was a platform to celebrate Schleyer's genius and linguistic virtuosity. Presiding over its first session was the German physician Rupert Kniele, an old subscriber to the *Sionsharfe,* and Schleyer's closest associate.[25] The hall was decorated with a bust of Leibniz and a painting that represented the children of the five continents, embracing the globe. All sessions began with the children of the local choir singing the Volapük anthem, with nods to peace and brotherhood, and the congress was closed with a banquet, toasts, and fireworks.[26]

The friendly atmosphere of this small congress prompted Schleyer to agree to some small changes in the grammar, and after "urgent petitions from many people" he even considered using the official spelling of German instead of his own spelling system in his publications. More importantly, the congress decided to make further efforts to expand the movement internationally. To grow in an orderly manner, congressional delegates agreed on the publication of an official journal that would give the names of those who were going to hold official positions in the movement. The congress also approved a first detailed account of the formal hierarchy of the movement. At the top of the hierarchy were the national leaders, followed by world language instructors and local leaders, with rank and file supporters at the bottom. Towering above them all was Schleyer, who had made himself leader for life. As his confidant, Rupert Kniele, said, "Volapük was really put into motion" at this congress.[27]

Delegates made an important decision to emphasize Volapük as an "internationale Handelsverkehrsprache," a language for international, commercial communication, which explains Kniele's confidence in Volapük's future. Delegates hoped that this announcement would give Volapük a narrow field of application. They also added an important caveat in the official motto of the movement. Originally it read "Menade bal püki bal," or "One human race, one language," but the new motto was "One human race, one language—*without prejudice to the mother language*" (unbeschadet der Muttersprache).[28]

These changes were intended to assuage serious anxieties that Schleyer and his associates had already provoked. Volapük, it turned out, had powerful enemies.

CHAPTER 4

"Pandemonium in the Tower of Babel": The Language Critics

Kerckhoffs's Association française pour la propagation du Volapük was established in 1886, three years after the Association nationale pour la propagation de la langue française, later called the Alliance Française. The Alliance was an organization "éminemment patriotique," whose goal was to "propagate the [French] language in the world [in order to] ensure the purchase of our national products, and expand its political and moral clientele [of France]." If Kerckhoffs envisioned a diglossic international regime with French dominating in politics and diplomacy and Volapük in commerce, were not his efforts undermining the patriotic goals of the Alliance? By giving up French, was he not a defeatist? Was he really serious when he asserted that Volapük could derail German and English in the field of commerce, and consequently help French to restore its international reputation?

Given the unfamiliar and, to some, weird, qualities of Volapük, astonishment and ridicule was a common response to the confident claims of Kerckhoffs and fellow Volapükists. The language was depicted as a squeaky absurdity, an irksome nuisance or, as *Le Figaro* put it, a maddening "hodgepodge of languages, a potpourri of dialects, a Russian salad of different patois . . . the revenge of the Tower of Babel. Masonic signs put into words." Schleyer's language became the subject of popular and strident criticism, from the print media to songs in cabarets. This criticism targeted the language, and also the sanity of its supporters. Is it possible to seduce a woman speaking Volapük, asked *Le Soir*? French journalists could not hide their delight when reporting the main episodes in Volapük's short history. Thus when other artificial languages entered the scene to question Kerchhoffs's efforts, *Le Bien Publique* suggested new lyrics for the tune *Malborough s'en va en guerre* (Marlborough is going to war):

Kerckhoffs est dans la peine
Mirliton, Mirliton, Mirlitaine!
Kerckhoffs est dans la peine
Chez Sarcey il s'en va.

Bonjour, cher camarade,
Volapük, der Teufel, est malade
Bonjour, cher camarade,
Hélas! il en mourra[1]

And when rumors about the first squabbles in the Volapük camp reached France, a journalist felt compelled to "gravely announce to its readers that conflicts have irremediably mounted among the Volapükists. The Munich congress . . . far from being a concert was like a pandemonium in the Tower of Babel. The students have finally decided that they know better the new language than the one who invented it. Our article proposes, thus, to Volapük-ize French. It will suffice to prune some Chinese-cisms and simplify the syntax a little bit to make it the best Volapük."[2]

Music halls and café concerts joined in. As a Volapükist complained, the language had become a trendy topic, although less among the *sérieux* than among the *boulevardiers*, the clientele of the cabarets and café concerts of the boulevards.[3] Unfortunately for the Volapükists, even when some distinguished *citoyens*—such as the senator and president of the Chamber of Commerce, Charles Dietz-Monnin, or Fréderic Passy, member of the Chamber of Deputies and future co-founder of the Interparliamentary Union—had given a vote of confidence to Schleyer's language, Volapük became a rich source of entertainment, mockery, and ridicule in the operettas and vaudevilles. The *ballet volapük* performed in the *Folies Bergères*, one of the fanciest café concerts of the time, staged singers and actors dressed in colorful national costumes, and speaking different tongues. Unable to understand each other, Progress comes to their aid, it opens the doors of a Volapük Institute, and things return to "normal"—with everybody uttering a rational, though incomprehensible language.[4] If globalization, standardization, and progress called for an international language, many French people were only ready to accept it if it were their own language.

That some vedettes teased Volapükists was not so worrisome. After all, making fun of everybody and everything was their trade. More worrisome was the serious criticism coming from those who, no matter how slim the chances for the success of Volapük might be, felt that its inroads in some circles was a troubling example of the malaise and decadence of French society. Was not Volapük, with all its inflections and umlauted vowels, a broken Teutonic language? Now that the future of French was uncertain with the lost territories of Alsace and Lorraine, should French people give up and support a language invented by a German? Who was this so un-French sounding Kerckhoffs? Even if his reassurances about the limited application of Volapük were sincere, wasn't he doing more harm than good? Could Volapük ever rival the proverbial *clarité*, *simplicité*, and *précision* of Molière's language? As the physician and rabid anti-Volapükist, Jules-Michel Jasiewicz put it, should Volapük ever succeed, Frenchmen

> would be less inclined to study their language and, instead, they would teach their children these so-called useful languages! It is not difficult to understand that the day when the merchants and the industrialists will only need English or Volapük, the French people will put aside the study of French, which will become useless for the scholars, the diplomats, etc. . . . This is all about the integrity of our patrimony, as well as the preponderance, at least the intellectual preponderance of the French language. . . . Why commit ourselves to our own effacement? Why should we contribute to our own moral and intellectual decline?[5]

German Volapükists came in for their share of mockery and ridicule as well. As the editor of *Rund um die Welt* complained: "It is not long ago that the word 'Volapük' is sufficient to inspire ridicule and scorn when not, at best, a compassionate smile. The newspapers have made fun of this 'invention': they have pronounced a world language unnecessary and impossible, and their supporters complete fools."[6]

But worse than a token of foolishness, Volapük was also perceived by some as a symptom of enfeebled patriotism, as was true in France. Although the victory in the Franco-Prussian war and the very creation of the German Reich had proved that the new country had the potential to rank among the great European powers, for Germany to realize this potential the unified state had to have its own lingua franca. This not only meant the standardization of German and its spelling—only accomplished in the early 1880s with the emergence of Binnen- or Reichsdeutsch, or Common Standard German—but also and more critically the *Verdeutschung* or Germanization of the recently seized territories of Alsace and Lorraine, the Sorbian-speaking communities of Brandenburg and Saxony, and the Lithuanian- and Polish-speaking territories of East Prussia.[7] For the most sensitive nationalists, more important than the Volapükization of the world was the Germanization of Germany—two commitments apparently in conflict.

It did not help that Volapük's inventor was a Catholic priest, and that the language had mostly taken root in the Catholic regions of the country. Compared with that of the Lutherans, German Catholic loyalty toward the Reich was still questionable. Catholics were discriminated against in the new state. In the two decades preceding World War I, only eight of the ninety most senior positions of the Reich's civil administration were Catholics. There was only one Catholic in the Ministry of Finance, two in Education and Religious Affairs, and five in Foreign Affairs. The only Catholic in Internal Affairs was a messenger.[8] *Deutschtum* was definitely closer to Luther than to Rome, and there was something suspicious about an employee of the pope with such a peculiar, un-German language.

The political arguments against Volapük were occasionally quite explicit, as was true in Richard Hamel's book *Die reaktionäre Tendenz der weltsprachlichen Bewegung* (The reactionary bias of the international language movement). For Hamel, a journalist and literary critic, "the universal language is a recurring deception of our mind, which falsely conceives of humanity as a single and all-encompassing organism." It was one more example of the "charlatanism" that goes against "the German language and culture." Hamel's dangerous diatribes had their response. But it was not Schleyer, a Catholic priest, who delivered it. Geography professor Alfred Kirchhoff, in his article "Is Volapük antinational?" proceeded cautiously. While he agreed with Hamel's argument, positing that human progress has given way to human diversity, he contended that Volapük did not try to reverse this progress. It was not trying to deter the independent evolution of different national characters and their corresponding languages. Rather, he reassured critics that Volapük had "narrow practical goals." More important, since Volapük was a

German invention, national pride demanded that Germans promote it. Otherwise, English, "which has sufficiently proved its excellent qualities, can triumph in the international context."[9]

Kirchhoff's and other Volapükists' patriotic responses, however, did not prevent further criticism. "Harlequin-like," "a fool's cap," "absurdity," "a fantastic caper," "young monster," "human-fleshed arrogance," "insipid," "profane importunity," "most unbelievable philistinism," and "total impotence" were some of the niceties that Dr. Römer (a pseudonym) reserved for Schleyer's language in his *Volapük und Deutsche Professoren: Polemische Arabeske.* Schleyer was for Römer "a gawkish language idol" who had given birth to a dead language: dead because it had emerged "aus den Kirchhoff"—from the graveyard.[10]

If in France Volapük was commended as a weapon against English and German, and in Germany as a weapon against English, did English speakers feel threatened? Not much, although this did not prevent some from criticizing the new language. This was true of Alexander Melville Bell, father of Alexander Graham Bell. Like Sprague, the leader of the American Volapükists, Bell had been very active in the spelling reform movement. But contrary to the former, Bell did not make the transition from spelling reform to advocacy of an artificial language. Volapük, according to him, was too German, and unsuitable as an international language. Moreover, English was "itself reaching out toward universality, under the influence of commercial and social necessities."[11] For English to finally become the global language it was only necessary to remove some difficulties, particularly in its spelling, since "Nō laŋgwij kŭd bē inve'nted for intė́ŋna'ṣūnal yūṣ ḑat wūd suŋpa's iŋgliṣ in grama'tikal simpli'siti and in jenerėl fitnes tŭ bēku'm ḑi tuŋ ov ḑi wuŋld."[12]

Also, most linguists on both sides of the Atlantic opposed Volapük (as well as Esperanto and artificial languages yet to come), as they were trying to define their niche in the scientific division of labor and to obtain the respectability enjoyed by other scientists.

Basically, this meant the establishment of a research program that put aside philosophical speculations about the Adamic language and replicated the logic of discovery of the most advanced sciences. If astronomers had been able to discover the laws that govern the movements of the planets, and biologists the laws that determine the survival and extinction of species, then linguists could accomplish something similar if only they conceived of a language as a self-enclosed system governed by its own laws that can and must be discovered. This could be accomplished either by a comparative approach that illuminated the inherent regularities that pervade linguistic phenom- ena—in other words, through the field of linguistics—or, less systematically, by a descriptive approach on the historicity and evolution of languages, which was the specialty of philologists.

Linguists' chance to establish their own niche in the scientific division of labor hinged on their capacity to narrow down the content of general linguistics and disentangle it from the labors of the more philosophically minded—either those interested in exploring the connection between cat egories of thought and language, or those searching for a perfect, universal language.[13]

Working within these parameters, the idea of a *Weltsprache*, or universal language, as Schleyer called it, was alien to mainstream linguists. It reminded them of the dreams of the old grammarians in search of the *Ursprache*, all the more so when Schleyer hinted that his Volapük came about as a sort of di- vine revelation in the dead of night and when he presented himself as the "discoverer" (*Erfinder*) of *the* Universal language, as if there were such a thing waiting to be unveiled.

But the endeavors of late nineteenth-century linguists, however scientific, were not free of mystical postulates. If self-governing systems were endowed with laws waiting to be discovered, then languages were also carriers of national characters, much in line with the Romantic tradition of Fichte, Herder, and Humboldt. This scientifically clothed Romanticism was particularly prev- alent among German linguists, since, contrary to older nation-states such as the United Kingdom or France, the new German Reich needed language as a coagulant of the German spirit. The conjunction of language and national character also allowed German linguists to frame their research in one of the most popular scientific approaches of the age: evolutionary theory. In the same way that Darwin had liberated our understanding of man and other species from religious prejudices, German linguists claimed that their conception of "nation and language" as one and the same reality allowed for the transposi- tion of positivist, evolutionary theory to the field of linguistics. This break- through would finally release the discipline from the unsubstantiated philosophical and religious approaches of the past. As August Schleicher ex- plained, such a breakthrough meant conceiving of languages as "organisms of nature; they have never been directed by the will of man; they rose and develop themselves according to definite laws; they grew old and die out. They, too, are subject to that series of phenomena which we embrace under the name of 'life.' The science of language is consequently a natural science . . . [and] the *Origin of Species* . . . [does not] lie so very far beyond my own department."[14]

If as a living organism a language has its own genius or "inner spirit" that embodies the nation that speaks it, there is no room for artificial languages. A universal language cannot be anything but an oxymoron, a contradiction in terms. Being the language of everybody, a universal language would be the language of nobody. Without a *Geist*, an international language would be a body with no blood in its veins, a *Homunkulus*, to use the contemporary buzzword.[15]

The fact that an unnatural alliance of German linguists and Parisian vedettes ridiculed Volapük could not be overlooked. Fortunately for the Volapükists, there were some linguists who risked their reputations vis-à-vis their German colleagues to champion the possibility of an artificial language. Among them was the German-born Max Müller (1823–1900), professor of Sanskrit and modern languages at Oxford. Also a supporter of the English spelling reform movement, Müller thought it worthwhile to let the Volapükists carry out their experiment. More encouraging was French linguist, sociologist, and legal scholar Raoul de la Grasserie (1839–1914), who saw no reason to rule out the possibility of an artificial language, and ended up creating a new one: Apoléma. As one of the fathers of sociolinguistics, de la Grasserie disagreed with mainstream German linguistics. Rather than studying how languages use people—apparently to survive just like any other living organism—he preferred to study how people use languages.[16]

German-born Hugo Schuchardt (1842–1927), a professor of Romance languages in Graz (Austria), was more adamant against the German linguists' Romantic mood. By the time Schuchardt stood up for the Volapükists and, more precisely, for the possibility of an artificial language, he had already conducted substantial research on language contact and Creole languages, precisely the linguistic phenomena that deviate the most from the *Mystizismus* implied by the language-as-living-organism metaphor.[17] Also, living in the multilingual Austro-Hungarian empire, Schuchardt was a firsthand witness to a paradox. The most eager defenders of the view of languages as autonomous (*selbständige*), living organisms were working hand in hand with those trying their best to prevent their autonomous development by purifying them from foreign influences or establishing linguistic authorities that would dictate usage. Languages, according to Schuchardt, were not self-contained, self-developing organisms. Although they can convey a national identity and elicit a comforting sense of belonging, they are also instruments of communication, and, as such, are usually subject to purposeful human intervention. For Schuchardt, in sum, there was nothing in the domain of language that forbade the invention of a new tongue. Whether Volapük or any other artificial language was the best candidate was another question. In any case, Schuchardt claimed, the obstacles that a language, artificial or not, would have to surmount to become a world language were not linguistic but political.[18]

All in all, even when most late nineteenth- and early twentieth-century linguists believed that the link between language and nation had to be explored, not all of them were willing to camouflage the old Romantic philosophy of language in the positivist, but ultimately mystical, metaphoric garb of language as a living organism. Volapük was the first occasion, as Schuchardt put it, to discuss different notions of language. When some years later Esperanto took the lead, the same debate, with very much the same arguments, continued. To the recurrent argument that without history and a fatherland an artificial language would, like a *Homunkulus*, be unable to grow organically, the Polish linguist Jan Baudouin de Courtenay offered the same reply that Schuchardt had advanced some years earlier: *"A language is neither a self-contained organism, nor a sacrosanct divinity* (unantastbarer Abgott), *but a tool and a function.* And man has not only the right but also the social duty to improve his tools and make them more practical, when not to substitute them by better ones."[19]

Underlying these differences about the nature of language and the scientific approach to its study were important political issues. For de Courtenay, the "naïve Romantismus" and the associated *Volksgeist* rhetoric that he saw prevalent among his German colleagues was scientifically misguided and politically dangerous.[20] The French linguist Michel Bréal expressed these concerns most clearly. As he confided in a letter to his friend Schuchardt on the language wars (*Sprachkämpfe*) in Austria: "I would not be surprised if in that corner [the Austro-Hungarian empire] opens the fissure which will eventually cause the breaking apart of the old Europe. The philologists who have been involved in those quarrels could never exaggerate their responsibility! They have provided the arguments and the pretexts."[21]

Aside from the challenge posed by German linguists, there was another problem in store. This was the emergence of other language projects: Weltsprache, the Langue Internationale Néo-Latine, and Pasilingua, launched in 1885; to be followed by Bopal, Spelin, Myrana, Kosmos, and Lingvo Internacia, later called Esperanto.[22] For the Volapükists, this unending procession of artificial languages was a source of anxiety and embarrassment, since by attempting to solve the Tower of Babel problem, a new Babel of artificial languages had been created, as not a few people were happy to point out.

To make things worse, in 1887 the American Philosophical Society announced its plan to establish a committee to thoroughly evaluate Volapük, compare it with other new artificial languages, and issue a report about its suitability as an international language. This committee attests to the generic appeal of an artificial language, but given Volapük's detractors in some academic circles, the announcement was somewhat alarming to Volapükists.

The Society's eventual report confirmed Volapükist fears and concerns. The report was devastating. Contrary to most German linguists, the Society did concede that an artificial international language was possible and necessary, especially for scientific communication, hindered by nationalist sentiments and linguistic chauvinism. While an artificial, auxiliary language could serve this purpose, the Society concluded that it could not be Volapük, since it was too inflectional and its vocabulary unrecognizable. A suitable artificial language, according to the Society, should have a non-inflectional grammar, similar to that of English or most Romance languages, as well as a recognizable "Aryan lexicon," a vocabulary naturally derived from the roots of the Indo-European languages. A supplementary report also scrutinized Lingvo Internacia (Esperanto) and Pasilingua, and they were not given a formal endorsement, either. The Society held that an artificial language should not be the work of a single person, but of an international committee of experts, who would be in a better position to create such a language and, more importantly, to obtain international recognition and acceptance. A universal language, in short, could be created, agreed upon, and launched in the same manner as most other international standards. To this end, the Society invited other learned societies to join in a new international committee.[23]

The learned societies, however, showed little interest in the Society's proposal, especially after the Philological Society of London published a detailed refutation of the American report.[24] According to the Philological Society, the flaws in Volapük's grammar and vocabulary that the Americans had noted were minor, based on misconceptions and a bias in favor of inflectional languages. Though imperfect, the Philological Society of London found, Volapük was good enough to serve as an auxiliary language. However, much to the chagrin of Volapükists, the Society regarded Spelin as superior and alleged that if Spelin had been launched first, it would have been "far more widely accepted, and have become as its name implies the All-language." Consequently, although the Philological Society of London concluded its report with a ringing "lifomös Volapük, long live Volapük," this enthusiasm was not owing to the language's inherent qualities: since Volapük has "the ear of the public and is in possession of a vast organization highly interested in propagating it," expediency counseled its support."[25] The Society, in short, had countered the conclusions of the Americans, but for reasons that displeased Volapükists.

But for as much as some journalists, entertainers, nationalists, and scholars might have opposed Volapük, those most responsible for the language's collapse were the Volapükists themselves.

CHAPTER 5

"Strangled in the House of Its Friends": Volapük's Demise

When Volapükists met at their First Congress in 1884, they agreed that they needed to spread the language and movement outside of the German-speaking world. They were successful. Two years after their First Congress the number of Volapükists had increased substantially, and more than 100 supporters had earned the Volapük teaching certificate. Local organizations sprang up in France, the Netherlands, Belgium, the United States, Great Britain, Spain, Portugal, and Italy. In path dependence terms, Volapük had an important advantage as the first mover.

A growing membership, however, kindled competing views within the Volapük movement, both about the final purpose of the language and about the design of the language itself. These competing views and their inability to reach a working consensus within the movement undermined the advantage that the Volapükists had. The continuous succession of rival language projects, the interference of scientific societies, the opposition of the German linguists, and the apprehension of the most nationalist-minded only exacerbated the internal difficulties in the Volapükist camp. While conservatives took these external developments as evidence of the need to rally around the language as it was instead of tinkering with it, no matter how well intentioned or expedient the proposed reforms might be, the reformists radicalized their position. For them, the critique of outside scholars and the publication of rival projects only lent new urgency to reforms that would give the language its definite shape.

The Association française pour la propagation du Volapük was most critical of the language as Schleyer had outlined it. Its leader, Auguste Kerckhoffs, saw Volapük as something similar to a code system, where simple rules or the kind of one-to-one functions that governed cryptographic systems would allow for a precise and unambiguous translation between a natural language and Volapük. As he put it: "The international language of commerce [Volapük] is the complement to the [Maritime] Signal Code. It is a dictionary of 15,000 words, neither pleasant, nor unpleasant, but easy to learn for whoever has the key."[1]

Schleyer took a different approach, aiming at a complexity that would leave room for the smallest nuances and subtleties of human cognition. Kerckhoffs contended that this very complexity could ruin the language and the movement. Rather than perfect coverage and ornamentation, his goals were simplicity and practicality. To this end, Kerckhoffs had already introduced some simplifications in the language in the first edition of his *Cours*, and would add more in later editions. Among them was the elimination of four tenses from the conditional, and also of the genitive and dative suffixes, which he replaced with prepositions. He also proposed new rules for word formation.[2] In 1887, and right before the Second Congress of Volapükists, Kerckhoffs published his *Examen critique des simplifications qi'il y a introduire dans le Volapük*. His suggestions were not minor. They involved substantial changes in both the grammar and the lexicon, about which he was adamant. As he put it before the congress: "the Volapük that we have seen in some German grammars, with all its exuberance of grammatical forms and lacking clear word-formation rules, does not have any chance of being favorably accepted by the practical and intelligent minds."[3] Right or not, Kerckhoffs's reform proposals distressed Schleyer and many other Volapükists, since no matter how helpful or appropriate they might be, they surely had the potential to jeopardize the integrity of the language and the movement.

In early August 1887, the Volapükists met at their Second Congress. It was attended by around 200 delegates. The congress took place at the main hall of the Löwenbräu-Keller in Munich, where some years later Hitler would give his annual speech to celebrate his 1923 putsch. The congress was organized by the Munich Volapük club, which, along with the Nuremberg club, was one of the movement's two strongholds, and similarly inclined toward reform of the language. The German geographer Alfred Kirchhoff acted as the president, while Schleyer was honorary president. If the mood among the delegates to the First Congress was rather friendly, the delegates of the Second Congress, coming from the United States and different European countries, had to work thoughtfully in order to smooth out internal differences that could no longer be concealed. Kerckhoffs had openly challenged Schleyer's authority, and some wanted to reinforce his leadership. Leading them was Kirchhoff. In both his opening speech and in his capacity as president, Kirchhoff saw the opportunity to make some things crystal clear. As he stated, without explicitly mentioning Kerckhoffs: "Within the well-defined limits of our language a command of Schleyer is much more valuable to us than the seductive siren's calls of the jolly reform-embracing storm troopers. We do not follow commands as mindless slaves, but as a well-disciplined army under a leadership well aware of our end purpose."[4]

This time, reformers and conservatives were able to avoid an open confrontation by delaying important decisions. They decided to establish a language academy to study reform proposals, following the example of the Académie Française. Seventeen reputed Volapükists from ten different countries were elected to its governing board, among them Kerckhoffs, who was to preside. Expecting opposition from other Volapükists, Kerckhoffs accepted this position only after he was allowed to name seven other Volapükists of his choice to serve on the Volapük Academy board. For international cohesion, the delegates also agreed to set up a World Organization of Volapükists, which would fund the Academy. Still, conservatives were able to shield Schleyer's position: he was given the right to veto the decisions of both the Academy and the World Organization.

But the World Organization never materialized. The initiative to establish it came from the Munich club, inclined toward the reformists and, consequently, suspicious in Schleyer's eyes.[5] In contrast, the Academy became operative as soon as the Second Congress was concluded. It lacked a physical location, and its members worked by correspondence. The Academy deliberations, published in Le Volapük, made many people aware that approval of some of the proposals could change the language drastically. And although the Academy did not have an established procedure to sanction alterations, since its bylaws had to be approved in the next congress, its activities distressed Schleyer and the conservatives.

Opposing internal views about the language were dramatically illustrated in 1888, a year before the Third Congress, when an open battle between Munich reformists and conservatives caused a split into two vying, local Volapük associations. In other cities in Germany and abroad, Volapük clubs experienced similar conflicts. Some of these conflicts provoked defections, even among the most prominent Volapükists.

Julius Lott, a former leader of the movement in Austria, and Adolphe Nicolas, vice-president of the Association française pour la propagation du Volapük, launched two new languages: Mundolingue and Spokil, respectively.[6] Other Volapükists took even more radical positions. Under the leadership of Leopold Einstein (no relation to Albert), members of the Volapük club of Nuremberg shocked the Volapük world by switching their allegiance to Lingvo Internacia, which was to become Esperanto.[7] These skirmishes were sometimes played out in public exchanges, rife with scathing personal remarks and mutual accusations of treason. For example, Kniele did not hesitate to allude to Einstein's Jewishness in order to explain, as Kniele saw it, his duplicitous, treacherous, and hate-filled character.[8] For his part, Schleyer summoned his followers in May 1888. He was afraid of losing control of the movement and wanted to set the stage for the upcoming congress in Paris, Kerckhoffs's territory. The meeting's conclusion, published immediately in the official journal, *Volapükabled zenodik*, was a straightforward *ipse dixit*: "Any resolution of the Academy that has not been accepted by the Inventor is null, even if the whole of the membership united against the Inventor."[9]

The Third Congress, much "expected, [and] even dreaded [since] many feared that dissension and collision were inevitable," as the American Sprague pointed out,[10] finally took place in mid-August 1889. By this time, and in spite of the defections of the former months, the Volapükist movement was at its peak, with 253 local clubs, 14 journals, and almost 900 certified teachers.[11] Kerckhoffs was president of the congress, and Sprague acted as one of the two vice-presidents. The congress took place in the headquarters of the Société d'encouragement pour l'industrie nationale, opposite the Abbey of Saint-Germain. It was the best attended ever. Also, and much to the satisfaction of the delegates, the official congress language was Volapük. If delegates used any other language, a translation into Volapük immediately followed. But notwithstanding their satisfaction, the delegates could not disguise the difficult situation, and the need to prevent outright collision between reformists and conservatives. In order to satisfy both parties, the congress agreed that every resolution made by the Academy should be submitted to Schleyer's approval. If Schleyer did not approve, there would be further discussion and a second vote by the Academy. If it obtained two-thirds of the votes, then Schleyer's veto would be overturned. This resolution allowed Schleyer, who had refused to attend the congress, to keep his position as the most powerful member of the movement, while it simultaneously deprived him of his veto power.

But Schleyer found this compromise unacceptable.[12] Although right before the congress he had hinted to Sprague that he would accept the congress's decisions, he chose not to do so.[13] He claimed Volapük as his intellectual property, formally rejected the authority of the Academy, and established a new one, restricted to his most loyal supporters.[14] Schleyer and the reformists parted ways, and Volapükists all over the world were forced to take sides. As an American Volapükist saw it:

> The next few years are to decide the future of Volapük, and especially whether it is to have a future, or whether this magnificent world-wide structure, built with so much care and toil and expenditure of time, labor and money, shall be shattered by internal strife. . . . We should remember . . . the greatest political fabric the world has ever seen, the great Roman Empire [which,] torn by internecine strife, fell, and left no trace of its former greatness. . . . Let us trust that Volapük will not meet a similar fate. Its enemies have been powerless to harm it. . . . Let it not be strangled in the house of its friends.[15]

Freed from Schleyer's rule, Kerckhoffs quickly put the Academy to work to give the language its final shape and to keep other projects, especially Esperanto, from gaining ground. Immediately following the congress, he sent his reform proposals to Academy members and asked that they discuss them with the societies of their countries. But instead of clear answers, he received nine other reform proposals. Weary, he resigned in July 1890. The next year he lost his teaching job in the École des hautes études commerciales, after criticizing the French Ministry of Education's administration of the modern languages exams. This forced him to move out of Paris to find a job. Kerckhoffs was definitively lost for the movement. After his resignation, the Academy had remained idle, since their members could not agree on a new director. Only in 1893 did they find a replacement: Waldemar Rosenberger, the leader of the movement in Moscow.

As soon as he took office, Rosenberger changed the decision-making process. Instead of asking Academy members to discuss the proposed reforms with rank-and-file Volapükists, he restricted the decision-making power to Academy members. This move deprived grassroots supporters of any influence over the final shape of the language. But by that year, their number had shrunk considerably in any case. In February 1892, the general assembly of the local organization of Vienna, which published the influential *Rund um die Welt*, decided to discontinue all activities, after many other local clubs had already disbanded, their members disillusioned by the lack of tangible results from the Academy.[16] They had volunteered to learn, teach, and expand an artificial language, and there was not much to do if the language remained under perpetual construction. Some of them returned to Schleyer's flock, and a few changed their allegiance to Esperanto, but most apparently gave up. For Schleyer, Kerckhoffs's defection and those of likeminded reformists was a relief, and he took it as an opportunity to purge discontents and tighten his control on the remnants of the movement. The purge was easily achieved. He simply deleted the names of the troublemakers from the list of Volapükists published in the official journal. As he explained it, he could not conceive of any different course of action: "Christianity is better than my discovery, and there too there were conflicts. The apostles disputed about whom among them was best qualified. And then came Jesus who settled the quarrel."[17]

Along with the purge, Schleyer strengthened the movement's organizational muscle, in keeping with the strict hierarchical principles he had imposed at its inception. This meant refining the organization's pyramid-like structure with a more detailed distribution of the privileges and responsibilities of each hierarchical level. At the lowest rung were the students or *julans*, who could correspond with other Volapükists (as *spodels*), and/or join a local club informally (as *kopanels*). Full membership in the movement, however, could only be obtained by earning a diploma in the language. Graduate Volapükists could correspond with other members (as *spodals*) and compete for leadership positions in their clubs in their new capacity as *kopanels*. On the rung above club leaders (*cifs*) were the regional or national leaders (*cifels*) and federal-level leaders (*lecifs*). The position of continental leader, or *lecifel*, was also defined although never filled. Similarly, there was a hierarchy among language instructors, which encompassed club instructors (*tidels*), city instructors (*löpitidels*), and country-level "professors" or *plofeds*. *Xamels*, at the country level, would be responsible for granting teaching certificates. In a higher position were the *kademals*, or members of Schleyer's Academy. It was possible to be a *kademal* and a *cifel* at the same time. Even higher on the ladder were the *senatäns*, or members of the Senate, a small body of Schleyer's personal advisers, appointed at his discretion. And finally, in his capacity of *cifal*, or permanent and supreme leader of the movement, Schleyer could repeal the appointments made by clubs and organizations by not ratifying them in the official journal, the *Volapükabled zenodik*, where Schleyer published his decisions, or "edicts," which were binding for all.[18]

In the period immediately following the Paris Congress, Schleyer managed to retain a substantial part of the remaining membership, but this purge and organizational tune-up ultimately failed to stem the tide of disillusionment in the movement. Many members could not withstand the mockery of journalists and linguists, echoed by a large portion of the educated population. But even more were alienated by the authoritarianism of the *cifal*, which made the organization more closely resemble a religious sect. Neither was it helpful that Schleyer himself began to make changes in the grammar and vocabulary, which obliged his loyal supporters to purchase new dictionaries and unlearn old words. Unsurprisingly, there were more desertions, first among the now disillusioned supporters, such as Kirchhoff, and later among the most loyal, such as Rupert Kniele, Schleyer's designated successor and most ardent devotee, who in 1895 gave up and abandoned the movement.[19] In 1894 only fifty local associations remained active of the two hundred and fifty that had flourished the five previous years. In 1905, nine were still operating, but the last two were dissolved four years later. At that time, Volapük was practically dead.[20]

CHAPTER 6

"My Troubled Child": The Artist and the Kulturkampf

What accounts for Volapük's demise? In the battle of artificial languages that it initiated, Volapük had the incumbent's advantage. In a short time it had kindled the enthusiasm of a large number of educated people, willing to endure criticism and mockery from their peers and firmly convinced that the definitive international language had arrived. In addition, Volapük had prevailed over upstart rivals such as Spelin and Pasilingua. For many, its ultimate triumph seemed assured. In the words of the younger Edgar de Wahl, whom we meet later:

> I remember when I came into contact with Volapük. I did not like it at all. I was really unhappy with every aspect of it. However, the fact that by that time Volapük had 28 journals and 283 associations all over the world looked so remarkable that, somehow, one was paralyzed. I had the feeling that matters had already been settled and that it was pointless to raise objections. . . . The idea that something else might emerge, that something better could be proposed, did not occur to me even in my dreams.[1]

And yet, the Volapükists failed. Instead of exploiting their position as the first movers, they squandered it. Reformists and conservatives had been playing a classic coordination game, and even when both could have benefited from mutual agreement, it was impossible to attain. As Ludwig Zamenhof himself admitted to his supporters, had the Volapükists been able to cooperate internally to fix or standardize their language in time, "we all would be probably speaking Volapük today."[2]

But this was not the case. The Volapükists had cleared a path that adherents had only to follow. Internal movement dynamics, however, impeded their attempts to lengthen that path and encouraged other potential rivals to open a new one. Contemporaries blamed Schleyer for this failure, and probably rightly so. He had been granted the most powerful position in the movement, from which he would have been able to delay and force the reconsideration of any reform proposal, but this was not enough: nothing less than absolute control could satisfy him.

Schleyer certainly could have acted differently and helped reach a compromise satisfactory to all. So why did he choose instead to place his entire project in jeopardy? One explanation is rooted in his self-regard, his attachment to his language, and what Volapük meant to him. This was in direct contradiction to Kerckhoffs's position. While the latter viewed Volapük in strictly utilitarian terms, Schleyer stressed its aesthetic dimension.[3] He was particularly inclined to experiment with language, to stretch and distort its limits. He enjoyed experiments with German spelling, reflected in his writings, much to the chagrin of his supporters.[4] He was also a polyglot. He had not learned other languages to obtain material or career advantages, but merely to explore the plasticity of language. He saw himself as a poet, an artist who worked with words. Artists do not negotiate colors or materials, or let a democratic assembly make decisions about aesthetics issues. Artists do not allow others to make brushstrokes on their paintings. Volapük was his creation. It was to be admired or imitated, but he alone had the right to make it more graceful or beautiful. It was his masterpiece, in constant need of protection. As he put it: "Volapük is my troubled child, my needy child, my bullied child."[5]

The archbishop of Freiburg used this cliché of the artist as a passionate, immature, and childish character in Schleyer's obituary:

> For anyone who knew Schleyer superficially, it was hard, when approaching him, not to be startled by the ebullience of his personality. It was not difficult to notice that one was not dealing with an ordinary man, and that a different yardstick from that used for measuring most mortals was needed to address his genius and excitable nervous system [that blended] geniality with naïve childishness. Schleyer was in many ways, and even in his old age, a child. It was his childishness that made him speak so often and in

such a self-congratulatory manner about himself, boasting about his work, his titles, and reputation. Or was it perhaps that he made this child the center of his small world? He was not aware of being pretentious. He never looked down on other people. On the contrary, he always extended his hand to other people. And was not he also grateful, like children are? Anyone who visited him in his studio could read in his face how happy your visit made him, and no one could leave without carrying in his hands a small parcel of literary samples of the inventor of the world language. Happy like a child![6]

But there is a second, more powerful explanation, unrelated to Schleyer's personality, which has to do with his membership in the Catholic Church and his past experiences in the Kulturkampf. They imprinted the distinctive authoritarian ethos on his movement and framed his strategies when he found himself confronted by reformists.

Schleyer invented his Volapük when he was serving in the small town of Litzelstetten. By then, he was no longer a subject of the Grand Duchy of Baden, but a citizen of the new and more secularized German empire. With the unification of Germany in 1871, its first chancellor, Otto von Bismarck, faced important new challenges. A particularly pressing one was the Catholic Church, most prominent in the southern states. To offset the influence of Rome, and to win the unconditional loyalty of German Catholics to the new state, Bismarck embarked on a political campaign against the pope that soon escalated into what contemporaries dubbed the Kulturkampf, or culture war.

The Kulturkampf was a reaction to Pope Pius IX's ultramontane stance, designed to counter the doctrines he so vigorously propounded, such as the condemnation of liberalism, free thought, modern science, secular education, civil marriage, the right of Protestants to worship in Catholic countries, and any interference by the state in Church matters, which were set forth in the 1864 *Syllabus*, and cemented by the dogma of papal infallibility in 1870.[7] To match that of the pope, Bismarck's position was no less radical, and it found expression in the expulsion of the Jesuit, Franciscan, and Dominican orders, the assertion of the right to appoint and dismiss Catholic clergy, the seizure of Church property, the expulsion of ultraconservative priests, the limitation of freedom of speech for Catholic priests (the "pulpit paragraph"), and an end to school supervision by the Church. Thanks to Bismarck's anti-Catholic laws—which Pope Pius declared null and void[8]—all Prussian bishops had been imprisoned or exiled by 1876. By the time the Kulturkampf ended, some 1,800

Catholic priests throughout Germany had been fined or sentenced to prison.[9] One of them was Schleyer.

The Kulturkampf erupted in southern Baden, in the region of Messkirch, where Schleyer was serving. More important, Messkirch was also the center of the Old Catholics movement, a schismatic group of liberal-leaning Catholics who allied with Bismarck and opposed the pontificate of Pius IX.[10] While liberal Catholics sought a more conciliatory position that would spare them from having to choose between Church and state,[11] the Old Catholics were vehement in their animosity toward the pope. They defiantly rejected not only his teachings, but his very position at the top of the Catholic hierarchy. The Old Catholics wanted to replace the centralized and hierarchical structure of the Catholic Church with a different organizational model based on the old diocesan episcopate, which was believed to be more in keeping with the traditions of the first four centuries of Christianity, when the bishop of Rome had no primacy over his peers. Although not strong in numbers, their earnest Catholic beliefs and Bismarck's support placed the Old Catholics at the forefront of the Kulturkampf, and local authorities usually chose them to replace Catholic priests as inspectors of schools.[12] Their open cooperation with state authorities earned them very harsh penalties from Rome.

As a young priest in Messkirch, Schleyer took an active part in the Kulturkampf by implementing the repressive measures the pope decreed against the Old Catholics. When he refused to give a proper burial to an Old Catholic in his parish, he was sentenced to four months in prison, after which his superiors commissioned him to serve in the small and more peaceful town of Litzelstetten. During the Kulturkampf, Schleyer positioned himself among the most loyal Church members, in sharp contrast to the position taken by Kerckhoffs, his most outspoken rival in the Volapük movement, and also a Catholic. As a doctoral student at the University of Bonn, he had supported the Old Catholic movement (although Schleyer appears not to have been aware of this).[13]

In his confrontation with Kerckhoffs, Schleyer did not bother to devise a new strategy, but instead envisioned this confrontation as a new battle in the war between the revealed truth and its enemies. First, he wielded an organization that closely resembled the Church itself.[14] Rigid and hierarchical, it even included a Senate, analogous to the Roman prelature (to which he would be promoted in his final years), whose members were selected on the basis of personal loyalty rather than merit. Second, he pursued the same strategies he used during the Kulturkampf. Like Pius IX, he asserted his own infallibility in all matters relating to the language, and when reformists challenged his authority, he ex-communicated them by striking their names off the official journal. Like the pope, Schleyer demanded unswerving loyalty. Voice was out of the question, and exit was the sole path open to those who wanted to contribute their ideas to the movement. Volapük, Schleyer hinted, had come to him as a sort of revelation, and in the same way that the pope was the Vicar of Christ, he saw himself as the ultimate guardian of Volapük.

Although he spent his entire life in monolingual Baden, Schleyer was a polyglot. He had learned many languages, but he had done so in the same way he had learned Latin, the lingua franca of the international organization in which he worked: by studying grammars and dictionaries. Unexposed to the evolving and adaptive character of living languages in multilingual settings, he thought that, very much like Latin, a language is a closed system materialized in a grammar and dictionary. If this is the nature of a language, then it is possible to create a language, contrary to the opinion of German linguists. One only needs to write the necessary textbooks and dictionaries. The idea that a language can be satisfactorily contained in a handbook and a dictionary naturally leads to the conclusion that, for that language to expand, disputes about words or rules should be suppressed. Thus, Schleyer's conception of language as a self-contained system fit very closely with his authoritarian strategy. Theoretically, he admitted, Volapük could be reformed, but not in a manner that could undermine the hierarchical principles inherent in this conception, and embodied in the printed word.

The language was Volapük, but the meta-language was authority. And authority he learned from his decades of service to the Catholic Church.

As he explained in his anonymously published *100 Gründe warum ich katolische bleibe* (100 reasons why I remain a Catholic), the Catholic Church is superior to other churches not only because of its doctrine but, more important, because it has "the highest and most sacred regard for unity and unanimity, [as well as] a visible leader . . . who has never made a mistake . . . and has a powerful central office in Rome."[15]

When Schleyer came across Volapük that memorable night in 1879, he did not think much about the possible applications of his language. Satisfied with his own genius, he let his supporters think about the problems his Volapük could solve.

To his surprise, these problems were many. As his supporters showed, Volapük could help solve the problem of scientific communication and facilitate international transactions. Volapük could also be the language of peace, or even a literary language capable of the most accurate and creative translations of the most important literary works of humanity. Volapük could deter the spread of English or, depending on national interests, German and French. Volapük could have expanded in many different directions and for different purposes. But this did not happen.

Esperanto was the opposite case. Its inventor created the language as a solution to a pressing problem: the preservation of the rights, dignity, and integrity of the Jewish people, and, by extension, of all peoples in an era dominated by international rivalries, ethnic hatred, and tribal nationalism. And, contrary to Schleyer, he was able to solve the coordination problem posed by the reformists and let his language spread in the different and sometimes contradictory directions that had begun to appear within the Volapükist movement before Schleyer decided to purge it.

PART II

Esperanto

CHAPTER 7

"The Purpose of My Whole Life": Zamenhof and Esperanto

In 1937, the Soviet Esperanto movement was liquidated. Some of its leaders were shot, and many others were sent to the Gulag. There is some evidence that Jews were overrepresented among the Russian Esperantists. One-third of the leading Esperantists of Petrograd who fell victim to the 1937 purge were Jews.[1] This connection between the Jewish people and Esperanto did not go unnoticed by the Nazis. In 1939, the German Esperanto association was dismantled under the conviction that the language was the "weapon of the Jews" in their struggle for world dominance.[2]

Hitler had already made much the same charge in *Mein Kampf*: "As long as the Jew has not become the master of the other peoples, he must speak their languages whether he likes it or not, but as soon as they become his slaves, they would all have to learn a universal language (Esperanto, for instance!), so that by this additional means the Jews could more easily dominate them!"[3]

Although by the early 1930s the association between the Jewish people and Esperanto was somehow diluted, it was quite strong in the language's early years. Ludwig Zamenhof (1859–1917), the inventor of Esperanto, was a Jew, and his language first flourished in the Jewish milieu of Eastern Europe. It is precisely because of his Jewishness, as Zamenhof confided in a letter to fellow Esperantist Alfred Michaux, that he acquired the necessary determination and obstinacy to launch a new international language:

I am a Jew, and all my ideals, their birth, maturity and steadfastness, the entire history of my constant inner and external conflicts, all are indissolubly linked to my Jewishness. . . . If I had not been a Jew from the ghetto, the idea of uniting humanity either would never have entered in my head or it would never have gripped me so tenaciously throughout my entire life. No one can feel more strongly than a ghetto Jew the sadness of dissension among peoples. . . . My Jewishness is the main reason why, from earliest childhood, I gave myself wholly to one overarching idea and dream, that of bringing together in brotherhood all humanity. . . . That idea is the vital element and the purpose of my whole life. The Esperanto project is merely a part of that idea; I am constantly thinking and dreaming about the rest of it.[4]

Ludwig Zamenhof was born in Białystok, a relatively prosperous and industrialized town in what is today Poland but at the time was part of the Russian empire.[5] Białystok was a multi-ethnic but predominantly Jewish town. Ethnic Germans, Poles, Russians, Lithuanians, and Belarusians constituted 30 percent of its inhabitants, while the rest were Jews. Culturally, it was a center of the Haskalah movement, the Jewish version of the German Enlightenment.[6] Russian *maskilim*, or supporters of Haskalah, had a difficult challenge. They were against superstition, opposed to both traditional Judaism and mystical Hasidim, and in favor of political and religious tolerance. Convinced that there was room for a distinct Jewish culture in Imperial Russia, provided that Jews embraced a more secularized worldview, they promoted the emancipation and integration of Jews. Among many other measures, they sought reform of the existing Jewish school curriculum in order to give more emphasis to occupational training and instruction in science, philosophy, Hebrew, and Jewish and Russian history. They were confident that progress was inevitable even in fairly backward Russian society, and that some changes in Jewish mores and folkways would grant them full recognition as loyal Russians, albeit distinctively Jewish.[7]

Zamenhof's father was a maskil. His loyalty to the tsar and condemnation of the 1863–64 Polish uprising won him a teaching position in a Warsaw gymnasium and the opportunity to become a civil servant.[8] This professional advancement placed him among the very few Jews who could give their children a university education.[9] In 1879, his son Ludwig began his studies in medicine at the University of Moscow. But two years later Ludwig had to return to his parents because of the wave of pogroms that began in Ukraine and reached Warsaw by Christmas 1881.

The pogroms had a tremendous impact on Ludwig Zamenhof. They were concentrated in the territories of the Pale of Settlement—present-day Poland, Belarus, Lithuania, Latvia, and Moldova—where the Jews where confined, and did not subside until September 1882, when the government finally decided to act against the perpetrators. All in all, from April 1881 to September 1882, several hundred Jews were killed, mutilated, or raped, and thousands lost property. The pogroms were a grim landmark in the history of Russian Jewry.[10] They shattered the confidence of the maskilim and made the prospect of emancipation within Russian society seem unattainable. It was certainly troubling to see the Russian government blaming the Jews for the violence, and further punishing them with new antisemitic measures. More disturbing was the silence and indifference of the liberal Russian intelligentsia.

The 1881 pogroms were a litmus test for the maskilim and Haskalah ideals. To many, and more particularly to young Jewish intellectuals, the pogroms illustrated the futility of the old dream of Jewish integration into the Russian empire. In fact, driven by the antisemitism of tsarist officials and an enduring economic crisis, from 1881 to 1914 around a quarter of the Jews living in the Pale emigrated to other countries, mostly to the United States. The pogroms made evident the need for new ideas and leadership, and the Jewish press, printed in Russian, Yiddish, and Hebrew, was crucial in this new period. Two articles written by Moshe Leib Lilienblum, an old and now-tormented maskil, changed the orientation of a divided Jewish press, then undecided about mass emigration. According to Lilienblum, it was a mistake to explain the pogroms as a transient phenomenon, or the natural consequence of the relative backwardness of Russian society. As long as Jews were aliens in their hosting societies, be they in Eastern or Western Europe, they would always be endangered. Lilienblum was convinced that assimilation was unrealistic. The more the Jews advanced in their societies, the more resentment they aroused. Nationalist movements in Europe and the "universal antipathy" that this ideology conveyed against anybody who was not considered a member of the hosting nation meant that the Jews could never dream of a safe place. Their only hope was to claim their own territory. For Lilienblum, that territory was Palestine.[11]

Lilienblum's articles convinced many, particularly young people, of the urgency of mass migration, a "new exodus," as the more Orthodox interpreted his argument. But even when historical and religious reasons recommended Palestine, some thought it should not become the final destination of the Jews.

If the old Haskalah agenda could not be realized in Russia, it could still be possible in the United States, where Jews could become loyal American citizens with a distinctive Jewish identity.

This was the position of the renowned Hebrew poet Yehuda L. Levin (pseudonym Yehalel); Yehuda L. Gordon, also a poet; and Lev O. Levanda, a poet and a formerly convinced Russifier and Russian patriot. It was also the position of Zamenhof, who made his views public in *Razsvet*. By early 1882, the debate between the supporters of America and the Palestinophiles, as they were called, was already over: the last Christmas pogrom in Warsaw made all of them—Levin, Gordon, Levanda, and Zamenhof—change their views and rally for Palestine.[12]

In February 1882, Zamenhof co-founded Warsaw's local Hovevei Zion chapter.[13] Hovevei Zion, a proto-Zionist organization, raised funds and helped colonists establish the foundations of a new society in Palestine. By 1883 there were only a dozen Hovevei Zion chapters in Russian territory. Until 1890, when the Russian government granted them legal status, Hovevei Zion chapters had to operate semi-clandestinely. In these conditions, they could hardly coordinate with each other, which prevented them from gaining political momentum. Although they were a failure in the eyes of many contemporaries, Hovevei Zion and its activities kept alive the Palestinian dream in those years, paving the way for the enthusiastic reception of Theodor Herzl's vision of Zionism in Russia.[14]

But only two years after the founding of the Warsaw Hovevei Zion society, Zamenhof was already disillusioned. He was not alone. By the mid-1880s, when the violence was over and the emotionally charged atmosphere of the previous years had dissipated, Gordon, Duvnov, and other former advocates of the Palestine project were reconsidering it to be an unattainable utopia, an escapist response to terrifying events.[15] But Zamenhof's disillusionment was perhaps deeper. His chapter had focused on helping young BILU members establish colonies in Palestine.[16] They were a self-proclaimed vanguard of university and gymnasium students, imbued by agrarian communalism and nationalist ideas. Baron Rothschild's refusal to support them, their lack of experience with agricultural labor, and personal rivalries ruined the experiment. In 1885, only around twenty of the fifty or sixty Biluim who moved to Palestine settled there. The rest either returned to Russia or emigrated to America.[17] Although a legend in Zionist historical memory, the BILU experiment was hardly a source of pride among contemporaries, Zamenhof included.[18]

Even more disillusioning to Zamenhof was the drift in Hovevei Zion toward a Jewish nationalism.[19] By 1884 Zamenhof had run out of patience with proposals of this kind. In Warsaw intellectuals including his friend Nahum Sokolow, the director of the newspaper *Ha-Zefirah,* were also critical of this nationalistic inflection in the movement and with the concessions that the new leadership was making to the Orthodox rabbinate for the sake of national unity.[20] If the problem was nationalism, they reasoned, the solution was not more nationalism, but less.

Certainly, while a student at the University of Moscow, Zamenhof had fallen under the nationalist spell, as had many other representatives of national minorities in Central and Eastern Europe. Influenced by the linguistic Romanticism of Herder, Fichte, and others, nationalist intellectuals were busy reinventing and standardizing their languages. By 1884, Czech, Slovak, Lithuanian, Serbo-Croatian, and Rusyn nationalist movements were relatively advanced in the standardization of their national languages. Now the Romanians, Finns, Norwegians, and Estonians wanted to have their own literary corpus.[21] The young Zamenhof contributed to this trend. During his studies at the University of Moscow, and in order to provide Russian Jews with a common language and identity, he crafted a proposal for the standardization of Yiddish as the language of the Jews.[22] But not much later he decided to end this project, since, as he explained, "I thought that the awakening of a sort of national patriotism among the Jews could be detrimental for them, as well as for the ideal of the unity of the human race."[23]

A leading figure of the proto-Zionist movement, Zamenhof later became rather critical of nationalism, Jewish or otherwise. Manipulating a language to draw a firm line between us and them, purifying it from foreign words, and choosing an appropriate script to convey a suitable historical memory was, for Zamenhof, a dangerous and divisive game. He was an idealist, but not naïve. He did not think that a common international language would bring peace among nations. There were other sources of conflict, such as economic interests, and countries with a common language have also endured civil wars.

But being a Jew and living in Eastern Europe, he thought that ethnic conflicts were equally if not more dangerous than economic ones. He thought that a neutral, non-national language could reduce the antagonism among peoples that ethnonationalism fueled. It could prevent majorities from imposing their language on ethnic minorities. More important, communication in a non-ethnic language could help promote a non-national, cosmopolitan identity. As an adherent of Haskalah, he pursued assimilation. But not to a

Herderian type of society, a patchwork of homogeneous nations differently colored by their languages or religion.[24] Assimilation should take place in a new society where kinship, religion, and language were not used to discriminate among people. And a non-national language could help advance this ideal.

This conception of the role of an artificial language departed from those of Schleyer and most Volapükists. Whereas for the latter an artificial language would basically serve an instrumental, communicative function, for Zamenhof it had a political mission. He understood that, strategically, it was advisable to emphasize the benefits of an artificial language for international trade or scholarly exchange, but he never concealed his idea that a non-national language had to have a soul, a moral mission. Paradoxically, then, Zamenhof, was replicating the strategy he witnessed among Eastern European nationalist movements, although for quite the opposite intention. If nationalists were reinventing languages out of the linguistic varieties present in their territories to create separate national communities, Zamenhof invented a neutral language from the larger stock of Indo-European tongues to create a non-national community of speakers who could relate to each other as autonomous moral agents, and not as passive recipients of inherited or invented traditions.

In any case, Zamenhof's rejection of Zionism was not exceptional among the most educated Jews of Central and Eastern Europe. In his autobiography, and reflecting on his youth in Vienna, for example, the philosopher Karl Popper claimed that "all nationalism or racialism is evil, and Jewish nationalism is no exception."[25] Living between cultures, and feeling insecure in the countries where they were born, many Jewish intellectuals resorted to the cosmopolitanism embraced in the Enlightenment ideal. Popper found his cosmopolitan *Heimat* in the international community of scientists and philosophers committed to reason and the pursuit of truth, and in the never fully realized and always precarious institutions of an "Open Society," which might elevate man above the boundaries of his ethnic or religious tribe.[26] Others found their *Heimat* in the supranational ideals of socialism and the promise of universal brotherhood. Zamenhof's cosmopolitanism was also a reaction against the ethnopolitics of his time, always prone to put the Jews at the losing end. But his cosmopolitan solution to the Jewish question was quite novel: it involved the creation a new language.[27]

CHAPTER 8

"Let Us Work and Have Hope!": Language and Democracy

In a technological contest dominated by positive feedback mechanisms, it is important for a potential challenger to enter the contest as soon as possible to prevent the incumbent from gaining further ground. This was Zamenhof's intention when he learned of Volapük, but he did not publish the first handbook of Esperanto until 1887. He could have entered the contest earlier, as he had been working on an international language since he was nineteen, but his involvement in Hovevei Zion and lack of funds made it impossible to launch his project earlier. Only after he severed links with the proto-Zionist movement and prepared a final version of his manuscript did he search for a publisher. For two years his search was unsuccessful. Volapük was already there, not to mention its offspring language projects, and no publisher thought it a good idea to invest his own resources to add another language to the list. Only after Zamenhof married and decided to use his wife's dowry to cover publishing costs did his manuscript go to press.

The first Esperanto brochure, the *Unua Libro*, as it was later called, was published in Russian, and shortly thereafter translated into Polish, French, and German, followed by English, Hebrew, and Yiddish the next year.[1]

The *Unua Libro* was a forty-page textbook. It had a long preface, a description of the grammar, a small vocabulary, samples of translations, original poetry, and blank forms that readers could send to the author to demonstrate their intention to learn the language.[2] The book was published with the title *International Language: Preface and Complete Grammar*, under the pseudonym Dr. Esperanto, meaning "the one who has hope," which later became the language's official name. The book included the most essential elements of the language. The description of its grammar, less inflectional than Volapük, took only six pages. Esperanto grammar has only one case, the accusative, whereas Volapük has four. In accordance with the ideas of Alberto Liptay and Paul Steiner, the author of Pasilingua, root words were chosen according to their frequency among Indo-European languages, which resulted in an ascendancy of Latin words. For example, *domo*, from "domus," is the Esperanto word for "house," and *patro* means "father." As with Volapük, spelling is phonetical. The Esperanto alphabet is Latin-based. It contains twenty-eight letters: twenty-three consonants and five vowels. Like the standardized Lithuanian, which borrowed diacritics from the Czech alphabet to distinguish itself from the Polish language and nation,[3] Esperanto incorporates diacritics in five consonants, ĉ, ĝ, ĥ, ĵ, and ŝ, and the semivowel ŭ. To give a glimpse of the language, "Je la komenco Dio kreis la ĉielon kaj la teron" means "In the beginning God created the heavens and the earth."

Equally important as the structure and qualities of the language, for those willing to volunteer their time and energy to create a public good such as an international language, was the strategy outlined in the *Unua Libro* for Esperanto's expansion. By 1887, when the *Unua Libro* was published, the conflicts between Schleyer and the reformists were beginning to surface. Aware of them, and eager to declare Esperanto a better project, Zamenhof presented himself as Schleyer's opposite. For example, on the second page of his book, and in bold letters, he declared: "The international language, as any other language, should be a common property, for which its author resigns forever to all personal rights to it."[4]

Whereas Schleyer insisted on his genius, Zamenhof claimed that his language could be amended or improved: "I am but a man, and may easily fall into error."[5] To emphasize his receptivity he asked interested people to give him feedback and send their suggestions. He promised to reflect on them and make public a more definite version of the language the next year. If this new version was not entirely satisfactory, Zamenhof proposed that a representative body of language users make final decisions. The *Unua Libro* was advancing not only a new language, but also a different, potentially more engaging and participative strategy to spread the language.

Participation for the purpose of refining the language and giving it its final shape was not Zamenhof's primary directive to his future supporters, however. He was honest when he asked for feedback to improve the language, but he also wanted to prevent future Esperantists from getting involved in fruitless and potentially damaging nitpicking about this or that word or grammatical rule. Rather than being involved in amateur linguistic discussions, he was asking his readers not only to learn, but, more urgently, to use the language right away. Whereas he was the only Esperantist, there were thousands of Volapükists, and the sooner a community of speakers emerged, the more likely Esperanto was to survive.

Since it was inconceivable that everybody would agree on all aspects of his language, he knew that sooner or later he would face the same coordination problem that was poisoning the Volapükist community. But the later, the better, he thought; and when necessary or unavoidable, conflicts could be resolved democratically. In the meantime, and instead of pondering its qualities and defects, the language should be used, either to translate from other languages or to produce original work. Like the nationalist movements around him, but contrary to many Volapükists who did not think that their language was useful for literary purposes, Zamenhof wanted to create a literary corpus.

His repeated insistence to learn and use the language right away, "whether the language receives a universal approbation or not," and "independent of others making the same" decision, became a pivotal component of Zamenhof's strategy.[6] It was later condensed under the buzzword "Antaŭen!" or "Go ahead!"—meaning "go ahead no matter the odds or the presumed strength of its rivals."

Zamenhof could not predict the extent to which Esperantists would heed his request to act spontaneously, or what the future held. But to facilitate things, he made it clear that he did not have a big ego or a personal interest in the language. His only interest was to provide the human race with a common good. The nature of this good was somewhat ambiguous. He made a passing reference to the political benefits of a non-national lingua franca,[7] but prudence recommended that he focus on more pragmatic issues, such as the dissemination of ideas and the advancement of science and commerce.

In any case, it was necessary to identify those most willing to learn the language: either because they were convinced that it could help advance the human race, or because they felt that Esperanto was something other, and more, than a language—perhaps a new initiative very much in line with other modernizing ideas opposed to tsarist rule. To do this, Zamenhof added blank forms in his *Unua Libro* and asked readers to send them back, to express either their disbelief or their willingness to study the language, no matter how many others followed suit. This last group of respondents, the *senkondiĉuloj*, or "unconditional," was Zamenhof's target. They were the building blocks of the new movement, provided that they communicated with each other and created a community of speakers.

And this was precisely the next step: to put language users in contact with each other. Zamenhof began the series of address books, which included the names and addresses of Esperanto users. The first address book was released in 1889, two years after the publication of the *Unua Libro*.

Retrospectively, Zamenhof's strategy looks like the masterwork of a brilliant tactician. Aware that he had entered a contest where positive feedback mechanisms were working for the incumbent, Zamenhof urged his potential followers to learn and use the language as soon and as much as possible, and no matter the prospects of Esperanto vis-à-vis Volapük. This strategy activated the "quasi-irreversibility of investment factors," to use Davis's terms, that can best create a hard core of loyalists.[8] Just as a skilled QWERTY user is not likely to shift to a different keyboard absent certainty about the new keyboard's ultimate success, a skilled Esperantist would be equally disinclined to forgo his initial investment in the language, either by shifting to another project or pursuing radical reforms. Also, Zamenhof's open invitation to participate and offer feedback, his withdrawal of any personal rights, and his insistence that the language was a common property further increased its appeal. His subtle indication that Esperanto could also serve political goals could only help him enlarge and diversify the movement base by attracting yet another interest group, even if this strategy would later cause tensions. Although he was asking his followers for their feedback, Zamenhof was more concerned about their willingness to learn and use the language than their potential criticisms.

Zamenhof's work plan, though, is better explained not as the product of a farsighted strategist but by his democratic convictions and his ideas about how languages work. He elaborated these beliefs in the *Dua Libro*, or second textbook, and its supplement (*Aldono al la Dua Libro*), published in 1888. They were the first books printed entirely in Esperanto and are critical to understanding Zamenhof's mutually reinforcing ideas about politics and language. According to him, languages are not autonomous, self-contained systems that can live independently of their speakers. Languages do not have lives of their own. Rather, they can only exist and possibly change and evolve through continuous interactions among speakers. It is always possible to arbitrarily arrange the blueprint of a new language, as he did, but this does not mean that the language has been brought to life. For a language to exist there has to be a community of speakers that creatively uses it to produce meaning and set in motion its ongoing evolution. This explains why Zamenhof preferred to portray himself as the "initiator" rather than the "creator" of Esperanto.[9] A language, Zamenhof writes, is a democratic, self-governing cultural product, where only the communicative needs and literary skills of its speakers can affect its future course.[10] A language, thus, cannot be governed. It develops "step by step," not through a formal decision-making process but as the by-product of an ongoing process of imitation and creativity, of incorporation of new words or conventions and the obliteration of old ones.[11] According to him, formal decision-making bodies are unnecessary for a language to sustain itself and develop, as the history of languages demonstrates. It is the community of speakers, not an ad hoc organization that ensures the consistency and future of a language.

Things are a little bit different with artificial languages, however. Artificial users might think that this or that rule is better and request a procedure to settle the issue. But such a request would violate the very essence of an artificial language since, although non-natural, it is still a language: the byproduct of an ongoing communicative interaction and not a series of formal, authoritative decisions. Thus, if not for the language itself, it is for the need to prevent discordance that those demands have to be attended. Discord and disagreement about usage would best be dealt with through democratic procedures, Zamenhof felt. These procedures reflect the communal nature of a language, and are also more likely to help build a shared commitment to its foundations, or *fundamento*. Further support for democratic procedures comes from the idea that right and proper decisions about the language and its foundations are not necessarily those that come from linguists. As Zamenhof also made clear, he was not a trained linguist, but a person "with no merits, and unknown to the world":

> I am not looking for praise. I only want people to help me eliminate the mistakes I have made; and the more severe their criticism is, the more I will appreciate them. . . . I am very aware that the work of *a single person* cannot be free from errors, even if this man is the most brilliant, or much more educated than me. Therefore, I have not given to my tongue its final shape. I cannot tell you "Here you have the language: finished and ready; and this is the way I would like it to be and remain."[12]

Since languages attain consistency and evolve by adapting to their speakers' communication needs, intuitively right and proper decisions are more likely to come from speakers than from theoretical arguments advanced by linguists, professionals, or dilettantes. Hence Zamenhof's call to learn and use the language: to better capture its inner nature and make informed, empirical, democratic decisions when and if the time came for improvements.

Zamenhof's strategic recipe, advanced in his *Dua Libro* and reasserted throughout his life, was straightforward: one should let Esperanto "live, grow, and progress according to the same rules that apply to any other language."[13] The blueprints of this language, already set up in the *Unua Libro*, should serve as the foundations of this undertaking. If necessary, these could be changed according to the opinion of its community of speakers. But to avoid possible mistakes and obtain informed opinions, Esperantists should, first of all, develop as much familiarity with the language as possible, which required the production of original work and translations.

And this should be done as if there were no other contestants in sight. There was a battle of artificial languages, no question about it, and Zamenhof commonly referred to Esperantists as *batalantoj*, or combatants. This battle, however, was not so much against other language projects as against the temptation to introduce reforms rashly, and against the indifference of the general public. *Ni laboru kaj esperu!* "Let us work and have hope!" was Zamenhof's rallying call.[14]

CHAPTER 9

"The Menacing Thunderstorm of Reforms": First Esperantists and First Crises

It might seem that Esperanto entered the artificial language contest late, and at the wrong time. But the opposite is true: Had Zamenhof published his *Unua Libro* in 1885, as he intended, we would probably not be speaking about Esperanto today. In 1888, a window of opportunity opened, and Zamenhof happened to be there. That year, the splinter Volapükist club of Nuremberg was looking for an alternative. They could not credibly adopt any of the other previous language projects that they had severely criticized, so they chose the next in line, and that happened to be Esperanto.

Had Zamenhof been able to publish his first textbook when he intended, most probably he would have shared the same destiny as the authors of Spelin or Pasilingua. In 1888, fortune was on Zamenhof's side.

Critical for the Nuremberg Volapükist club's shift to Esperanto was its president, the journalist and teacher of Judaism Leopold Einstein (1833–1890). Einstein was probably the Volapükist with the most profound knowledge of old and contemporary artificial language projects. Among others, he corresponded with Bauer and Lott, whose proposals he had also discarded. In 1888, Einstein read the *Unua Libro* and saw in it the perfect substitute for Volapük. That same year he published *La lingvo internacia als beste Lösung des internationalen Weltspracheproblems* (The lingvo internacia as the best solution to the world language problem) and managed to sway the Nuremberg club to Zamenhof's side. As he saw it, Volapük was hopeless. Not even "the most resourceful and careful reparations and patchery can ever make [the Volapük house] habitable."[1] Einstein was taken with Esperanto not only because of the problems he saw in Volapük. Equally important seemed to be Zamenhof's unassuming character, as opposed to Schleyer's authoritarianism and "mystical obfuscation."[2] Notwithstanding his "ceaseless . . . bragging" about his love of humanity, Schleyer had not refrained from including in his dictionary words such as *jüdeln* and *Jüdelei*.[3] When Einstein shifted to Zamenhof's project, he was rather sick. He died in 1890. By then, he had become close friends with Zamenhof, who, hearing of his death, acknowledged his friend's fearless defense of Esperanto, no matter the "abuse" he had to endure in his last years from his former fellow Volapükists.[4]

The example of Einstein and other members of the Nuremberg club, however, did not reverberate far. With the exception of some other ex-Volapükists in current North Rhine-Westphalia, very few supporters of Schleyer's language shifted to Esperanto. Thus, from a total of 1,709 Volapükists included in the official records of Schleyer, Kerckhoffs, and the editorial board of *Rund um die Welt*, only about 20 of them appeared in the first *Adresaro*, or address book, containing the names and addresses of the first 1,000 Esperantists.[5] In fact, and as might be expected, the membership of Volapük and Esperanto at this time was quite unevenly distributed. Volapük had mostly taken hold in Germanic-speaking and/or Catholic territories (with Bavaria, Baden, the Rhineland, Flanders, present-day Austria, and the Netherlands amounting to 60 percent of the Volapükists), while 92 percent of the first 1,000 Esperantists were living in Russian territories. Such a non-uniform distribution of the two language movements reflects the quasi-irreversibility factor: only those most committed to the idea of an international language were willing to forgo their investment in Volapük and learn a new language, but Russia was unexplored territory for those making their first commitment.[6]

If the German ex-Volapükists were insignificant in terms of membership numbers, they were crucial in other ways. Like Schleyer, Zamenhof wanted to have a journal, which would serve as a meeting place for the emerging community of Esperantists and as a written record that would help Esperanto establish its literary standard. For this purpose, he planned to launch *The Internationalist*, but the tsarist authorities rejected his request. The Nuremberg club stepped in and offered to launch *La Esperantisto*. They believed, correctly, that it would be easier to circumvent the tsarist censorship if the journal were published in Germany and later distributed in Russia. The ex-Volapükists' offer, however, was not unconditional. In exchange for their offer, they requested that Zamenhof consider a radical reform in the language. Zamenhof accepted the challenge, and in September 1889 the first volume of *La Esperantisto* was published.[7]

In December 1889, *La Esperantisto* announced that its purpose was to create an International League of Esperantists and asked its readers to contribute ideas about the bylaws of the future organization, and, more concretely, about the rules that would allow the league to introduce changes in the language. Zamenhof made the announcement, even when he clearly indicated that, at this stage, he thought it more useful to produce a body of literature than ponder potential reforms. But as long as there were people who thought otherwise, he was determined to settle the issue and proceed with the creation of the league.[8] Three months later, *La Esperantisto* published the bylaws of the league and, to the surprise of many readers, also announced that the league was already operative. According to the bylaws, annual elections would be held to choose the ten members who would compose a future language academy. The electorate would be composed of local clubs, and each club would have one vote for every twenty members. The ten members of the Academy could introduce reforms, which would only require the approval of six members. If a local club objected to a reform, it would be submitted to a referendum, in which all local clubs could vote.

Although democratic, these statutes were not acceptable for Zamenhof. He had been discussing with members of the Nuremberg club different drafts of the bylaws, the prerogatives of its academy, and the mechanisms to introduce reforms, but the bylaws finally published in *La Esperantisto* were not the result of a common understanding. They only represented the ideas of the German ex-Volapükists and had been published without Zamenhof's agreement. As he confided to a Russian Esperantist: "I had drafted completely different bylaws, but Mr. Schmidt [the president of the Nuremberg club after Einstein's death], without telling me a single word in advance, changed the whole spirit of my bylaws, and, under my name, he gave them their current form, which is something that I cannot approve of."[9] Zamenhof could not accept such bylaws because an electorate comprising local clubs would place the Russian Esperantists at a disadvantage, given their difficulties in establishing legal Esperanto associations under tsarist rule. The German ex-Volapükists might not have been aware of these difficulties, but Zamenhof was. He claimed that, if the published bylaws were accepted, the local club of a little German town, comprising people who might have not learned the language but current with their fees, could be more influential than a much greater number of isolated but active Russian Esperantists.[10]

It took four months for Zamenhof and the Germans to restore trust and reach a cooperative agreement, during which time *La Esperantisto* was dormant.[11] The terms of the final agreement, outlined in the November 1890 issue of *La Esperantisto*, included setting aside the creation of the league in exchange for a serious consideration of some radical reforms in the language. Thus, from April 1891 on, the journal began inserting reform proposals sent by the readers and opened a public debate about them. In January 1893, *La Esperantisto* announced that, in order to make a decision about those proposals, it would hold a referendum, in which all journal subscribers would have the right to vote. For the sake of transparency, and to facilitate private communications among subscribers, the journal included their names and addresses. For a year and half, Esperantists were using a language to discuss whether that same language should or should not be reformed. Two opposing views emerged from this debate. On the one side were those convinced that the ultimate victory of Esperanto hinged on its proximity to the ideal of a perfect language.

On the other side were Zamenhof and likeminded Esperantists, who were convinced that building a community of speakers and a literary corpus was more important than trying to perfect the language. These opposing principles embodied two different conceptions about the nature and goals of an international language. If primarily considered as an instrument of communication, then the more fine-tuned or technically perfect language should, ultimately, prevail and be accepted by the international community. Its fate can be foretold by its grammar and vocabulary. But if conceived as a political instrument, then the larger a language's community of speakers, the more likely it would triumph. For Zamenhof and likeminded Esperantists, the fate of an international language could not be predicted by its technical merits and attributes, since it depended on the more fluid factors of the number and commitment of its speakers.

These contrasting views were tested in the November 1894 referendum, when only a sub-sample of the Esperantists—namely, the subscribers to *La Esperantisto*—had to decide whether or not to reform the language. The ballot gave the victory to Zamenhof and the anti-reformists, but not an overwhelming one. Whereas 157 voted against reforming the language, 107 wanted reforms, and many more abstained. More important, and as Table 1 shows, the referendum disclosed a clear-cut divide in the Esperanto community: following Zamenhof's advice, most of the Russian Esperantists had voted against the proposed reforms, while most of the German ex-Volapükists and West-

Table 1. Results of the 1894 Referendum on Reforms in Esperanto

	Abstain	For reforms	Against reforms	Total
Unknown residence	10	9	4	23
Residents in Russian territories	176	12	117	305
Residents in Western Europe	71	86	36	193
Total	257	107	157	521

Source: *La Esperantisto* (November 1894): 161–62.

ern European Esperantists were convinced that only a reformed Esperanto had a chance to succeed.

Zamenhof was quite relieved with this result. As he confided to a fellow Russian Esperantist: "As a result of this debate about reforms we have wasted the whole year. But I cannot complain, since the final result has been quite positive. The menacing thunderstorm of reforms has disappeared, and the atmosphere has cleared once and forever. . . . Our cause is now safe, and we can apply all our energies to extend [Esperanto]."[12]

But his was a Pyrrhic victory. In the first place, the long, open discussion in *La Esperantisto* about the need for or, contrarily, the danger of reforms had drastically reduced the number of supporters. If in 1893 *La Esperantisto* boasted close to 900 subscribers, by the 1894 referendum, only half of them were still current with their subscriptions. Second, and more important, as a result of the ballot, many reform-minded Esperantists abandoned the movement. In 1894, ninety-eight Germans subscribed to *La Esperantisto*, but the next year there were only ten. The referendum had certainly cleaned up the atmosphere, but there were many fewer people to breathe it.

To stop the attrition, Zamenhof made a desperate move. He reached an agreement with the Posrednik publishing group, which allowed him to reproduce articles from Tolstoy in *La Esperantisto*. He calculated that this arrangement would increase the appeal of his journal, but the tsarist regime could not tolerate his alliance with the Tolstoyans. The Russian government prohibited the circulation of *La Esperantisto* in its territory, where three-quarters of its subscribers lived. This was the *coup de grace*, and in June 1895 *La Esperantisto* published its last issue.

Zamenhof's eagerness to strike an alliance with the Tolstoyans did not surprise fellow Russian Esperantists. As Zamenhof explained, the

Tolstoyans also craved universal justice and fraternity far above and beyond national or religion affinities.[13] This demonstrates the extent to which Zamenhof's political vision of Esperanto was shared in the region, in contrast to the more instrumental position of western Esperantists.

Of particular significance is the embrace of Esperanto in Jewish circles. In his private correspondence, Zamenhof confided that there were many Jews among the first *senkondiĉuloj*, or unconditional Esperantists.[14] In fact, 64 percent of the first 1,000 Esperantists included in the first *Adresaro* lived in the Pale of Settlement. Also, a brief look at the biographies of the first Esperanto writers illustrates the kind of people living in Eastern Europe who felt attracted to Esperanto: mostly, people driven by ethical and political commitments rather than by an interest in the advancement of commerce and science. Thus, out of the first six Russian Esperantists who published original work in this language, three had a political résumé that could only make a tsarist official raise his eyebrows. They were Leo Belmont (1865–1940), a Jewish lawyer who had served five terms in jail before being permanently removed from the bar; Vasili N. Borovko (1863–1913), who had learned Esperanto in Siberia in 1889, where he was exiled; and Aleksandras Dambrauskas (1860–1938), a Catholic priest who translated and smuggled copies of *Unua Libro* into Lithuania, since the Russian government had prohibited publications in Lithuanian.[15]

A vague, quasi-messianic idealism, heralded with broad appeals to universal fraternity and justice, had helped the language overcome its first crisis, but it could not keep it alive. A year after *La Esperantisto* was forced to close, a new journal, *Lingvo Internacia*, published in Uppsala, was launched, but the dwindling number of Esperantists did not provide a solid platform for takeoff. Also, Zamenhof had to set aside his work on Esperanto and concentrate his energies on making a living from his private practice as an eye doctor. Languishing in Eastern Europe and about to disappear in Germany, it seemed that Esperanto was going to share Volapük's fate. Under these circumstances, Zamenhof asked French Esperantists for help.[16]

CHAPTER 10

The French Resurgence

In 1898, a year after Zamenhof turned to French Esperantists for help, Louis de Beaufront launched *L'Espérantiste*, a bilingual French and Esperanto journal. A man of humble origins, de Beaufront was very ambitious. He had managed to climb the social ladder and become the private tutor in a wealthy family. Well connected, de Beaufront concentrated his campaign for Esperanto among the intellectuals and the upper echelons of French society. He quickly recruited to the cause a small clique of highly regarded public personalities who became the center of the international Esperanto movement until the outbreak of World War I. They were Émile Boirac, professor of philosophy and rector of the University of Dijon; Carlo Bourlet, professor of mathematics and mechanics; Théophile Cart, professor of foreign languages at the École Libre de Sciences Politiques; and General Hippolyte Sebert, a scientist and artillery specialist, managing director of a public shipyard company, secretary of the French Academy of Sciences, president of the Association française pour l'avancement des sciences, and member of the International Institute of Bibliography. Another prominent French Esperantist was Émile Javal, a twenty-year member of the National Assembly, head of the Ophthalmology Laboratory at the University of Sorbonne, and member of the Academy of Medicine. Like Zamenhof, Laval was of Jewish origin. He was the son of Leopold Javal, former vice-president of the Alliance Israelite Universalle. Javal became Zamenhof's closest confidant until his death in 1907. Gaston Moch, a former military officer and leading member of the international pacifist movement, was also an assimilated Jew.[1]

Founded when the passions unleashed by the Dreyfus Affair were still very much alive, *L'Espérantiste* did its best to portray Esperanto as a purely neutral, technical solution to the problem of international communication. It

silenced Zamenhof's political mission for Esperanto, explained in his fa-
mous letter to Borovko and published in 1896 in *Lingvo Internacia*. The
rampant antisemitism of key sectors of French society convinced the leading French Esperantists that it would be expedient to misrepresent Zamenhof as a Polish eye doctor. Concealing Zamenhof's Jewish identity was also a
convenient way to avoid internal conflicts between the Dreyfusards Moch
and Javal and the anti-Dreyfusards de Beaufront and Bourlet. This approach
required teasing apart the language and the political agendas that Zamenhof thought it could serve. As *L'Espérantiste* made officially clear: "Regarding the opinions and parties in which the world is divided, and available to
anybody who wants to use it, as it is the case with any other language, Esperanto remains and will remain independent."[2] Esperanto was thus portrayed
in narrow terms as the best realization of the long-awaited international language that the law of Progress demanded to promote the advancement of
science, commerce, finance, industry, and improved international relations.[3]

This instrumental depiction of Esperanto fit very well with the mainstream
political tradition of a République that presented itself as the embodiment of
universalism, secularism, rationalism, positivism, and faith in science and
progress.[4] Unlike Zamenhof and his quasi-messianic goal of bringing together
in brotherhood all humanity, as he expressed in his published letter to Borovko,[5] the leading French Esperantists portrayed themselves as respectable and
practical *citoyens*, allergic to any kind of utopianism. If Gaston Moch, René
Lemaire, and many other pacifists were attracted to Esperanto, they were
mostly moved by practical concerns, such as the establishment of an international arbitrage system, and worked through the official, well-respected
channels of regular politics.[6]

Catholics and freethinkers, military officers and pacifists, Dreyfusards and
anti-Dreyfusards: There was room for all of them in the eclectic ranks of the
French Esperanto leadership. More Eurocentric and cosmopolitan than internationalist, and characterized by practical and well-connected people, the
French Esperantists could safely work for the cause so long as they were not
stigmatized as hopeless dreamers, which occasionally required exiling the potentially embarrassing Zamenhof to the backstage.

They were very effective at their task. Originally promoted in scientific
circles and through the local press, Esperanto rapidly obtained some popularity among the educated elite. By the turn of the century, more French than
Russians sent their names and addresses to Zamenhof to be included in the
Adresaro, or address book (see Figure 2), and by 1902 there were more Espe-

Figure 2. Percentage of Russian and French people in the Esperanto movement, 1889–1901. Source: *Adresaroj*, 1889–1902, reprinted in Ludovikito, *Ludovikologia dokumentaro, IX. Adresaroj I, 1889–1902* (Tokio: Eldonejo Ludovikito, 1992).

ranto clubs in France than in any other country. In a short time, Esperanto had shifted its center of gravity from Russia to France.

A milestone in this process was the 1900 Universal Exposition, held in Paris. The Exposition was a bold celebration of the advancement of science and technology, and a privileged site to promote the idea of a standard, artificial language. Among the many scientific meetings that the Exposition had planned, there was the general conference of the French Association for the Advancement of Science, where de Beaufront made a presentation on "The Essence and Future of the Idea of an International Language," based on an unpublished article of Zamenhof's.[7] With the help of the Russian Esperantists, the Paris Esperanto group set up a permanent stand on the premises of the Exposition.

A more important but less visible milestone in the French popularization of Esperanto was the contract the following year that the French Esperantists managed to sign with the Hachette publishing group. Founded in 1826, Hachette's niche was affordable textbooks for the middle and working classes. Since 1860 it had also been the publisher of *Le Tour du monde*, a periodical that focused on travel and international issues. This was also a good platform to promote Esperanto. The deal with Hachette allowed Zamenhof to publish his manuscripts and also edit and approve the publication of dictionaries, handbooks, translations, and literary pieces written by other Esperantists.

Since Hachette had a scholarly department, the Esperantists aspired to give their language some academic stature. Hachette also had commercial ties in the most important European cities, which helped improve the visibility of the language across the continent. More important, the Esperanto book series published by Hachette became the main literary corpus of the language, facilitating the standardization of the language consistent with the 1894 referendum. All in all, the collaboration with Hachette helped protect the language against potential reformists and other contenders.[8]

The main contender by this time was not Volapük. In 1896, too busy rewriting his dictionary, Schleyer transferred the day-to-day business of the movement to his most loyal disciple, the Catholic teacher Carl Zetter (1842–1912) of Graz (Austria), who took over the editorial office of *Volapükabled zenodik* and published a third edition of Schleyer's handbook. Zetter was able to breathe some life into the movement, but Esperanto had effectively ruined it.[9]

This was, at least, Schleyer's interpretation. In 1910, when Volapük was an extinct linguistic species, he anonymously published a brochure against Esperanto: *Über die Pfuscher-Sprache des Pseudo-Esperanto* (On the botched, pseudo-Esperanto language). In this, his last word in the international language movement, Schleyer exuded bitterness. He drastically misrepresented the characteristics of Esperanto, conveying the idea that Zamenhof's language was a poor imitation of Volapük—an imitation that, according to Schleyer, was doomed to disappear, as had other imitations. "On Volapük a greater Genius, impelled by a long and deep study of languages, has revealed and manifested itself," he wrote. But "on the language systems proposed by its imitators, only simple capriciousness, vagaries and the sheer desire to get money or a name."[10]

The main challenger to Esperanto at the time was not Schleyer, however, but the Volapük Academy that his rivals still controlled. Led since 1893 by Waldemar Rosenberger, a German-speaking engineer who lived in Moscow, and after some years of inactivity, the Academy got down to work. Rosenberger's initial idea was to reform Schleyer's vocabulary, and to this end he began sending lists of new words to other Academy members, to vote on them. He soon realized that it would take years to complete a dictionary, so Rosenberger decided to put aside Volapük's word construction rules and create a brand new lexicon based on the same principles that Zamenhof and Liptay had proposed: namely, to use the most common roots of the more important natural languages.[11] This idea, however, also implied the construction of a new grammar. Since Volapük words began and ended with a consonant, and grammatical prefixes and suffixes were marked with vowels, the introduction of a common word such as "animal" demanded a new grammar. For Rosenberger, this realization meant that the whole Volapük edifice had to be dismantled and that, consequently, a new language had to be created.

In 1902, Idiom Neutral came into the world.[12] Almost immediately, the ex-Volapükists-turned-Esperantists of Nuremberg, disgruntled by their defeat in the 1894 referendum, changed their allegiance to Idiom Neutral.[13] But Idiom Neutral was not much different from Esperanto, and it had arrived too late. Esperanto kept growing, and dictionaries, handbooks, and literature could be ordered from any European bookstore. As Guérard put it, as if he were reminding us of the importance of timing in path-dependent processes: "Idiom Neutral never achieved a corresponding degree of popular success: it remains the 'Illustrious Unknown' among artificial languages. Had the Academy been a little more active, a little less conscientious, perhaps, the language could have been made public much earlier, about 1898, before Esperanto had taken a tremendous lead. In 1903 Esperanto was no longer a project but a fact."[14]

The 1905 First Esperanto Congress, held in France's Boulogne-sur-Mer, was critical to Esperanto becoming "a fact" more than a project. The congress was organized by the local Esperanto group, led by the Jewish lawyer Alfred Michaux. Interestingly, the First Esperanto Congress was not the byproduct of a scientific or political initiative, but of an earlier sporting event: a motorboat race that had brought together Esperantists from both sides of the Channel. The fact that participants were able to communicate in Esperanto encouraged Michaux to organize an international Esperanto congress to show the world that the language was also suitable for face-to-face communication. He obtained the support of the Touring Club de France, a mixture of a sport, tourist, and conservationist society, founded in 1890, which only five years later had 22,000 members, mostly urban professionals and qualified workers. The Touring Club had been promoting Esperanto since 1901. It let Esperantists use its premises, inserted articles about Zamenhof's language in its monthly *Revue du TCF*, and published Esperanto tourist guides, dictionaries, phrase books, and abridged manuals.[15] But as Michaux was soon to learn, the support of the main Esperanto leaders was not as easy to obtain as the Touring Club's.

Personal animosities rankled among these leaders, and more conspicuously between de Beaufront and Bourlet. Everyone knew that Bourlet and de

Beaufront were not on speaking terms, and the personal relationships among other leaders were not much better, largely stemming from problems around the Hachette publishing deal. Only after Zamenhof's direct intervention and Michaux's diplomatic maneuvering was it possible to set aside personal quarrels and get everybody working for the congress.

To put an end to these quarrels, but also to personally detach himself from the movement in order to pursue his philosophical and political agenda more freely, Zamenhof suggested that the congress should approve an international formal organization to establish some order in the movement, act as the official representative of the Esperantists vis-á-vis national governments and international organizations, and deal with other contenders and potential demands for language reform. The Tutmonda Esperantista Ligo that Zamenhof envisioned was going to be democratically governed. In his proposed bylaws, which he sent to the French leaders for discussion, he envisioned an annual convention or congress of Esperantists, which would elect a representative body. This body's decisions would only be provisional. Final, authoritative decisions regarding language and organizational matters could only be approved by the whole Esperanto community attending its annual congress. This scheme involved the definition of positions of formal authority within the movement, which proved thorny. Acting unilaterally, the French leaders rejected Zamenhof's plan, mutually afraid that some other rival would end up filling an important position.

As important as their personal rivalries were differences about the language and the movement, which made it impossible to agree on an organizational template. Viewing Esperanto as similar to any other language, able to evolve endogenously, Cart was against any formal organization that would interfere in its natural development. On his side, and following the example of the International Peace Bureau established in 1892, Moch proposed a loose confederation of Esperanto groups that precluded any centralizing or authoritative body. More bureaucratically minded, de Beaufront advocated an international federation with national organizations as its pillars; Bourlet and Sebert had in mind a more centralized organization.[16] If Zamenhof's goal behind the establishment of a permanent organization was to step back and transfer his authority to a formal body to pursue his own philosophical and political ideas, he attained the opposite result. The eventual rejection of his plan and open rivalries among the French Esperantists made more visible Zamenhof's position and informal authority in the Esperanto movement.

If not Zamenhof's projected Tutmonda Esperantista Ligo, the Boulogne Congress did accept the foundation of a Lingva Komitato, or Language Committee. To a large extent, the Lingva Komitato was a replica of the Volapük Academy. Like the latter, it was a large body entrusted to deal with language questions, and its members would work by correspondence. But unlike the Volapük Academy, the Lingva Komitato did not have any power to enforce reforms. It could only make suggestions, provide advice to speakers, think about new words, and examine reform proposals. Zamenhof's bylaws of the Tutmonda Esperanto Ligo included stipulations on how reforms could be implemented. But since his organizational scheme was rejected, nobody really knew how Esperanto could be reformed, should anybody request it.

To let the language develop naturally, as Zamenhof thought both inevitable and desirable, the congress agreed on a grammatical and lexical baseline, a starting point that would let the language evolve and adapt to speakers' needs. This was the *Fundamento de Esperanto*, a manuscript edited by Zamenhof and published by Hachette immediately before the congress.[17] The *Fundamento*, which the congress decided to make *netuŝebla* (untouchable), was prescriptive, meant to function as an abbreviated literary corpus, ideally reflecting the substance and spirit of the language. Also, and at the insistence of Sebert, the congress accepted the establishment of a Central Office, privately financed by Sebert and Javal. This office did not have an official character, and had no decision-making power. It was designed to be a clearinghouse of statistics and information. Finally, the congress agreed to set up a committee that would organize the next congress in Geneva.

CHAPTER 11

"Bringing Together the Whole Human Race": Esperanto's Inner Idea

Planning his participation in the Boulogne Congress, Zamenhof sent a letter to Michaux, also of Jewish origin. In this letter, Zamenhof explained his worldview and Esperanto's role in it. As he told Michaux, it was precisely because of his Jewishness that he had committed to the idea of "bringing together the whole human race," and Esperanto was only an instrument toward the realization of that ideal.[1] More troublesome for the assimilated and secularized Michaux was Zamenhof's warning that he intended the congress to be a "heart-warming," quasi-religious experience, for which he would write and read a prayer.[2] Busy as they were with the preparations of the congress, the French leaders did not pay much attention to this. But when they received Zamenhof's opening speech and the prayer he intended to read at the congress, they were shocked.

For some years, Zamenhof had been working on a philosophical and political program and discussing it with fellow Jewish intellectuals. Basically, he elaborated the basic tenets of Reform Judaism, which, according to the prophets, claimed that the historical mission of the Jews was to bring forth the reunification of humanity. As Zamenhof explained, the solution to the Jewish question and, by extension, to ethnic hatred was to deethnicize all peoples by establishing a linguistic and religious common ground that could help individuals to recognize one another's humanness: their standing as autonomous moral agents rather than as carriers or instruments of a narrow national or religious program. Though not included as such in his planned opening speech, these were the ideas that inspired Zamenhof.[3]

But in his planned speech, Zamenhof's invocation of a "spiritual Force," and his ambition to reunite the human race beyond all national and religious creeds, sounded to the ears of the French leaders like the words of a new Jewish messiah. They feared that if Zamenhof read his speech, the movement would be ridiculed and Esperanto would disappear. The night before the congress, they tried to convince Zamenhof to change his speech. In Warsaw, he was occasionally admonished by his Jewish friends. As a journalist and the owner of the daily *Ha-Zefirah*, Nahum Sokolow wrote to him: "Always the same Zamenhof. . . . We are in 1905—revolutions, military rule, political murders, big changes in the world, and still you are sitting down in Dzika Street improving your international language, while funeral processions of Jewish victims are walking by your door."[4]

It was difficult for Zamenhof to accept that his new friends in Western Europe censored his idealism, too. He was almost brought to tears. But he decided not to change the spirit of his speech. He agreed only to omit the last verses of the prayer, the most religious or mystical to the French leaders' ears. When the congress opened and it was Zamenhof's turn to talk, he was received with thunderous applause, the waving of Esperanto flags, and cries of *Vivu Zamenhof!* (Long live Zamenhof). In his speech Zamenhof ignored any mention of the presumed utility of Esperanto for science and commerce. He had a more important message, and as the speech progressed, its emotional and religious tone grew stronger. He began talking about the new age that was announcing itself, not audibly, but "manifest for any sensitive soul." For many years, "prophets and poets dreamed of some distant and misty era when people could, once again, understand one another, and be united in one family; but this was just a dream. We talked about it, like some sweet fantasy, but . . . now for the first time, this thousand-year dream comes true. . . . In this Congress . . . we all feel like members of one nation and of one family; and for the first time in human history we, the members of the most different nations, stand next to each other not as strangers or rivals, but as brothers. . . . Today, within the hospitable walls of Boulogne-sur-Mer, we are meeting not Frenchmen with Englishmen, not Russians with Poles, but men with men."

He then paid homage to Schleyer, the first man to launch an international language, and mentioned Leopold Einstein and other deceased fellow Esperantists. At this point, he asked the audience to stand and declared: "To all dead Esperantists, the First Congress of Esperanto expresses its sincere respect and regard." He finished: "I feel that at this moment that I do not belong to any nation or religious creed; I am only human. And at this moment, only that high moral Force, which every human being feels in his heart, stands before my eyes . . . and to this unknown Force I give my prayer."[5]

When Zamenhof finished his prayer, the audience gave him a long standing ovation. His emotional speech became a memorable event in many participants' lives—"a stirring time," as one British Esperantist reported.[6]

Zamenhof's enthusiastic reception clearly showed that side by side with the instrumental view of Esperanto, there was room for a more idealistic conception. The French leadership thought it important to downplay the latter. Right after the congress, they launched a public relations campaign to obscure Zamenhof's ideological zeal, and, more important, its source; namely, his Jewishness. The campaign succeeded. As Javal reported to Zamenhof after the congress: "I have read more than 700 hundred articles related to Esperanto after Boulogne. *Only one* commented that Dr. Zamenhof is Jew. We have used remarkable discipline to hide to the public your origins. About this issue, all the friends of Esperanto agree that we have to hide it until we win the final battle [the acceptance of Esperanto as the international language]."[7] Helping this campaign was the "declaration about the essence of Esperanto," passed by the congress. The declaration, tactfully approved by Zamenhof, stated that "Esperantism is an effort to spread throughout the world the use of a neutral language for all; which . . . while not aiming in the least to force out the existing national languages, would give to men of different nations the possibility of understanding one another. . . . Any other idea or hope which this or that Esperantist connects with Esperantism is his purely *private* affair for which Esperantism is not responsible [and, consequently,] every person is called an Esperantist who knows and uses the language exactly, whatever the objects for which he uses it."[8]

Aside from the formal meetings, the Boulogne Congress included many other events. Those who attended had a chance to enjoy a play of Molière's *Le Mariage forcé* (The forced marriage) in Esperanto, performed by actors from nine countries. Balls, banquets, poetry readings, concerts, comic performances, comedies, and outdoor excursions were also organized for everybody's entertainment. Catholics could attend a morning service in Esperanto at the local church. All told, close to 700 Esperantists from twenty countries attended the congress. The media attention proved its success. *The Daily Mail's* correspondent, for example, wrote that "in the streets and cafes, in the railway stations and shops [of Boulogne], one hears the hum of the language [but] the theater . . . is the great rendezvous of all, and during the whole of yesterday presented a scene of dramatic animation; and here it was that fully came home to me the force, the significance and the potentiality of the new language. . . . The ease, the fluency, and the facility with which [Russians, Japanese, Englishmen, Germans, French, and Norwegians] spoke to each other struck me forcibly." Like the British journalist, the correspondent of *La Van-guardia*, a Barcelona daily, was also most astonished by the representation of Molière's play. But after conceding that Esperanto had made great strides, he ended his report with some skepticism, the memory of Volapük still fresh: "Who can tell that Esperanto is the longed-for language which will facilitate international relations, and not one more project?"[9]

For the Esperantists, the Boulogne Congress proved something more important. During the months before the congress, Esperanto leaders had aired their disagreements about the organization and strategy of the movement. This had weakened the *society* of Esperantists, but face-to-face interaction among people from different nationalities, their common participation in the entertaining events and working sessions in a language that they had chosen to learn, strengthened the *community* of Esperantists.

Theirs was a multifaceted movement, and members had different ideas about the ultimate purpose of the language. But they also understood that they depended on each other to learn and practice the language, to let it grow. Beyond their local organizations, their professional, national, or religious affiliations, the congress's atmosphere helped forge a network of personal ties and shared emotions, a distinctive identity minted by a common language and a new community or country, as Zamenhof named it: *Esperantujo*, or the country of the Esperantists.

We find an example of the community-building properties of the language and the annual congresses in the recollections of the German philosopher and physicist Rudolf Carnap (1891–1970). He learned Esperanto when he was fourteen. Three years later, in 1908, he attended the international Esperanto Congress in Dresden: "It seemed like a miracle to see how easy it was for me to follow the talks and the discussions in the large public meetings, and then to talk in private conversations with people from many other countries while I was unable to hold conversations in those languages which I had studied for many years in school."[10]

A member of the Vienna Circle connected with Bertrand Russell, Rudolf Carnap worked in the new field of symbolic logic. He explored the possibility of an ideal, scientific language, a research program that resembled those of Dalgarno, Wilkins, and Leibniz. In Carnap's view, such a language would let us translate common expressions into their logical relations. Although not useful for common interaction, a language of this sort would help us distinguish between real, empirical problems and pseudo-problems (namely, statements not logically translatable and, as such, dispensable as metaphysical or illogical). This language would advance scientific knowledge, and, consequently, social welfare. Carnap was not a detached philosopher. He was a socialist and a pacifist, very involved in political debates. For him, Esperanto was a natural way of extending his political ideas. He fled to the United States in 1935, having previously helped his friend Karl Popper escape from Vienna. But before moving to the United Stated he had the chance to attend another Esperanto congress, this time in Helsinki. There he met

> a Bulgarian student; for four weeks we were almost constantly together and became close friends. After the Congress we traveled and hiked through Finland and the new Baltic republics of Estonia, Latvia and Lithuania. We stayed with hospitable Esperantists and made contact with many people in these countries. We talked about all kinds of problems in public and in personal life, always, of course, in Esperanto. For us this language was not a system of rules but simply a living language. After experiences of this kind, I cannot take very seriously the arguments of those who assert that an international auxiliary language might be suitable for business affairs and perhaps for natural science, but could not possibly serve as an adequate means of communication in personal affairs. . . . I have found that most of those who make these assertions have no practical experience with such a language.[11]

If not every Esperantist shared Carnap's motives or was as sociable as he was, the extent to which likeminded idealists joined the movement shows that Zamenhof's agenda had gained a hearing among the Esperantists, easily driven to transform a formal meeting into a memorable and emotionally charged experience.

The enthusiastic reception of his 1905 speech in Boulogne gave him new energies to popularize his ideas in *Esperantujo*. In anticipation of the Second Congress, to take place in Geneva, he sent a philosophical manuscript to Émile Javal, who was, like Michaux, an assimilated Jew. He asked Javal for comments and to distribute it among those who might have an interest in his ideas. Writing to a fellow Jew, Zamenhof confided to Javal that Esperanto was only a fraction of a larger project, namely, the "unification of humanity in one fraternal family"—a project that, he made clear, is the "mission" or "raison d'être" of the Jewish people.

As he explained it, his ideas were beyond common cosmopolitanism. He proposed an ethical and political program based on the assumption that state borders are arbitrary, and, consequently, that "every country belongs to everybody who lives there, no matter their language or religion. . . . It is the identification of the interest of one country with the interests of one religion or language group . . . which is the cause of most wars."[12]

Zamenhof's first intention was to make public his program at the next congress, which was going to take place in Geneva, as his private, non-official initiative. But again, Zamenhof's plans caused alarm, if not open hostility, among the French leaders, including Javal. Zamenhof was the most relevant Esperantist, and it would be practically impossible for public opinion to distinguish between his personal ideas and Esperanto. For them, the movement should be completely neutral and avoid entanglements in any political debate. As de Beaufront put it: "Esperanto is not a political party, a religion, or a philosophical or social program, but only a pure language; *only a language*, which people will use for the most diverse and sometimes conflicting purposes."[13]

As had happened the previous year, before the opening of the Boulogne Congress, Zamenhof and the French leaders had to find common ground. After some doubts, Zamenhof was invited to the congress and allowed to give the opening speech on the condition that he did not detail his philosophical and political ideas. Although modified, Zamenhof's opening speech at the Second Esperanto Congress in Geneva was no less stirring than the one he had delivered in Boulogne. He rejected the official definition of "Esperantist" inserted in the Boulogne Declaration and phrased for the first time the concept of the "inner idea" of Esperanto, broadly defined as the pursuit of peace and mutual respect among ethnic and national groups. As he explained to the audience, there might be Esperantists who only see in the language

something of practical utility . . . an instrument for international comprehension, similar to the maritime signals, although more perfect. . . . If such Esperantists ever come to our congresses . . . they do not participate of our joy and enthusiasm, which might look to them naive and childish. But the Esperantists who are among us not through their heads, but with their hearts, they will always feel and recognize in Esperanto, above all, its inner idea. They will not be afraid when the world jeers at them and calls them utopian, and when the chauvinists attack their ideals as criminal. They will be proud to be called utopians. At every new congress, their love for the internal idea of Esperantism will be stronger, and little by little our annual congresses will be a constant celebration of humanity and of human brotherhood.[14]

Most probably, had Zamenhof been given the opportunity to associate Esperantism with the ideological scheme that he had been elaborating for the last years, which implied the establishment of a new ethical and religious society, he would have created a commotion.[15] But he had not. Instead, he resigned himself to advance broad appeals to human brotherhood, justice, peace, and mutual respect, and blend them in the handy and intentionally ill-defined motto of the "inner idea," which any Esperantist could interpret "in different forms and degree."[16]

It is impossible to prove that this idealism helped recruit more people to Esperantism, but it is relatively safe to say that at least it did not impede recruitment: Right after Boulogne and Geneva, membership increased.[17] In 1906 a record number of more than 3,000 sent their names and addresses to the *Adresaro*. That same year there were 434 Esperanto groups around the world, 756 the following year, and close to 1,300 in 1908. And in the same period, the number of Esperanto periodicals increased from 18 to 59.

Significantly, the increasing number of periodicals mirrored the greater diversity of people and specialized interests in the movement: Catholics, Protestants, socialists, Monists, pacifists, vegetarians, excursionists, and even photography aficionados and stamp collectors.[18]

But before we turn to the inhabitants of *Esperantujo*, we should pause and reflect on Zamenhof's strategies and accomplishments. In many respects, Zamenhof was the opposite of Schleyer. He also was a polyglot, but, contrary to Schleyer, he had learned many languages by being exposed to them. He believed that a language was a constantly evolving, adaptive entity. For a language to exist and grow, it does not need to be fixed or codified in a printed grammar. Such was the case with Yiddish: spoken in its different varieties by millions of people, there were no Yiddish grammars or textbooks. Zamenhof believed that for a language to exist we only need a community of speakers who can change and adapt it according to their communication needs. Hence, his insistence that, more important than disputes about this or that word or grammatical rule is the mastery of the language, to communicate with fellow speakers. Setting up a formal organization to discuss words or grammatical rules was an unnatural way to proceed. But since a language belongs to its users, a democratic organization had to be created if users requested it.

Thus, as was true of Schleyer, there was a close fit for Zamenhof between his conception of language and the strategy he used to spread Esperanto. Differences among the Esperantists before the Boulogne Congress made it impossible to agree on an organizational template for the movement. But this was not a great source of concern for Zamenhof, since more important than any organization was the community of speakers. And he concentrated his energies on community building.

At this, he did not fail. An "imagined community" of people who shared a language did emerge. In its central core, this was a value-laden community, based on the inner idea. But since this inner idea could be interpreted in different ways and even rejected, the community of Esperantists was not a homogeneous one. Forged by the drastic social and political transformations of the period, the community of the Esperantists was rife with divergent ideas about the possible applications of the language.

PART III

The Esperanto Cluster: Same
Language, Different Communities

CHAPTER 12

The Demographics of *Esperantujo*

Since an international language such as Esperanto is a public good, rationality dictates free riding rather than volunteering to promote its success. Another factor that might discourage cooperation was personal reputation. Like the Volapükists before them, the Esperantists were harassed and ridiculed by the media as hopeless fools, when not more vehemently as people of questionable patriotism. Who were they? What motives drove them to invest time and money and to risk their personal reputations to learn and champion a barely spoken language?

A review of contemporary journals gives us some answers. Also, the *Adresaroj*, or address books, provide some basic information about the Esperantists. The most comprehensive source of information, however, is the data collected by the American Reuben A. Tanquist in 1927, for his master's thesis.[1] Supervised and encouraged by his mentor, the sociology professor and Esperantist Edwin L. Clarke, Tanquist launched an ambitious research project to profile the Esperantists, their motivations to learn the language, and its diffusion mechanisms. To do this, Tanquist sent 1,800 questionnaires to Esperanto clubs and journals in the United States, the United Kingdom, and continental Europe.

A total of 505 individuals returned the questionnaire, 162 from the United States, 207 from Britain, and 136 from continental Europe. Since 109 of the latter come from Germany and Austria, we can broadly label them "German-Austrian Esperantists." If we compare Tanquist's data with the statistics on the distribution of the international Esperanto movement in 1926 provided by the Germana Esperanto Instituto,[2] it is evident that Tanquist's sample was not representative. It did not include members of the working-class Esperanto movement, and it offers only a snapshot of the English- and German-speaking Esperantists in 1927. Notwithstanding these biases, it is the best source for studying the Esperanto movement in the interwar period. Table 2 shows the distribution of these three sub-populations according to gender, age, education, and occupation.

As Table 2 shows, slightly more than one-third of Esperantists were women. Women were better represented among Esperantists in the United Kingdom (41 percent) and the United States (37 percent) than in Germany and Austria,

Table 2. Percentage of American, British, and German-Austrian Esperantists by Gender, Age, Education, and Occupation in 1927

	American	British	German-Austrian	Total
GENDER				
Women	37	41	26	36
Men	63	59	74	64
AGE				
< 20	27	21	19	25
21–30	19	32	34	29
31–40	24	27	20	24
41–50	17	15	15	13
51–60	10	5	8	7
> 60	3	0	4	2
EDUCATION (LAST SCHOOL ATTENDED)				
Primary	19	48	24	31
Secondary	43	28	40	36
University	28	9	17	17
Teachers school	4	2	10	5
Commerce school	3	1	5	3
Other prof. school	4	12	4	7
OCCUPATION				
Un- and semi-skilled workers	7	8	5	6
Skilled workers	5	15	11	11
White collar	26	33	11	25
Professionals (incl. teachers)	26	21	41	28
Students	24	8	16	16
Housewives	10	13	10	11
Others	2	1	4	3

Source: Tanquist, "A Study."

where they were only 26 percent of the movement. Still, this compares favorably with other social movements and organizations of the time. Even after the incorporation of the Women's Labour League in the Labor Party after World War I, only 32 percent of Labour Party members were women. Similarly, in 1928 Germany, women were only 21 percent of the total membership of the SPD.[3] Women's contributions to the Esperanto movement also compared well with the Volapükists (10 to 15 percent) and the Idist movement (11 percent according to the *Yarlibro Idista 1922*). (We examine the Idist movement in Part 4.) This relatively high number of women among the Esperantists did not go unnoticed by contemporaries, who sometimes underlined the effeminate character of the movement: more emotional than rational, and lacking virile values such as patriotism and militarism.

Compared to their co-nationals, Esperantists were younger. Whereas 53 percent of American Esperantists were between 20 and 40 years old, this age group amounted to only 27 percent of the American population overall. Like their American counterparts, the British Esperantists were also younger than the general British population (59 versus 31 percent in the 20–40 age group). The same can be said of the German-Austrian Esperantists: 54 percent of them were between 20 and 40, but only 36 percent and 30 percent of the German and Austrian populations were, respectively.

Esperantists were also better educated than their corresponding national groups. Only 1.2 percent of Americans were attending a university or a professional school, but among the Esperantists they represented 28 percent. In the United Kingdom we have a similar scenario: less than one percent of the British population was enrolled in a university, whereas nine percent of British Esperantists had a university degree. While less than one percent of Germans and Austrians were attending a university or a technical Hochschule, 17 percent of the German and Austrian Esperantists had a higher education degree. Tanquist's data, thus, indicate that the Esperantists concentrated on the early working age group and were relatively younger and better educated than their co-nationals.[4] But, again, Tanquist's survey underrepresents the working-class portion of the movement.

Students were particularly well represented in the movement, especially in the United States and the German-Austrian group, where they amounted to 24 and 16 percent, respectively. But more important, perhaps, is the percentage of professionals and teachers in the German-Austrian group, around 40 percent of Tanquist's sample. Among the professionals (not showed in the table), public employees (24 percent), and scientists and clergymen (7 and 6 percent, respectively) dominated. Overall, 15 percent of Esperantists who reported their occupation were teachers or enrolled in teaching schools. Given the predominance of women in the teaching profession, this might explain the movement's higher percentage of females. By this time, Esperanto had been experimentally introduced in primary and secondary schools in different European countries. For example, by 1922, Esperanto was a compulsory subject in thirteen primary schools and four secondary schools in the United Kingdom, and a positive report of the British Board of Education indicated that the teaching of Esperanto could be extended. A similar thing happened in Poland, Scandinavia, and the Baltic countries.[5] This created a demand for qualified Esperanto teachers, who had to have a strong command of the language. Data from *The British Esperantist* from 1920 to 1930 indicate that this demand was mostly met by women: around two-thirds of those who passed the upper-level Esperanto exams were women. (Another factor that might explain the relatively high proportion of women activists in the movement might be ideological, as we see below with regard to the feminist branch of the pacifist movement.)

There is one demographic group that Tanquist's survey does not capture: the blind. Since printing a book in Braille was, on average, fourteen times more expensive than in regular type, only rarely would Braille publishers cover costs, which reduced the availability of reading material for the blind. One solution was to reduce the printing costs by making books smaller by means of a stenographic system. But this solution was far from perfect: blind children would have to learn the stenography rather than the orthography of their language, and people who had become blind late in their life would have to learn a new writing system. Another solution was to increase the potential number of readers by publishing the book in an international language such as Esperanto. The deaf-blind Swede Harald Thilander endorsed this solution. With the financial support of the Frenchman Émile Javal, an ophthalmologist, who, by a sad irony, went blind after contracting glaucoma, the French Théophile Cart (1855–1931) and Thilander adapted the Esperanto alphabet to Braille. In 1904, Cart launched the monthly *Esperanta Ligilo*, an Esperanto journal printed in Braille. The journal was a success. Local clubs and national organizations of blind Esperantists emerged, and in 1923 the Universala Asocio de Blindaj Esperantistoj (Universal Association of Blind Esperantists) was created.[6]

Table 3 shows two waves of recruitment: before and after World War I. Particularly important was the second category. Thus, in 1912 there were

Table 3. When, How, and Why American, British, and German-Austrian Esperantists Learned the Language, and How the Language Was Diffused (percent)

	American	British	German-Austrian	Total
WHEN THEY LEARNED ESPERANTO				
Before 1910	27	21	20	23
1910–1919	18	20	16	18
1920–1926	55	59	64	59
HOW THEY LEARNED ESPERANTO				
Private class	33	28	42	33
Self-study	44	28	44	37
Esperanto group	7	24	5	14
Night school	0	11	0	5
School (incl. university)	12	5	5	8
Radio lectures	3	0	4	2
Unclassified	1	4	1	2
DIFFUSION MECHANISMS				
Social Networks				
Friend	28	36	22	31
Relative	5	11	12	9
Fellow worker	5	7	1	5
Total	38	54	35	45
More Formal Mechanisms				
Teacher	8	2	2	4
Newspaper articles	32	19	32	26
Esperanto propaganda literature	10	15	13	13
Esperanto propaganda meeting	4	8	7	7
Radio talk	3	1	4	2
Other	4	2	6	4
Total	61	47	64	56
WHY THEY LEARNED ESPERANTO				
Peace	24	31	30	28
Political propaganda	3	6	2	4
Religious propaganda	7	2	0	2
Interest in languages	25	24	30	26
Travel, correspondence, collecting	30	29	22	28
Novelty	6	5	3	5
Other	5	3	13	6

Source: Tanquist, "A Study."
Note: The sum of percentages is sometimes higher than 100 because some informants chose more than one answer.

273 Esperanto clubs in Germany, but by 1928 there were 441. Similarly, between 1923 and 1931, the French Society for the Propagation of Esperanto almost doubled its membership, as did the Swedish association, while the British increased by 30 percent. The Netherlands witnessed the highest increase, from 300 to 1,300 members. Similarly, the Universala Esperanto Asocio, the most important umbrella organization of the Esperanto movement, saw an increase from 6,300 to almost 9,000 in the same period. These figures do not reflect the real growth of the movement, since they do not include SAT, the international working-class Esperanto organization that by 1927 had more than 5,000 members.[7]

Regarding learning the language, one-third of the Esperantists said they had learned it by self-study, which is congruent with their higher educational level. Also congruent with the social networks mechanisms that diffused the movement (see below) is that another third learned Esperanto through private classes.

Tanquist did not include in his dissertation a cross-table indicating the diffusion mechanisms through which the respondents learned the language. Such a table would have let us examine the relative weight of formal and informal mechanisms in the prewar and the postwar periods. It is important to note, however, that 45 percent of the Esperantists active in 1927 reported that they had learned the language because of people in their own social networks, such as friends, relatives, and co-workers. In fact, when taken separately, friendship with an Esperantist or with somebody interested in the language is the most influential factor (31 percent) to becoming an Esperantist, followed by a newspaper article. Thus, slightly more important for the expansion of the movement than being "out there" (i.e., mentioned in a newspaper or in a talk on radio) was that Esperanto was "in here"—within preexisting social networks. Interpersonal networks are more critical in the early phase of social movements, since a nascent social movement that lacks an organizational infrastructure is more dependent on interpersonal ties. Hence, it is somewhat surprising that even in the late 1920s interpersonal ties were so important for recruitment.

Table 3 also shows that one-third of respondents associated Esperanto with the pursuit of peace or other political or religious purposes. The data indicate that, for some other Esperantists, the language had less idealistic and more instrumental purposes. It was clearly a hobby for some who were interested in languages or in traveling and collecting. These Esperantists, however, were neither the most active nor the core of the movement, as a simple overview of the general and specialized Esperanto press indicates.

* * *

It is sometimes possible to conceive of a social movement as a unitary entity whose members share a common goal or a set of beliefs. When a social movement fits this model, a researcher might apply a linear or natural perspective to explore it. This perspective entails visualizing the movement as if it were a living entity and studying its original goals, internal organization, and strategy, emergence, growth, and decay. Other social movements, however, hardly fit this self-contained image. Rather, they are a collection of social networks, individuals, and organizations, which, even when they share a common goal, interpret it in different and sometimes opposite ways. In these cases, researching a social movement as a sort of organic entity can only impede a proper understanding of the movement.[8]

As we see in the next chapters, the Esperanto movement is closer to the collection of social networks than to the unitary actor model; what the movement lacked in a centralized organization it gained in diversity. Certainly, all active Esperantists were working for the dissemination of the language, but for quite different, and sometimes divergent, reasons. The eclecticism of the Esperanto movement mirrors the challenges and uncertainties spawned by the rapid disruption of the old order, manifested by the emergence of new nation-states and national movements, the questioning of democratic principles by a new brand of authoritarian ideologies, the political organization of the working class, a strong secularizing thrust that questioned the authority of old churches, as well as by the economic and social transformations brought about by the second industrial revolution.

Up to the mid-1930s, when most Central and Eastern European countries abandoned democratic principles and nationalist and authoritarian regimes emerged, the Esperantists were able to increase their numbers and pursue different goals, which they materialized in specialized organizations. Wherever political conditions were favorable, a colorful array of specialized Esperantist organizations blossomed. These organizations had their own agendas and were governed by their own internal dynamics. Sometimes they were subordinated to other international organizations, such as the Comintern or the Holy See, but most often they were loosely coupled with the official national and international organizations of the movement.

In the next chapters we see the Esperantists participating, in sometimes contradictory ways, in the public debates of their times, nested in a variety of social groups and phenomena, such as pacifists, free thinkers, teachers, old and new religious or quasi-religious movements, and movements that catered to the needs and expectations of new social groups (such as young people) or new lifestyles (vegetarians and theosophists, for example). Diverse as they were in their views and social composition, Esperantists gathered to create specific organizations in order to prove that their language could help assuage the anxieties that were afflicting the European and world societies.

CHAPTER 13

Pacifists, Taylorists, and Feminists

In a standardization battle where positivist feedback mechanisms operate, the number of adopters is critical: the more that people adopt technology A instead of B, the more likely next adopters will also choose A rather than B. But equally and perhaps more important than the number of adopters is the variety of places and social settings where adoptions occur. If adoptions concentrate within the boundaries of a specific location or interest group, the door is open for rival technologics to gain a foothold elsewhere and offset the progress made by the first adopters. Also, if for whatever reason the social group where adoptions concentrate loses economic, social, or political leverage, the more difficult it will be for their adopted technology to obtain visibility and expand, for in the same way that rational investors diversify their portfolios in order to minimize risk, technologies competing in a standardization battle can better sustain it the more diverse the social settings they have been able to infiltrate.

In preceding chapters we have seen that the Volapükists had the potential to spread in different directions. Some saw in Volapük an instrument to facilitate international commerce, while others were more interested in its capacity to advance scientific research, a new literary corpus, or a closer understanding among nations. This potential, however, was radically curtailed given their failure to agree on the basics of their language. On the contrary, the Esperantists were able to reach such an agreement, which let their language find shelter among different and sometimes diverging social groups: from humanists to supremacists, from scientists and engineers to people looking for a new spirituality, and from social conservatives to anarchists. Spread in different directions, the Esperantists made it practically impossible for later rivals to crowd them out.

Among the different groups that compounded the Esperanto movement, the pacifists were probably the most visible. As we saw in the last chapter, around 30 percent of Esperantists learned the language because they associated it with pacifism. A quick glance at the international Esperanto press of the years leading up to World War I indicates that this association was rather strong. The international pacifist movement, however, was far from uniform. Different strands of pacifism coexisted, cooperating with each other most of the time, and working diligently to avoid open conflict. The most important of these strands was the realist pacifism of the French positivists and German Monists. Theirs was a quasi-determinist pacifism, based on a grand narrative that envisioned the convergence of peace and progress in the near future. For this strand of pacifism, which some supporters called "scientific pacifism," organization was the buzzword: peace could only be guaranteed through the organization of the world, which required the promotion and planning of scientific research working against religious prejudices. Some pacifists of this school took the primacy of science over religion to its extreme, embracing one or another version of Social Darwinism. Side by side with this scientific or positivist pacifism was the old brand of religious pacifism of Quakers, Mennonites, and Tolstoyans, as well as representatives of the Catholic and Protestant churches. Finally, a new strand of pacifism, not necessarily associated with the socialist movement and particularly important in the interwar years, was represented by women who linked their subjugation to militarism and military spending. Some of the leading representatives of these three branches of pacifism were also reputed Esperantists.

*   *   *

Advances in the chemical and electricity industries had changed the living conditions of many people. More and more cities substituted electric for horse-drawn cars, and electricity for kerosene. An increasing number of city dwellers had access to a telephone, and new methods for producing paper increased the number of periodicals, making it easier for political and industrial entrepreneurs to publicize their ideas and products. Also, the electrification of factories accelerated the introduction of the assembly line, mass production became increasingly common, and advances in medicine (such as new vaccines and X-rays) also improved the living standards of many people. For many contemporaries, the definite triumph of science over superstition and metaphysics was only a question of time. History and progress were two sides of the same coin, and more powerful advances in science and technology could make people happier and healthier. Underpinning this grand narrative were Auguste Comte and Positivism in France and Ernst Mach and Monism in the German-speaking world.[1]

The changes in the economic and social environments that the second industrial revolution had brought about, however, also created new problems, which, following the positivist grand narrative, demanded rational solutions. A first challenge was to rationally organize science and technology. A second problem was the destructive potential of that science and technology, for if progress could bring humanity closer to Eden, it could also destroy it. Given the lethal power of the new weaponry, many were convinced that a European war would be tantamount to total annihilation. As Bertha von Suttner put it: "Every village will be a holocaust, every city a pile of rubble, every field a field of corpses, and the war will rage on."[2] For some of the most important public figures, these two problems, ensuring an orderly progress of science and making the world a more secure place, were also linked to a particular view of the role of an artificial language.

We find an example of this combination of scientism, pacifism, and support for an artificial language in the German Monist and Nobel laureate in chemistry, Wilhelm Ostwald (1853–1932), first an Esperantist and later an Idist. Shortly before World War I, Ostwald founded Die Brücke (The Bridge: Institute for the Organization of Intellectual Work). Understanding the human race as a living organism, Ostwald thought that this organism required a brain, able to coordinate the scattered efforts of scientists, engineers, artists, and industrialists. The Bridge was going to be this brain. As he explained to his American colleagues, The Bridge's goal was to apply scientific management to scientific research.[3] This required the normalization of scientific technology, the publication of bibliographies, directories, encyclopedias, international catalogues, and the like. It also required the creation of international research institutes, to maximize scientific efficiency by sidestepping inefficient national research institutions. An international institute for chemistry, for example, would standardize chemical nomenclature, establish an international committee on atomic weights, host a universal library of chemical works, and publish an international register of chemists and research projects. The Bridge promoted the universalization of the Dewey cataloguing system and also a "World Format" for scientific communication, which encompassed from the standardization of scientific reports and abstracts to the size of scientific journals in order to save shelving space.[4]

Needless to say, a rational, artificial language was part of this program, since efficiency required that scientists, called by history to lead the progress of civilization, be spared the trouble of learning different languages.[5]

Ostwald's plans, however, were not very innovative. Before the turn of the century, Belgians Henri La Fontaine (1854–1943) and Paul Otlet (1868–1914) had been engaged in a similar project. A very wealthy socialist, freemason, professor of international law, senator, and member of the Belgian Esperanto League, La Fontaine was, above all, a passionate bibliographer and pacifist, very much like his friend Otlet, a lawyer.[6] As ardent positivists convinced of the need to promote the social sciences that Comte had placed at the top of the hierarchy of scientific disciplines, La Fontaine and Otlet cooperated with the Belgian Society of Social and Political Sciences to create a bibliography of sociology. In 1895 they received a copy of Dewey's classification system, which inspired them to expand their interests to all scientific fields. With financial assistance from the Belgian government, they convened the first International Conference on Bibliography and established the International Institute for Bibliography, with headquarters in Brussels. This institute would collect bibliographical repertoires from all countries and fields and create a Universal Bibliography Repertory, which would use an expanded version of the Dewey system: the Universal Decimal Classification.[7]

La Fontaine and Otlet's bibliographical commitment had a philosophical basis. By facilitating cooperation among scientific societies, mutual knowledge among nations would improve and the likelihood of war among advanced nations would be minimized. Like many of their contemporaries, they believed that science supported peace, not only because an armed conflict among developed nations would be suicidal, but also because science and the pursuit of truth conspire against the two main sources of war: irrationalism and chauvinism. Pacifism and scientism were, for both friends, soul mates. Thus, in 1910, they brokered the creation of the still extant Union of International Associations, a sort of international civil society composed of international organizations of all sorts (scientific, professional, technical, religious, commercial, and so on), which reflected the current "universal synthesis of knowledge" and the "organic nature of the movement towards internationalism [and] the world community."[8] Also, the Union of International Associations would sponsor the construction of a World City, able to accommodate one million people. Devoted to the pursuit of peace, the World City would be the brain of the world. It would host an International Library, a World Museum, international societies, and, ultimately, a future League of Nations. For the plans of this city, Otlet had enlisted Le Corbusier, equally concerned about efficiency, rationality, and standardization in architecture.[9]

This combination of scientism, universalism, and pacifism attracted other Esperantists, such as the engineer and retired general Hyppolite Sebert. In 1898 Sebert established the Bureau bibliographique de Paris, and the next year he became president of the Association française pour l'avancement des sciences. In close contact with La Fontaine and Otlet, Sebert was also the most important advocate of Esperanto in French scientific circles. He also was instrumental in the creation of the Esperantist Internacia Sciencia Asocio (International Scientific Association), which launched the journal *Internacia Sciencia Revuo* (1904–1923).[10] A leading Esperantist, he ran the Centra Oficejo, the Central Office of the Esperanto movement, which, very much like La Fontaine's and Otlet's International Institute for Bibliography, was a bibliographical information center on Esperanto for Esperantists.

This link between bibliography or information studies and pacifism might sound strange. Remembering the antiwar movement of the 1960s and 1970s, we tend to associate pacifism with other kinds of protest movements. But the pacifism of people like Sebert, Otlet, and La Fontaine (who was awarded the Nobel Peace Prize in 1911) was of a very different nature. They were representatives of a liberal, "patriotic" pacifism, to borrow from Sandi Cooper, which recognized full sovereignty to nation-states, accepted "just wars," and worked for the establishment of an international court of justice, an international arbitration system, and, more ambitiously, a League of Nations able to enforce international agreements.[11] This pacifism was the driving force behind the Universal Peace Congress of 1899, which became an annual event from that point forward, as well as the International Peace Bureau, established in 1891, in which La Fontaine served as president from 1907 to 1943. This was the pacifism of the upper echelons of society: journalists, scientists, industrialists, and intellectuals. They were men who had access to kings, emperors, diplomats, and prime ministers and understood power relations and the meaning of Realpolitik.

A central figure of this strand of pacifism was the French Esperantist Gaston Moch (1859–1935). The son of a German Jew of the Saarland, Moch studied at the École polytechnique to pursue a military career. Alfred Dreyfus was a classmate. In 1891 Moch married a young woman from wealthy Parisian Jewish society. His wife's dowry of one million francs allowed him to quit the army and pursue his reflections on the need for reconciliation with Germany on the question of Alsace-Lorraine. When the Dreyfus Affair came to light, Moch helped found the Ligue de droits de l'homme, which at the turn of the century had 200,000 members. In the polarized political environment of the Dreyfus Affair, the Ligue forged close contacts with Emile Arnaud's Ligue international de la paix et de la liberté, and from 1896 Moch became a prominent figure in the international peace movement.[12]

An ex-Volapükist, Moch thought that an artificial language could play a critical role in the pursuit of peace. Right after he joined the pacifist movement, he submitted a report that recommended the use of Esperanto.[13] He also brought to the Esperanto camp the Briton W. T. Stead, editor of the *Review of Reviews*, as well as Felix Moscheles, chairman of the International Arbitration and Peace Association. In 1905, Stead and Moscheles founded the first Esperanto society in the United Kingdom. Moch also co-opted for the Esperanto cause the Austrian journalist Alfred Fried (1864–1921), co-founder with Bertha von Suttner of the German Peace Society.[14] In 1905, Moch's Esperantist network created the Internacia Societo Esperantista por la Paco (International Esperantist Society for Peace), which launched the monthly *Espero pacifista* (1905–1908). In December 1905, it had 300 members from twenty-three countries.

Moch's positivist pacifism was more consistently elaborated by his friend Alfred Fried, also a Nobel Peace Prize winner.[15] Very much like Ostwald, La Fontaine, Sebert, and Moch, Fried portrayed the history of humankind and international relations as a preordained process leading to ever more efficient organization: "What we call the world history is nothing but a continuous organization process, a step by step progress in the transformation and regulation of the energy components, a progressive transformation of power into law."[16] For Fried, this organizing process would inevitably lead to the end of anarchy in international relations and the beginning of a coordinated world system, in keeping with the demands of science. But whereas Fried and Moch stopped there, other Esperantists went further and conflated this positivist, organizational-driven conception of world history with Social Darwinism. Leading exemplars of this amalgamation of pacifism, Social Darwinism, and Esperanto were the Frenchman Charles Richet (1850–1935) and the Swiss neurologist Auguste Forel (1848–1931).

A Nobel laureate in medicine and a supporter of the rights of women and the elevation of the working classes, Richet was a well-known pacifist. He presided over the Ninth Universal Peace Congress, which took place in 1900 in Paris, and was president of the French Society for International Arbitration. But there was something about Richet that seemed not quite right to other

Esperantists. It was not his interest in spiritism (see Chapter 14) but his plans for the betterment of society. Contrary to the continuous chatter of well-intentioned humanists, Richter thought it incontrovertible that the human species was hierarchically ordered. Crowning the natural hierarchy was the white race, undoubtedly superior to the "yellow" and to black people, the latter of which have "not made any contribution [to civilization] and are at the very bottom."[17] He opposed intermarriage and favored eugenics: "If the amputated, the hare-lipped, the club-footed, the poly-fingered, the hydrocephalic, the idiots, the deaf-mutes, the rickety and the cretins were eliminated (*supprimés*), human societies would not miss anything. There would be fewer unhappy people. That's all."[18] The promotion of science and the organization of society, Richet claimed, demanded the adoption of Esperanto and a program of human selection. If consistently implemented, the breeding of the fittest and the sterilization or the feeble and unsavory could deter the degeneration of society and bring closer *l'humanité future*, composed of wiser, healthier, and happier men. If, given their primitive stage of development, war is expected among uncivilized nations, among Europeans it is not. Still, it has to be prevented, since it "makes a selection, but in the *opposite* direction. It eliminates the brave, the young, the strong, the vigorous, the noble, and it doesn't let survive, for the perpetuation of the species, nothing but the scum (*le rebut humaine*)."[19]

Auguste Forel was also a Social Darwinist and a pacifist Esperantist. A staunch defender of women's rights, he also opposed discrimination against homosexuals. He advocated free trade, but was not against the socialization of land and industries provided that it improved the living conditions of the working class. He was also a convinced anti-nationalist. European nations, according to him, were artifacts. As he expressed to a colleague: "Our cultural nations are an utterly artificial product, created by wars and what the conquerors imposed to the conquered. . . . It is a deeply rooted scientific lie when, for example, the German nation defines itself as being 'purely German.' It is full of Celtic, Slavic and mixed blood. Therefore, I utterly reject this artificially produced nationalism." But there was an important caveat to this anti-nationalism: "Of course, one should not misunderstand me. In no way I doubt true racial differences, according to natural science, nor do I agree with mixing in inferior races such as Negroes."[20] To neutralize nationalism, Forel proposed a United States of the Earth, an international parliament, army, and court of justice. Esperanto should be compulsory in every school.[21] The advancement of civilization, however, also required racial and eugenic measures. Whereas the interbreeding of European races had been the most beneficial to the progress of civilization, the "laws of evolution and the fight for existence" have also produced peoples with "smaller brains." Examples of these are the Weddas in Ceylon and the Akkas in Congo. Weddas and Akkas, however, live far away and do not represent a biological hazard. More threatening are other

> races, above all the Negroes, who are physically strong and robust, extraordinarily fertile, but mentally inferior, who have learned to adapt to our culture extremely well. When they have adapted to our culture they corrupt it and our race through sloth, lack of ability and by creating such awful, mixed races as the Mulates. By carefully observing the situation in the southern states of the USA it is easy to be convinced how negatively the Negro element, as it increases, affects our culture.[22]

Cooperating with positivist pacifists like La Fontaine, Fried, and Moch, and Social Darwinists were humanist and religious pacifists, particularly important in the United States and the United Kingdom, as well as the feminist branch of the international pacifist movement, also well represented by leading Esperantists.

Like the positivist pacifist, the religious or "absolutist pacifists," to use Eloise Brown's terminology, also supported the development of international law and a system of international arbitration. But religious pacifists went further: they campaigned for mutual disarmament and rejected the concept of "defensive war," which Moch wanted the International Peace Bureau to accept. In fact, it was the well-known British Esperantist Priscilla Peckover (1833–1931), also a member of the International Peace Bureau, who most forcefully opposed Moch's resolution, and eventually ensured its rejection.[23] The daughter of a wealthy banker, Peckover was raised a Quaker. She learned Esperanto at a late age and made a name in the Esperanto movement thanks to her financial support for the translation and publication of the Bible.[24]

The Quaker Montagu C. Butler was an absolute pacifist and an Esperantist. Even his recommendation of conscientious objection during World War I did not prevent Butler's election as secretary of the British Esperanto Association in 1916, which attests to the relative strength of this radical pacifism among British Esperantists.[25]

Also militant against positivist pacifists were the feminist branch of the pacifist movement that began to emerge in the United States and Europe at the end of the century. Like their religious counterparts, pacifist feminists advocated for disarmament, something that positivist pacifists were reluctant to contemplate for fear of being accused of treason. In their more radical version, pacifist feminists supported an anti-militarist agenda, on the premise that military values and spending contributed to the subjugation of women. Women peace activists were particularly strong in France. In 1896, the Ligue des Femmes pour de désarmement international (Women's League for International Disarmament) was created, as was, shortly later, a more radical splinter group, l'Association "La paix et le désarmement par les femmes" (Women's Association for Peace and Disarmament). This latter association was led by Sylvie Flammarion, also a member of Societo Esperantista por la Paco.[26] Similar organizations were set up in the United Kingdom, Germany, and Italy, and in April 1915 they merged in the International Committee of Women for Permanent Peace—or the Women's International League for Peace and Freedom (WILPF), as it was later named.[27] Like the International Peace Bureau, the WILPF supported and used Esperanto for international correspondence and meetings.[28] Finally, in 1929, the Unuiĝo de Esperantistaj Virinoj (League of Esperantist Women) was founded. Highest on their agenda was peace: they supported the WILPF and Einstein's League.[29]

The connections between Esperantism and pacifism, in all its varieties, show the different ways the language was interpreted and appropriated. Pacifism was certainly a privileged platform to make Esperanto visible. In fact, in 1905, six of the twenty-six members of the International Peace Bureau were also leading Esperantists.[30] But, although important, pacifism did not exhaust Esperantist activism. As we see in the following chapters, they were a restless tribe, dispersed and much involved in the social and political challenges of their time.

CHAPTER 14

"Hidden-World Seekers":
Esperanto in New Wave and Old Religions

If the celebration of science and the search for organizational efficiency were part of the spirit of the times, equally characteristic was the reaction by some against the dehumanizing character of scientific and technological progress. For many, it looked like a new tyranny had triumphed: the tyranny of the mechanical and the artificial, which was about to cut man off from nature and suffocate the true, spiritual character of humanity. The blind materialism and consumerism brought about by mass production and embodied in a continuously expanding plague of department stores should be resisted. The first decades of the twentieth century revived a search for new lifestyles, which ranged from more trivial return-to-nature movements, such as vegetarianism or the wandering societies, to more radical new spiritual movements which, critical of science's manipulative power, searched for truth elsewhere.

Among the latter were the theosophist and spiritists. Founded in late nineteenth-century New York, the Theosophy movement expanded to Europe in the early twentieth century, particularly to the United Kingdom, Germany, and the Austrian empire. Theosophy, or Anthroposophy, as its splinter movement was called in German-speaking lands, liberally blended Western and Eastern philosophy, Buddhism and Christianity, mysticism and spiritualism.[1] It promised its followers a mystical avenue to the ultimate and transcendental truths, a plea to liberate the Dionysian forces of human nature (at odds with bourgeois values) and, perhaps more important, a method to communicate with the beloved dead ones, which appealed to both the educated and non-educated. Among the former, most significant were the members of the British Society of Psychical Research, founded in 1882. Presided by promi-

nent people such as William James, Henri Bergson, the Esperantist and Social Darwinist Charles Richet (whom we met in the last chapter), and Arthur
Balfour (also prime minister of Her Majesty's government from 1902 to 1905),
the Society sought to disclose charlatans and imposters while hoping to find
scientific proof of the afterlife and the possibility of communicating with the
dead.[2] Also in Fabian quarters the occult and the paranormal had their followers.[3] Thus, in 1902, Frank Podmore published a two-volume treatise on
the subject, *Modern Spiritualism*, and on more than one occasion he convinced
fellow Fabians Edward Reynolds Pease and George Bernard Shaw to escort
him in his research into haunted houses.[4] By 1911 the British Theosophy movement had 16,000 members and the interest in the occult and the paranormal
only increased after the butchery of World War I and the Spanish flu, which
left many new mourners trying to contact their loved ones.[5] Sharing the troubles and anxieties of their time, it is not surprising to find Esperantists in these
circles. Thus, in 1911, the Teozofia Esperanta Ligo (Theosophycal Esperantist League) was created with an eye to facilitating contacts among European
and American theosophists, and two years later the official journal of the
league, *Espero Teozofia* (1913–1928), was created.[6] Among the Esperantist occultists, the most popular was perhaps the pacifist and journalist William T.
Stead, who in 1905, the same year he co-founded the first Esperanto club in
the United Kingdom, published *After Death*, which detailed his exchanges
with his beloved dead friend Julia Ames. But spiritualism and Esperanto also
intersected in continental Europe. The French philosopher and rector of the
University of Dijon, Émile Boirac, also president of the Lingva Komitato, never
hid his strong interest in psychism. In 1908, he published *La psychologie
inconnue. Introduction et contribution à l'étude expérimentale des sciences
psychiques* and, in 1919, the year of his death, *L'avenir des sciences psychiques*. Also, in 1907 French booksellers could display in their windows the
Esperanto translation of Gustav Fechner's best seller *On Life After Death*. In
neighboring Belgium the Spiritualist Federation published the *Revuo de
Esperanta Psikistaro* (1912–1913), and in the prewar years spiritualists held
special meetings on the occasion of the World Esperanto Congresses. In 1934,
a new international organization, the Psihan Esperanto-Ligon (Psychic
Esperanto League), was created.[7]

Less exciting, although no less popular avenues for alternative lifestyles
than theosophy and spiritism, were vegetarianism and wanderism. And as
was the case with the occult seekers, the Esperantists were also well represented in both movements. A religiously inspired vegetarian movement had

existed in the United Kingdom since the mid-nineteenth century. In the following decades, the movement expanded to other corners of Europe and
particularly to Germany, gaining new momentum in the first decades of the
1900s. But it was not until August 1908 that vegetarians combined efforts
and created the International Vegetarian Union. Interestingly, this association was set up by the Esperantist and secretary of the Friends of the
Vegetarian Society, the British Quaker J. Arthur Gill, who almost simultaneously created the corresponding International Union of Vegetarian Esperantists (Esperantist Internacia Unuiĝo de Esperantistaj Vegetaranoj), which
in 1914 launched its official journal: *Vegetarano*. As he expressed to fellow
British vegetarians after the launch of both international organizations, Esperanto could be invaluable for the exchange of information and community building:

> At the recent International [Esperanto] Congress in Dresden there
> was opportunity for observing the part which language can play in
> the spread of a movement. The present writer is an Esperantist and a
> vegetarian who attempted to attend both series of meetings [the Espe-
> rantist and the non-Esperantist vegetarian meetings]. After one of
> the vegetarian meetings, he found a German regarding him with
> friendly eyes, and at once tried to fall into conversation with him.
> But no! After each had cudgeled his brains for a few stray words in
> the other's language, the whole and sole result was the following
> scene: "Vegetarian? Yes!" "Vegetarian? Yes!" Violent and delighted
> handshake. When this had been repeated two or three times . . . the
> interest waned. How different was the case [among vegetarian Espe-
> rantists]. Picture a little group of half-a-dozen sitting round a table
> and vastly amused with everything around, and especially one another,
> all speaking with interest and animation. From the conversation it
> was impossible to learn of their nationality, yet one would be a Finn,
> another a Tyrolese, another a Frenchman, and so on.[8]

Also in search of different life experiences was a new social group. With
the expansion of educational and professional training institutions, and the
parallel extension of the formative years, young people emerged in the first
decades of the twentieth century as a distinct social category, trying to find
their place in a rapidly changing world. All over Europe, young people organized and banded together. They searched for social recognition not simply

as adults in the making.[9] The scouting movement illustrated the emerging youth movement. In Germany it was the Wandervogel movement (Wandering Bird movement), founded in 1896, while in Bohemia and Moravia it was the Sokol movement (Falcon movement), founded in 1862. Although these movements promoted the exploration of nature and the experimentation with a new kind of freedom, unburdened by conventional life, they could also operate as schools of patriotism and national pride, since a healthy nation always requires a healthy youth.[10] It is not too surprising that some Bohemian Esperantists, uncongenial toward the German-speaking Esperantists of their country, tried to forge ties with the nationalist Sokol movement.[11] The Boy Scouts movement, established in 1908 in the United Kingdom, was more transnational and, thus, more attractive to Esperantists. In 1918, the Briton Alexander W. Thompson, who had been a corpsman in World War I, created its Esperantist counterpart: the international Skolta Esperanto Ligo (League of Scouts Esperantists). This was the first international scouts organization. The non-Esperantist scout movement had to wait two more years to launch their World Organization of the Scout Movement. Occasionally both international organizations, the Esperantist and non-Esperantist, convened together the international camp gatherings (or "jamborees," in Scout jargon).[12]

Spiritualists, theosophists, vegetarians, and wandering young people were *Hinterweltler*, or hidden-world seekers: people searching for meaning and authenticity not in a distant heaven, but right now and here, or just "behind the wallpaper," as the popular German journalist Carl Bry remarked. They comprised a new breed of believers, people who thought that the unattainable could be reached with the proper amount of conviction and commitment. They were members of a kind of pseudo- or disguised (*verkappte*) religion, brought about by the accelerating pace of modern life.[13]

But side by side with these new religions were the traditional ones, and Esperantists were also active in Catholic and Protestant circles. In their case, and mirroring the universalist message of the language, ecumenism and interconfessional dialogue were important concerns in their agenda.[14]

Catholic Esperantists were the first to organize. In 1902, the French Emile Peltier (1870–1909), the parish priest of a small town near Tours, tried to create a Catholic Esperanto organization. But instead of an organization, he had to content himself with a journal: *Espero Katolika* (Catholic Hope). Already in its first issue of October 1903, Father Peltier made it very clear what kind of Catholicism he stood for. Contrary to the authoritarian and condescending shepherd-and-flock paradigm of conservative Catholics, Peltier pledged to the Esperanto community his willingness to cooperate on an equal footing with other Esperantists, Catholics or not. As he put it: "We are happy to see that Socialists, Jews, Protestants, and Freemasons have their [Esperanto] journals. . . . We will go further: we will open our journal to everybody. In all fairness, we do not think that we own the universal truth, and are ready to concede that people whose religious ideas diverge from ours can teach us many things."[15] Statements like these could attract an audience among the more liberal and social Catholics, but they also distanced traditional Catholics from the Esperanto movement, as some contemporaries pointed out. In any case, the more involved Peltier and likeminded Catholics became in the Esperanto movement, the more they drifted away from mainstream, official Catholicism to embrace ecumenism. Very much enthused after his participation in the Boulogne Congress, Peltier went so far as to publish in *Espero Katolika* a call for the creation of an Esperantist group of ecclesiastics of all Christian faiths. This group, according to his plan, would reunify all Christian religions. But Peltier was too far ahead of his time, and his ecumenical visions did not materialize. He died in 1909, and the next year the Internacia Katolika Unuiĝo Esperantista (IKUE), which Peltier had first envisioned, was created.[16]

From 1911 to 1914, IKUE organized its own annual congresses, and in 1920 it resumed its international activities after the interruption of World War I. By this time the organization—weaker and more tightly controlled by the Catholic hierarchy—faced a strong competitor in the German priest Max Josef Metzger (1887–1944). In 1916, and while IKUE was almost inoperative, Metzger created the World Peace League of the White Cross (for the white cross usually imprinted on the sacred host in the Eucharistic). This was a pacifist and Catholic organization, which promoted the creation of a league of nations based on democratic and Christian principles of truth and justice. The White Cross wanted to unify the scattered groups of progressive Catholics that mushroomed during the war in Germany and abroad, as well as joining forces with other Catholic and non-Catholic pacifist organizations. Since it was an international organization, and Esperanto was widely used in the pacifist movement, the working language of the White Cross was Esperanto. In 1918 Metzger also founded the Peace League of German Catholics (Friedensbund deutscher Katholiken), a non-Esperanto branch of the White Cross. Pacifism, however, was not Metzger's only concern. As a Catholic theologian, he was also involved in the German ecumenical movement, the Hochkirchlich-Oekumenischer Bund (High-Church Ecumenical League), created at the initiative of some progressive German Protestants, to whose journal *Una Sancta* Metzger regularly contributed.

In 1920, when IKUE was able to convene its first postwar conference, Metzger proposed the merger of IKUE and his World Peace League of the White Cross into a new organization: Internacio Katolika (IKa). Although his proposal meant the dismantling of IKUE, it was accepted, and in May 1921, the monthly *Katolika Mondo* (1921–1928) was founded. More conservative Catholic Esperantists, however, were less than happy with this outcome. With the assistance of key members of the Church hierarchy they were able to relaunch *Espero Katolika*, which did not spare criticisms of Metzger, and shortly after they reestablished the old IKUE. Metzger's involvement with the progressive High-Church Ecumenical League most likely explains the Catholic hierarchy's disaffection toward IKa. Ecumenism was still not very popular in Rome, as the *Mortalim animos* encyclical of 1928, which called for the return of Protestants "to the one true Church of Christ," made clear to everybody.

But it was not the lack of support of Rome that put an end to IKa. A pacifist and a deeply religious person, Metzger did not survive the hostile environment of Nazi Germany. His Peace League of German Catholics was in fact among the first victims of the new regime, and IKa followed suit shortly after.

These setbacks, however, could not stop Metzger's activism. Unlike most of the Catholic hierarchy, which opted for accommodation when not for open support of National Socialism, Metzger chose open confrontation. [17] "My worst fears were surpassed," he wrote in private letter of February 1933, after hearing a radio speech of Hitler. "He is a completely hysterical maniac or a thug of the worst sort. After the lecture I said I would have no qualms about shooting him if I could thereby save the lives of the thousands of men who will have to die because of him. Even if I were torn apart in the process . . . I have a very pessimistic view of the future for Germany."[18]

A few months later, Metzger wrote and anonymously published *Die Kirche und das neue Deutschland* (The Church and the New Germany), a mimeographed pamphlet in which he discussed the opposition between the Nazi worldview and the Christian faith. When it became known that he was the author, he was arrested. In 1939 he was behind bars a couple more times, but he served short terms. When the war broke out, Metzger became bolder. He worked on a memorandum that he wanted to send to the Lutheran

Archbishop of Uppsala for distribution in Allied countries. In his memorandum, Metzger urged the Archbishop of Uppsala to act in concert with other religious leaders to put an end to the war, and he advanced his ideas about a postwar democratic Germany and a federalized European Union. But his plan failed, since the person entrusted with handing over the memorandum to the Archbishop of Uppsala was an undercover Gestapo agent. Metzger was arrested for the last time and executed in April 1944. For the Esperantists, Catholic or not, his death was a hard blow to the movement in postwar Germany.[19]

Somewhat more ecumenically oriented than the Catholic IKUE was its Protestant counterpart, KEL (Christian Esperantist League, or KELI, Kristana Esperantista Ligo Internacia, after 1923). Established in 1911, KEL emerged from readership of the Esperanto journal *Dia Regno* (Godly kingdom), which gave voice to Anglicans, Lutherans, Calvinists, and other non-Catholic Christians unconcerned about denominational boundaries. The man behind *Dia Regno* was the German engineer Paul Hübner (1881–1970). Originally, KEL Esperantists aimed to cooperate with the YMCA (Young Men's Christian Association, an international organization with headquarters in Geneva) and the American Christian Endeavour Society to promote these two organizations' international agendas. KEL's membership, however, was never sizeable. In 1912, *Dia Regno* had 410 subscribers, mostly Germans, and twenty years later KEL's total membership amounted to 420 members, most of them Dutch. From 1914 to 1928, KEL was languishing and not even able to issue its journal. Like Catholic Esperantists, Protestant Esperantists were regularly chastised by conservative Protestants for their association with pacifists, freethinkers, leftists, and even Catholics. In reality, KEL preferred to confine itself to the fulfillment of its Christian mission, preferably through the YMCA, rather than forge ties with other Esperantists. KEL felt obliged, however, to cooperate with Catholics and Quakers in the Esperanto translation of the Bible (published in 1926), but, in fact, ecumenism was not high on KEL's agenda. Hence, the quarrel between KEL's president, Paul Hübner, and Livingstone Jenkins, the Quaker and editor of the Esperanto ecumenical journal *Inter Ni* (Among us). The latter was willing to get involved in an open debate with non-Christians, and this was too much for Hübner. Nor was KEL much inclined to exchange points of view with IKUE, all the more so when the latter was controlled by the more conservative Esperantists. Only in 1968 did both Catholic and Protestant Esperantists convene their annual meeting at the same time and place.

Largely marginal in the Esperanto community, KEL could have improved its popularity among fellow Esperantists on the occasion of the Twenty-fifth World Esperanto Congress that took place in the summer of 1932 in Cologne, when the mass persecution against leftists after the Reichstag fire was still in full swing. But in 1932, Paul Hübner was under the spell of National Socialism, like many among the German Evangelical pastorate.[20] Much to the outrage of Dutch KEL members, he encouraged Esperantists to attend the Cologne Congress, even when many of them, particularly the Jews and leftist-oriented, were expressing strong reservations not only because of personal safety but also because of the possibility that the Nazis would try to exploit the Esperanto Congress to save face. Hübner, however, saw things differently, and encouraged fellow Esperantists to attend the congress so that when they returned back home, they could expose the "lies" (*kalumnioj*) that the international press was mounting against the Nazis.[21] His stance certainly did not increase KEL's popularity in the Esperantist community. Only after the Nazis forced him to stop his Esperanto activities did Hübner change his mind about National Socialism, but by then the damage had already been done.

CHAPTER 15

Freethinkers, Socialists, and Herderians

The emergence of new lifestyles and "disguised" religions, as the journalist Carl Bry called them, was not the only front that the established churches had to contend with. Darwinism and, in general, the scientism of positivists and Monists also posed a serious threat to the privileged position that Catholic and Protestant churches had long enjoyed. This challenge was exacerbated when freethinkers and socialists created their own cross-border internationals that mimicked those of traditional religions. And also in this direction the Esperanto movement spread.

In 1880, British, French, Dutch, Belgian, and American freethinkers established the International Freethought Federation.[1] Since 1905, the International had been considering the introduction of Esperanto as a co-official language in its annual meetings, under the assumption that it could strengthen universal fraternity and international relations. Although always regarded sympathetically, the plan to adopt Esperanto never obtained the necessary support.[2] The Esperantist freethinkers, however, were undaunted. In 1908, on the occasion of the third World Esperanto Congress in the United Kingdom, the freethinkers in attendance created their Internacia Societo Esperantista de Liberpensuloj (International Society of Esperantist Freethinkers) and launched *Libera Penso* (1908–1914). After World War I, the organization was reestablished under the name Internacia Ligo de Liberpensuloj (International League of Freethinkers), and *Libera Penso* became *Liberpensulo* (1925–1927).

While freethinkers broadly defended the separation of church and state, they focused on education as their battleground with organized religion. Freethinkers not only opposed the public funding of religious schools but also their very existence. In their fight for the laicization of the school system, freethinkers were not alone. With the extension of public education since the last third of the nineteenth century, and in close relation with socialist and anarchist intellectuals, the freethinkers formulated a new pedagogical paradigm to replace the disciplinary education of traditional schools. Examples include the orphanages established by Janusz Korczak in Warsaw, as well as the Austrian Freie Schule (Free Schools) of Red Vienna, sponsored by freethinkers, freemasons, and socialists.[3] More radical were La Ruche (The Colony), a school founded by the anarchist Sébastian Faure; the experiments of Paul Robin with the *éducation intégrale*; and the Escuela Moderna (the Modern School) of Francisco Ferrer (more about him later). Although too radical for many, these experiments shook the old educational paradigm and were a driving intellectual force for the new and enlarged teaching profession. To exchange ideas and educational experiences, an International Committee of National Federations of Teachers in Public Secondary Schools was created in 1912, and in 1923 the trade unions–based International Trade Secretariat of Teachers was founded. But by then, Esperantist teachers had already established their own international, the Internacia Asocio de Instruistoj (International Association of Teachers), created in 1910, which made the early-established *Internacia Pedagogia Revuo* its official journal.[4]

Freethinkers, progressive teachers, and socialists usually combined their anti-religious sentiments with a pacifism tinged by anti-nationalism. This was the case, for example, with Austrian sociologist Theodor Hartwig, who in 1925 established the International of Proletarian Freethinkers, which supported Esperanto.[5]

But a more vital example of this mix of anticlericalism, anti-nationalism, Esperantism, and pro-socialism is perhaps the Spanish pedagogue and freethinker Francisco Ferrer, the founder of the Escuela Moderna. Executed by the Spanish authorities in 1909 after being falsely accused of organizing the anticlerical and antimilitary riots in Barcelona that year, Ferrer became a martyr for both anarchists and freethinkers. Although Ferrer was not an Esperanto speaker, he was quite clear about his pedagogical and political approach toward the intertwined problem of language and nationalism in the working-class school network that he founded:

There were people who, enthused by the curse of regional patriotism, advised me that we should instruct in the Catalan language. . . . [To my mind, this] would have the effect of narrowing down the humanity and the world to the few thousand people cornered between the Ebro River and the Pyrenees. Not even in Spanish—I replied to the fanatical Catalan nationalist—if Progress had already endorsed the universal language, as it is known. I prefer a hundred times to introduce Esperanto than Catalan.[6]

If Esperanto had been able to infiltrate among freethinkers, in socialists circles it had a higher impact. For many socialists, an artificial language was of paramount importance. It would not only be instrumental for the extension of international revolutionary action; more important, it could help preserve the democratic and proletarian character of the working-class movement by preventing the educated polyglots (namely, members of the bourgeoisie *cum* revolutionaries) from controlling it. In fact, even before Schleyer invented his Volapük, some socialists were already toying with the idea of an artificial language. Thus, in the second congress of the First International that took place in Lausanne in 1867, the anarchist section persuaded other delegates to pass a resolution calling for the "concretion of a universal language, which will promote the unity and fraternity of all peoples."[7] A similar, although fictional, resolution was pictured by Cabet in his utopian novel *Voyage en Icarie*, where the Icarians initiate research to create a universal language.[8] In working-class circles, the idea of an artificial language had an old appeal and was a constant presence.

Following the Esperanto congress in Boulogne, some labor Esperantist associations sprang up in France, Germany, Sweden, and the Netherlands. In France, the Esperantist and the mostly anarchist group Paco-Libereco (Peace and Freedom) was born in 1905. The following year, it merged with Esperantista Laboristaro (Esperantist Workers) to create Liberiga Stelo (Emancipating Star). The new association, comprised of socialists, anarchists, and syndicalists, launched *Internacia Socia Revuo*, with the goal of establishing an international organization opened to all socialist leanings. By 1913, the journal had more than 600 subscribers in twenty countries. The creation of an international of Esperantist workers, however, had to wait until 1921, when, on the occasion of the annual Esperanto congress in Prague, and under the initiative of the French workers and particularly of Lanti (whom we met in the first pages of this book), the SAT (Sennacieca Asocio Tutmonda, or Universal Association of A-Nationalists) was created. SAT, which launched the journal *Sennaciulo* (1924–), had more than 5,000 members in 1927.

Lanti (whose real name was Eugène Adam [1879–1947]) was born in the small town of Néhou, in Lower Normandy, to illiterate parents. He became a cabinet maker and in 1903 settled in Paris, where he worked as an instructor in a vocational school. Raised as a Catholic, he became an atheist and a radical pacifist, with an affinity for the anarchist movement. He learned Esperanto while serving in World War I in an ambulance unit. In 1920, inspired by the success of the October Revolution, he joined the French Communist Party. Lanti was always a strange bird in the party, however. Although he admired the communists' revolutionary zeal and organizational efficiency, he was never a dogmatic Leninist and always remained close to the anarchists. His three-week visit to the Soviet Union in 1922 only reinforced his skepticism toward official communism.

As Lanti saw it, SAT was meant to be the working-class counterpart of bourgeois Esperantists. Indeed, between 1922 and 1924, SAT banned dual membership with non–working class Esperanto organizations, whose official neutrality in working-class issues, according to Lanti, only helped to reinforce global capitalism and camouflage the struggle between the proletarians and the bourgeoisie. Even worse, by accepting the existence of nation-states and claiming that Esperanto should not aspire to dislodge national languages, the neutral Esperanto movement was, according to him, reinforcing a sort of false consciousness that perpetuated the fetish of the national community and the exploitation of the working class. Hence, the critical role that Lanti envisioned for Esperanto: it could help dissolve those supposedly natural bonds that united the oppressors and the oppressed, and propel class struggle. Lanti's internationalism was more radical than Zamenhof's. Both of them were aware of the creative work of intellectuals and political entrepreneurs to artificially construct nations, but whereas Zamenhof still felt that an ethnic identity was inescapable and even necessary as the basis for an individual identity and thus for the possibility of moral action, Lanti believed it pernicious and ultimately disposable. Lanti's anti-nationalism can best be perceived as a flattening universalism, whereby the old national and linguistic identities had to be replaced by a new, transformative, and universal identity. As he once put it: "The anti-nationalists are against everything national: against the national languages, cultures, traditions, and customs. For them, Esperanto is the most important language, and their national languages only are auxiliary languages [condemned to] become archaic, dead things, like the ancient Greek and Roman languages and cultures."[9]

Because of Lanti's radical anti-nationalism, the SAT only accepted individual membership. At the same time, the new organization was not conceived for revolutionary action, but for instruction and debate. As stated in its bylaws, "Not being a political, but an enlightening, educational and cultural organization, it endeavors to make its members tolerant and broadminded regarding the different political and philosophical schools or systems [of the working-class movement]. By the exchange of facts and ideas and free discussion, it strives to counteract the dogmatization of the teachings instilled by their respective schools."[10] But neither such open-mindedness nor their common identity as Esperantists could spare SAT members from the internal fights that punctuated the entire history of the European socialist movement in these years, and more particularly between the Bolshevists and their rivals in the international socialist movement.

The leader of the Esperantist Bolshevists was Ernest Drezen (1892–1937). He became a Bolshevist in 1918 and was a high-ranking military officer and political commissar in the Red Army during the Civil War. An engineer by training, and in his capacity as deputy chief of the All-Russian Central Executive Committee from 1921 to 1923, he was entrusted with the implementation of Taylorism in the growing state apparatus of the new regime. In Drezen's worldview, there was room for Esperanto in a revolutionary, multilingual Soviet Union. In 1921, Drezen collected the remnants of the former Russian Esperanto movement and created SEU (Sovetrespublikara Esperantista Unio). The relatively less repressive environment that the just-adopted New Economic Policy heralded let Drezen enlist non-communist Esperantists. He hoped that this would strengthen the visibility of Esperanto in the Soviet Union. This open-minded strategy, however, put Drezen in a difficult position. As he knew very well, the survival of the movement in the new regime did not depend on its numerical strength, but on the difficult and perilous task of navigating among the different Bolshevist factions, and the Kremlin's shifting foreign policy. Given the public pronouncements of bourgeois Esperantists, Esperanto could be easily labeled as a counter-revolutionary language, a distraction in the march toward world revolution. As Drezen saw it, the most expedient way to give Esperanto a chance in the Soviet Union was to put SAT at the service of the Bolshevists and the Comintern.

Prompted by the "united front" policy adopted by the Third Congress of the Comintern, Drezen urged Western European communists to join SAT in order to take it over and align it with "the [proper] organizational form of international action [the Comintern] . . . , unmask its confounding idealism, and instill in it a more practical and Communist influence."[11]

The mass influx of communists in SAT immediately influenced the editorial line of its official journal *Sennaciulo*, which, in order to avoid an open confrontation with the Bolshevists, avoided any criticism of the Soviet Union and concealed the wave of arrests of anarchists and other "counter-revolutionaries" that intensified in 1923. This approach, however, did not please all SAT members. A sizeable number of anarchists abandoned SAT to create their own international: the Tutmonda Ligo de Esperantistaj Senŝtatanoj (World League of Stateless Esperantists), which published the bi-monthly *Libera Laboristo* (1925–1931).[12]

Conflicts between the SAT and SEU continued for some years. The SEU tried to win over the national Esperantist labor unions, with an eye to capture SAT, and in 1930 Drezen and fellow communists were able to take over the strong German labor association of Esperantists, but that was all. In 1931 Drezen gave up. He decided to part ways with SAT and, with the help of German Esperantists, create his own pro-Moscow Esperantist international, IPE (Internacio de Proleta Esperantistaro). IPE, however, had a short life. In 1933 the German government banned all communist activity, including that of the Esperantists. And at home, the Kremlin viewed Drezen's lack of success vis-à-vis Lanti and SAT with growing suspicion. Eventually, the internecine battles in the Kremlin reached Drezen, who, because of his "counterrevolutionary and terrorist" activities, was executed, together with some other members of SEU's Central Committee. Hundreds of rank-and-file Russian Esperantists were sent to the Gulag.[13]

Divisions among working-class Esperantists did not stop here. A third Esperantist labor international, of social democratic leanings, the Internacio de Socialistaj Esperantistoj, was established in 1933 under the leadership of Franz Jonas, who would later serve as president of Austria between 1965 and 1974. With primarily Austrian membership, the social democratic international of Esperantists disappeared five years later as a result of the Anschluss.[14]

As noted in previous chapters, nationalist and conservative circles opposed the idea of an international language. For the most radical among them, the Esperantist was an effeminate movement, a gathering of meek souls preaching pacifism and hysterical women. That important sectors of the working class adopted Esperanto and mobilized on either an anti-nationalist or a pro-Moscow basis only increased their misgivings toward Zamenhof and his language.

Interestingly, however, even in nationalist circles there was some thought that Esperanto could be useful to further their agendas. We might call them "Herderian Esperantists." As Herderians, they envisioned a world society comprising self-governing, equally worthy, and mutually respecting, albeit linguistically and ethnically homogeneous, nation-states.[15] As Esperantists, they thought that Esperanto could be the bulwark against the corruptive influence of the more powerful and aggressive foreign languages and, consequently, improve the vitality of their languages and nations.

In their view, Esperanto would minimize the need to learn any of the languages of the most powerful nations and, more important, make it easier to cleanse or purify national languages. The creator of Spelin, Georg Bauer (1848–1900), had already noted an artificial language's potential sanitizing, prophylactic power. In Bauer's Volapükist years he encouraged his fellow Croatians to protect their language against the filth (*Schmutz*) of foreign tongues by way of Volapük: "My people, love your language above all / Live in it, die for it / Adopt Volapük and you will save your language."[16]

But it was probably the German Esperantist Arnold Behrendt who in 1913 expressed this Herderianism most radically. Since it would be unrealistic, given the complexity and irregularities of the otherwise beautiful German language, to expect it to surpass French or English in the international arena, Behrendt thought that Esperanto could be of great service, since its extension would undermine the position of those two other languages. More important, by helping to cleanse the German language of foreign words, Esperanto could "strengthen the German national consciousness, deepen the comprehension and knowledge of the German language, nourish and invigorate Germandom abroad, and convey the appreciation and respect for the German essence in other countries. Esperanto can help all Germans preserve their leading role amongst the nations, which only of late and after great difficulties has transpired."[17]

Herderian Esperantists were more common in multilingual countries, however, and we find them working hand in hand with nationalist movements. For example, rather than cooperating with the German-speaking Esperantists for the establishment of an encompassing Austrian Esperanto League, the Bohemian Esperantists preferred to work autonomously by way of their Bohema Unio Esperantista.[18] And when the independent Republic of Czechoslovakia was created in 1918, the tensions between German- and Czech-speaking Esperantists eventually resulted in the establishment of two separate associations: the Germana Esperanto Ligo en Ĉeĥoslovakio (German Esperanto League in Czechoslovakia) and the Ĉeĥoslovaka Asocio Esperantista (Czechoslovak Esperantist Association). Similarly, a leading member of the Irish Esperantist Association, set up in 1909, was Joseph M.

Plunkett, one of the seven signatories of the Irish proclamation of independence that followed the 1916 Eastern Rising.[19] Also in 1929, some Flemish Esperantists launched the journal *Flandra Esperantisto*, the motto of which was "A free Flanders in a peaceful world," and one year later they founded the Flandra Ligo Esperantista (Flemish Esperantist League), which aimed at monopolizing the representation of the Flemish Esperantists vis-à-vis the Belga Ligo Esperantista.[20] By that time, the Herderian Esperantists of Catalonia had a long history. They were also more tightly connected with their respective nationalist movements. The founder of the Catalan Esperanto association Espero Kataluna (Catalan Hope), Frederic Pujulá i Vallés, was also a member of the executive committee of Unió Catalanista, an umbrella organization of Catalan nationalists that decided to use Esperanto as the means of communication with other nationalist movements.[21] As the Esperantist Pujulá saw it: "The great task is to divide the world into its natural regions. . . . We should encourage each other; the Finnish for Finland, the Castilian people for Castile, but also the Catalan [for Catalonia], since this is the first step to feel human."[22]

Although there is a clear boundary between Herderianism and National Socialism—which, contrary to the former, does not place nations on an equal footing—the potential of Esperanto to diversify and extend in different directions crossed that line. Even when Hitler had condemned Esperanto as the weapon of the Jews, in 1931 a young SA member established the pro-Nazi NDEB (Neue Deutsche Esperanto Bewegung, or New German Esperanto Movement). The NDEB, which by the mid-1930s had roughly 500 members, most of them also members of the Nazi Party, aspired to take over the Germana Esperanto Bund (German Esperanto League) and cleanse it of "Jews, pacifists and all kind of scroungers."[23] As the Nazi Esperantists saw it (at least Zamenhof was already dead and would not have to see this development), Esperanto could be instrumental for international propaganda, as well as for strengthening the Deutschtum by protecting the German language from the invasion of foreign words. But as we saw in Chapter 7, the Gestapo had a more accurate view of things. It declared Esperanto to be diametrically opposed to National Socialism, banned party members from joining any Esperanto organization, and finally dismantled all Esperantist organizations.[24]

The Nazi Esperantists were in no way representative of the movement. As we have seen before, the pursuit of peace had a more central position for the average Esperantist. But the fact that Esperanto could also be found, albeit temporarily, in the most unexpected and undesirable quarters proves the capacity of the language to expand and quite often to be appropriated by the most divergent sectors of society. Esperantists came from all walks of life and chose to learn the language for quite different reasons. They were Bolsheviks, anarchists, and socialists; atheists, and religious-minded people; Catholics and Protestants; feminists and conservatives; blind people; Social Darwinists and people convinced of the sacrality of all human life; Herderians and anti-nationalists; people exploring new life styles and "hidden worlds," and people concerned about real-world problems; scientists and Nobel Prize winners and workers with a basic education; librarians and Taylorist engineers; and radical and conservative pacifists. They attest to a diversity of interests only foreshadowed in the Volapükist movement.

But, since the Volapükists were not able to agree on the basics of their language, a precondition for a language to develop and move in different directions, they lived and died together, fighting about this or that word or grammar rule. The Esperantists, in contrast, were able to agree on their *Fundamento*, which let them explore the language's utility in different and sometimes opposing directions. This agreement did not make the community of Esperantists to be a thick one. On the contrary, it was traversed by different worldviews and lifestyles. Esperantists ended up speaking the same language, but not dancing to the same music.

It was precisely this diversity of interests and peoples within the movement, the potential of the language to infiltrate in different sectors of society, and its demonstrated utility as a means of verbal and written communication that made Esperanto not only look invincible vis-à-vis potential rivals yet to come, but also in some quarters a political threat that had to be contained. This potential to spread in different directions, the linguistic resiliency and adaptability created by Esperanto's diverse users, and the merits of emphasizing communities of speakers over technical perfection—all these prove to be critical when we consider Ido, Esperanto's most dangerous rival.

PART IV

Ido and Its Satellites

CHAPTER 16

"One Ideal International Language": Ido

In 1900, before the opening of the Paris Universal Exhibition, Leópold Leau, the ex-Volapükist and professor of mathematics at the University of Dijon, published *Une langue universelle est-elle possible?* In this brochure, the author did not position himself for Volapük, Esperanto, or any other language project. He was mainly deploring how a multiplicity of vernaculars impeded scientific progress. He anticipated that this problem was going to become quite visible at the international scientific meetings scheduled to take place in Paris. And, consequently, he proposed that national scientific societies and the recently created International Association of Academies name delegates to a committee that should try to find a solution. He commissioned some friends who would be attending international congresses at the Universal Exhibition to put this proposal on the floor. Some of them were successful, but not many. Unsurprisingly, the Congrès de l'enseignement des langues vivantes did not want to hear anything about an international language. The participants at the Congrès d'histoire comparée, the Congrès de l'enseignement technique, the Congrès de philosophie, and the Congrès des mathématiciens, were more enthusiastic. They agreed to name delegates—in the last case, Leau himself—for the proposed committee.[1]

Leau did not have to try hard to convince his old friend, Louis Couturat (1868–1914), about his scheme. Although with some resistance from fellow philosophers—more particularly, from those who thought that the use of different languages in philosophical investigations was a blessing, not a curse—participants of the Congrès de philosophie finally agreed to name Couturat for the projected committee.[2]

By this time, Couturat was already fascinated with the idea of an artificial language. With a major in mathematics, he had applied his interests to philosophy and symbolic logic. His dissertation on the problem of the infinite received a very favorable review from Bertrand Russell, with whom Couturat later forged a closed friendship.

Both Couturat's interest in symbolic logic and in the possibility of an artificial language originated in his research on Leibniz, many of whose works were still buried at the archives of the library of Hannover, waiting to be discovered. In his work *La logique de Leibniz*, published in 1901, Couturat devoted a lot of attention to Leibniz's ideas on the problem and possibility of a philosophical language. But, contrary to Leibniz, as well as to Dalgarno and Wilkins, Couturat did not think it possible to construct a philosophical language. He did think it possible, however, to approximate this ideal with the help of symbolic logic. The new field of symbolic logic, Couturat thought, could help adjudicate between competing artificial languages. By thinking in these terms, he and Leau were reproducing the agenda and spirit of the American Philosophical Society, which, as we saw in Chapter 4, thought that the construction and ultimate decision about the properties of an artificial language should not be left to aficionados. More important, the success of an international language, according to Leau and Couturat, as well as the American Philosophical Society, exclusively depended on its internal qualities, no matter the number of people who had been lured by one or another competing project.

Following their plan, in January 1901, Leau and Couturat established the Delegation for the Adoption of an Auxiliary Language. They wanted to convince the general public of the need to adopt an international, auxiliary language, and, more importantly, to adjudicate among different projects. To promote the Delegation, Couturat launched an intense campaign, mostly focused on scholars and scientists. This campaign had uneven results. For example, his friend and rising star Bertrand Russell was not very enticed by this idea. As he wrote to Couturat, he still preferred the Leibnizian project of a strictly logical language. Also, if the merit of an artificial language such as Esperanto is that "it saves us the trouble of learning two or three foreign languages, I wouldn't say that there is much utility in the project, since it only spares us of a little bit of trouble . . . and I think that learning foreign languages has a value of itself." Still, Russell thought that Couturat's plan could have some utility "if the Russians, the Dutch, and so on, were persuaded to adopt it; since, it would be intolerable that it became necessary to learn all these barbaric languages (*langues barbares*)." In the end, Russell agreed to help his friend and campaign for the Delegation.[3]

Like Russell, more than 1,300 scholars and around 300 scientific societies and academies gave their support to Couturat's Delegation. They expected that the International Association of Academies would pursue the matter. If not, the Delegation would name a commission that would choose among the competing language projects and give its official support to the winner. To help the cause Leau and Couturat published in 1903 the *Histoire de la langue universelle*, a 500-plus-page book that analyzes more than forty language projects originating from as early as the seventeenth century. Four years later, the *Histoire* was updated with the supplement *Les nouvelles langues internationales*.

But the International Association of Academies declined to take a position on this topic, under the assumption that the problem of an international language could only be solved empirically, in a Darwinian manner.[4] Leau and Couturat decided to proceed with their plans. Based on a list proposed by them, the scientists and societies who had supported the Delegation's plan voted for the members of the planned commission, which would choose the winning language. The Commission for the Adoption of an International Language was originally composed of fourteen members, and in late October 1907 it went to work. Since most of its elected members were not able to attend the meetings, they named substitutes. The Commission also co-opted other scientists and interested people to take part—most significantly, Giuseppe Peano. Peano's research in both fractal geometry and number theory—Peano's curves and Peano's axioms, respectively—had earned him an international reputation in scientific circles. From number theory, Peano moved to symbolic logic and ended up creating an artificial language: Latino sine flexione (or Latin without inflexions). Inspired by Rosenberger's Idiom Neutral, Peano took the de-morphologizing thrust of the latter to its limits, so much so that, to use his own words, he had constructed a "lingua sine grammatica" (a language without grammar).[5]

Aside from Leau and Couturat, the most active members of the Commission were two professors of linguistics (Jan Baudouin de Courtenay, from Saint Petersburg University, whom we met in Chapter 4, and Otto Jespersen, from the University of Copenhagen), the Esperantist (and spiritist—see Chapter 14) Émile Boirac, rector of the University of Dijon and president of the Lingva Komitato, and the chemist Wilhelm Ostwald (whom we met in Chapter 13). Never before had such a collection of knowledgeable and interested people held lengthy debates on the topic of an artificial language. The Commission finally met in 1907, two years after the Boulogne Congress. For two weeks, and on top of Volapük and Esperanto, the Commission examined Langage simplifié, Dilpok, L'Apolema, The Master Language, Logo, Universal, Novlatin, Spokil, Parla, Langue Bleue, Peano's Latino sine flexione, and Rosenberger's (reformed) Idiom Neutral.[6] The meetings were mostly conducted in French and occasionally in German. Peano, however, preferred to defend his Latino sine flexione in this same language. At Zamenhof's request, de Beaufront commended Esperanto, also supported by Boirac.

Most of these projects were summarily dismissed. A little more attention was given to Rosenberger's (reformed) Idiom Neutral and Peano's Latino sine flexione, but eventually they shared the same fate. Esperanto seemed to be the favorite.

In one of the last meetings, however, Couturat surprised Commission members when he presented a new language scheme. Apparently, this was an anonymous project, authored under the pseudonym "Ido," which nobody had ever heard of. Couturat explained to the members of the Commission that he knew who the author was, but he wanted to remain anonymous. He reassured them that the author was not a member of the Commission, as its statutes required.

After some discussion, the Commission examined Ido, as the language was later called. It became very clear that it was a radically reformed Esperanto. It incorporated some of the reforms rejected in the 1894 referendum, such as the suppression of the letters with diacritics (ĉ, ĝ, ĥ, ĵ, ŝ, ŭ) that looked too Slavonic. Ido also suppressed the accusative case, as well as the concordance of nouns and adjectives. More intriguingly, it also incorporated the objections to Esperanto's word formation rules that Couturat had thoroughly criticized in his *Étude sur la dérivation en Esperanto*, published only months before the Commission met.

In its last session, the Commission approved the Ido project. The only disapproving voice came from the pacifist Moch, who was substituting for Boirac. According to Moch, the Commission was exceeding its prerogatives, since its job was to adjudicate among competing artificial languages, not to change or create a new one.[7] For the sake of unanimity, however, Moch approved the Commission's final report, which agreed to accept Esperanto "in principle," meaning "on condition that it is changed . . . in the direction indicated by the secretaries' report and by the project called Ido, and if possible in agreement with the Lingva Komitato of the Esperantists."[8] To negotiate this agreement, the Commission established a Permanent Committee presided over by Wilhelm Ostwald.

Although disturbing, the Committee's final decision was one that many Esperanto leaders expected, since talk about language reform had never ended. They were taken aback, however, by the commanding tone of Couturat and the Permanent Committee. A frenzied epistolary exchange ensued in the next months between Zamenhof, leading members of the Lingva Komitato, and the Permanent Committee. This correspondence shows a remorseful Boirac, who had proved unable to prevent the Paris Commission from endorsing Ido, an astonished Zamenhof trying to find out what his closest associates stood up for—particularly de Beaufront, his trusted confidant at the Commission— and Couturat and Ostwald discussing how to twist the arms of Zamenhof and leading Esperantists. More important, this correspondence shows that underlying the unavoidable clash between Esperantists and Idists was a divergent interpretation about the nature of authority in artificial languages. Whereas for Zamenhof and the leaders of the Lingva Komitato, the Paris Commission lacked legitimacy to propose reforms, since it did not emerge from within the ranks of the Esperanto community, for Couturat and associates —the Idists— it was the only authoritative body to do so, given its scientific character. Thus, when the Esperantists invited the Idists to hold joint discussions within the Lingva Komitato, Couturat plainly refused. It did not make much sense for him to discuss scientific matters with lay people.

As we saw in Chapter 11, disagreements among the Esperantists at the Boulogne Congress had made it impossible to establish a stable, centralized organizational structure which represented the movement. This made things more difficult for Couturat. He was forced to deal with both the Lingva Komitato and Zamenhof, acting as the informal leader of the movement. This made interlocution with the Esperantists rather difficult: when addressed by Couturat, the Lingva Komitato deferred to Zamenhof, and when Zamenhof received a request from Couturat, he deferred to the Lingva Komitato. To end this situation, Ostwald demanded that Zamenhof act in an authoritarian manner to facilitate the transition from Esperanto to Ido. Zamenhof refused, insisting that he did not have the power to change the language,[9] but he agreed to exercise his moral authority, although in the opposite direction.

In an open letter and four circulars that he sent in December 1907 to local groups and journals, Zamenhof asked the Esperantists to ignore the Idists and their Permanent Committee and work through the official channels, namely the Lingva Komitato and the annual congresses, for whatever changes or reforms the Esperanto community would be willing to make.[10] Anyone who decided to work outside these channels, Zamenhof concluded, "does not deserve to call himself an Esperantist."[11]

Right after the publication of this letter, the Lingva Komitato conferred, asking its members about the reforms proposed by the Idists. Eight members refused to give a clear answer for lack of information, eleven wanted some changes to be introduced, eight approved of the Idists' proposals, and thirty-four completely disapproved them and refused to negotiate with an external body. These results and Zamenhof's position settled the issue and by January 1908 the Esperantists ended their conversations with the Permanent Committee. As Boirac explained to Ostwald in a private letter, the Idists' proposal to reform Esperanto was akin to the demand of a French person who is fluent in German that Germans change their language according to his preferences. Boirac found this insulting and unacceptable. And since the Idists based their demands on scientific grounds, he rounded off his argument using the language of sociology: "According to us, Esperanto is an already existing language, living, similar in this respect to natural and national languages, English, French, German, etc.; consequently it is like them a *fact*, even a social fact, which will evolve, like all social facts, by the action of humanity for the most part on its own initiative, whose life makes it possible in the same way."[12]

The end of the negotiations between the two camps compelled Esperantists to take sides. It is impossible to know for certain how many shifted to Ido. Different sources agree, however, that most rank-and-file Esperantists did not change sides. More precisely, it has been estimated that around one-quarter of the leadership—the most cultivated Esperantists, and hence the most sensitive to Couturat's scientific discourse—shifted to Ido.[13] Couturat had administered a severe blow to the Esperanto community, and relations between the Idists and Esperantists were rather bitter from the start. This bitterness was also fueled by suspicion on the side of the Esperantists toward de Beaufront: he had been entrusted by Zamenhof to defend Esperanto in the Commission, but ended up in the Idists' inner circle. Rumors were circulating that de Beaufront had been a double agent, and, more excruciating, that he was the author of Ido.

These rumors were corroborated in February 1908, when Jespersen received a letter from Couturat that was originally addressed to de Beaufront but put in the wrong envelope. The content of this letter convinced Jespersen that Ido was the collaborative undertaking of Couturat and de Beaufront. Jespersen had supported Couturat, and now he felt he had been manipulated.

Incensed, Jespersen informed Ostwald about this double game and asked both Couturat and de Beaufront to come out in open.[14] It took de Beaufront four months to come forward. In his public confession, and in order to save Couturat's reputation, de Beaufront assumed the entire responsibility for Ido's authorship. This satisfied Jespersen. As he retrospectively explained, progress and scientific advancement were more important than occasional upheavals in personal relations: "Despite my misgivings about the persons involved, I did feel that they were on the right track, in contrast to the bullheaded stand which the Esperantists were putting up against any improvement of the language."[15] And to some extent, it also satisfied the Esperantists. They had unveiled de Beaufront, the Judas of Esperantism, a villain whose last service to the movement was to unite all Esperantist against him and Ido.

Following the break with the Esperantists, the Idists' Permanent Commission set out to polish the new language according to Couturat's ideas about word formation rules, which were going to give Ido the highest possible degree of logicality and perfection. As he saw it: "There is only one ideal international language, being the current projects more or less proximate realizations of this ideal language . . . and [subsequently] dialects of the same [ideal] language."[16] Translated into practical terms, this search for higher degrees of perfection involved a permanent reform process, and, ultimately, a language in constant motion. Hence, rather than a standardization battle dominated by increasing returns mechanisms, Couturat and most Ido leaders perceived themselves working their way in a diminishing returns scenario where the best technology necessarily crowds out competing designs. In the words of a leading Idist:

The bicycle, the motor car, and the typewriting machine have undergone successive improvements till finally they have attained to their more or less definite form. We see from this that when inventions have once reached a certain degree of suitability they are not afterwards easily replaced by others. There is, therefore, only one adequate criterion of the stability of an international language, namely, that of suitability or adaptation to its purpose, and we maintain that it is only by means of continuous reforms and improvements that it will succeed in satisfying this criterion and finally attain stability.[17]

To implement this program, Idists launched *Progreso*, their official journal, in March 1908. That same year they established the central organization of the movement, the Uniono di l'Amiki de la Linguo Internaciona (Union of the Friends of the International Language). The Uniono was composed of two bodies, independent from each other: the Academy and the Central Committee. The Academy, composed of twelve to thirteen people, was entrusted to make changes in the language, and its decisions were binding. On its side, the Central Committee, which did not have veto power over the Academy's decisions, had to financially assist the latter and organize public relations campaigns. More significantly, membership in the Academy was restricted to scientists and linguists, while members of the Central Committee had to be elected according to their organizational skills and social status.[18] By mid-1909, both the members of the Academy and the Central Committee were elected by all registered members of the Uniono. Couturat was named secretary of the Academy, and Jespersen was president.[19]

Like members of the old Volapükist Academy, Ido Academy members worked by correspondence. But unlike the Lingva Komitato of the Esperantists, the Ido Academy was entrusted to make decisions on behalf of the speakers. This was exactly the same mistake that the Volapükists had made and the Esperantists had avoided. By agreeing on the basic properties of the language at an early stage, and letting speakers to develop the language according to their communicative needs, the Esperantists had established the mechanism that would allow their language to expand in different directions.

Couturat and leading Idists, on the contrary, were more than happy to reform Ido as they thought it necessary. And they did so at lightning speed, in order to perfect the language as soon as possible. To give an idea of the rate of these changes, the 1914 English reprint of Couturat et al., *International Language and Science*, first published in 1910, does not include specimens of the original edition, "since the difference between 1910 Ido and that of 1914 onwards is great enough that it may cause confusion for those learning the language."[20]

This reformist zeal and the philosophy behind it created problems. Not everyone was happy with the changes, or with Couturat's leadership style, sometimes perceived as disingenuous and manipulative.[21] For these reasons Ostwald stopped working with him, although he later agreed to be named honorary president of the Uniono.[22] Similarly, in 1908, Baudouin de Courtenay discontinued his contacts with the Idists, regretting the "fatal consequences" of a new movement for the international language ideal.[23] Otto

Jespersen, the other prominent linguist in the Ido ranks, and president of the Academy, quit in mid-1910 because of disagreement with Couturat's linguistic ideas.[24] For the same reasons, the British linguist Paul Hugon, vice-secretary of the Ido Academy, abandoned the movement, as did the German A. Haugg, editor of the Idist journal *Internaciona Pioniro*.[25] More aggravating to Couturat was that the Idist journal the *International Language* changed allegiance to Peano's Latino sine flexione, as had also been the case a year earlier with the Italian *Rivista della Lingua Internatiozionale*.[26]

Peano was a particularly menacing rival to Couturat. The fact that Peano was also applying the tools of symbolic logic to create his own artificial language eroded Couturat's scientifically based legitimacy discourse.[27] On top of this, Peano proved to be a tough nut to crack. In 1908 he took over Rosenberger's ex-Volapükist Academy, changed its name to Academia pro Interlingua, and began publishing the journal *Discussiones* the following year. Both his Academy and journal became instruments to promote Latino sine flexione and undermine Ido.[28] The confrontation between Couturat and Peano ended a twenty-year professional relationship. Their fight became so acrimonious that in the last letters they exchanged, Couturat stopped using French and shifted to Ido, to which Peano counterattacked by using his Latino—an interesting outcome coming from two people who had invented international languages to facilitate communication and understanding.[29] By February 1910, they were no longer on speaking terms, much to the chagrin of their common friend Bertrand Russell. As he complained to his longtime confidant Ottoline Morrel,

> I enclose 2 letters (which please return), one from Peano and one from Couturat, both occupied with the international language (or rather languages). First there was Volapük, then Esperanto, then an improvement on Esperanto called Ido (its proficients are called Idiots), then Peano's "Latin without Inflections." These various sects hate each other like poison, but Esperantists and Idiots hate each other most because they are nearest akin. Couturat is an Idiot. I am ashamed to confess that he was my earliest disciple.[30]

Furthermore, even though everyone agreed that reforms were necessary, frictions also arose around the pace of these reforms. On the one hand, some thought that if the very essence of Ido was its constant refinement, reforms should be introduced as swiftly as possible to prevent the language from getting "crystallize[d] by general usage."[31] For them, arresting reforms would be tantamount to stooping to the level of the irrational Esperantists and their fetishism around their *Fundamento*. Also, some held the idea that Ido's failure to surpass Esperanto could be explained because Ido was not perfect enough, and that its perfection required a stronger reformist commitment. Others, however, thought it necessary to slow down the rate of reforms, or even to temporarily halt them, since it was difficult to promote a language that was in constant motion and that required unlearning old words and rules to learn new ones.[32] According to the more conservative followers, the most urgent matter to promote the language was the publication of dictionaries and grammars, which necessarily meant restraining the Academy's perfectionist zeal. These frictions, or, in Couturat's words, the "state of war" among Idists, demanded prompt action, which he eventually took.[33] In 1911, he decided to establish a short stabilization period, which in 1914 was extended to ten more years.[34] During this period, two versions of Ido became official: the old, "klasika Ido," externally used to promote the language, and the continuously changing Ido that resulted from the official decisions of the Academy, still operative in this period of stability. This middle-ground solution, however, did not solve the problem, since some journals preferred to give preference to classic Ido, whereas others refused to use an outdated version. These tensions required Couturat to act in an authoritarian manner, according to some, by condemning both the "conservatives who refused to follow him [and] progressives who went one step ahead of him."[35]

More important still, if Ido was expected to automatically triumph over Esperanto and other rivals as a result of its technical superiority, which demanded its constant improvement and perfection, then the promotion of a community of speakers was thought to be secondary, if not counterproductive. Thus, contrary to Zamenhof—who constantly encouraged his followers to create an original literature in order to experiment with the language, facilitate its natural development, and nourish an emotional attachment with the language and its community of speakers—in Idist circles the perception was that an original literature could only strengthen the "love to the language" as it was and forge an irrational sentimental attachment to the language that could prevent it from constantly progressing. An original literature, they concluded, could only be pursued with caution, insofar as "love to the language remains within rational boundaries."[36]

Similarly, the chemist Ludwig Pfaundler, first vice-president of the Central Committee of the Uniono, argued against sociability. Even when balls, concerts, or plays, so common in Esperantist circles, could attract the curious, they were distracting. Rather than entertaining, Pfaundler recommended that local Idist associations be practical and fill their regular meetings with language courses, reading and discussion of journals, and so on.[37] This course of action was unequivocally endorsed in 1921, on the occasion of the First Ido congress, whose slogan was "We have come here to work, not to amuse ourselves."[38]

Correspondingly, any association of Ido with any kind of ethical or political program was plainly dismissed as inimical to what was ultimately meant to be a scientific research program.[39] Even though it would be inaccurate to conclude that this organizational strategy prevented Idists from forging their own identity and networks of interpersonal ties, this was what Couturat and his associates expected. To borrow from Forster's analysis, rather than a community of speakers composed by people emotionally attached to a language, they had chosen to become a society of learned "seekers."[40]

Applied in an increasing returns scenario, Couturat's strategy proved to be fatal. Inattentive to the power of language as a source of identity, and to the competitive advantage that a strong base of supporters could offer, he pinned all his hopes on the technical superiority of Ido. But being in permanent construction and hence never fixed or standardized, Ido could hardly win a standardization battle.

If Schleyer's meta-language was hierarchy and discipline, and Esperanto's was participation and commitment, then Couturat's was truth. As a scholar, he was confident that truth would ultimately assert itself. It was only necessary to set up the conditions for truth to reveal itself. Hence, the organizational primacy of the Academy over rank-and-file Idists, of research over sociability, of scientific progress over emotion. And when truth failed to assert itself, there was only one explanation in Couturat's mental model: irrationalism, fanaticism, or fetishism, when not pure wickedness on the side of the Esperantists. To quote from Bertrand Russell:

> In the last years I had lost contact with him [Couturat], because he became absorbed on the question of an international language. He advocated Ido rather than Esperanto. According to his conversation, no human beings in the whole previous history of the human race had ever been quite so depraved as the Esperantists. He lamented that the word Ido did not lend itself to the formation of a word similar to Esperantist. I suggested "idiot" but he was not quite pleased.[41]

Couturat died in a car accident right at the beginning of World War I. He had been the soul of Ido, for which he had traded his academic reputation. After his death, the Ido movement witnessed some temporary reprieve due to the decision to stabilize the language, at least temporarily. But it was short-lived, and compared with the Esperantists the Idists never developed a wide base of support.

To begin with, and very much like the Volapük, the Ido movement was male-dominated: women only represented between 11 and 15 percent of total membership.[42] This small percentage can probably be explained by Couturat's emphasis on concentrating his propaganda on the fields of science and commerce, where women were underrepresented. If we consider the counterexample of the Esperantists, the relative absence of women seriously curtailed the growth potential of Ido.

Also, Couturat had always resisted any link between Ido and moral or political messages that he feared could alienate the support of influential organizations or governments. This hands-off strategy excluded Zamenhof's admittedly never well-defined "interna ideo" and its pacifist message. As he saw it, and notwithstanding their moral appeal, "vacuous and chimeric ideas" could do more harm than good to the language.[43]

In the postwar years, this policy was somewhat relaxed and, as a consequence of the decision to temporarily stabilize the language, some specialized organizations (Catholics, teachers, anarchists, communists, and even vegetarians) emerged in the Ido camp. These organizations, however, did not last long. By 1925, the Uniono had only 500 members, and the following year, at the international congress in Prague, the movement split into a reformist and conservative camp. By the second half of the 1920s most of the specialized Idist journals had ceased publication.[44]

Certainly the Ido episode was a hard blow to the artificial language cause in general, but retrospectively the Esperantists benefitted from the experience. By abandoning Esperanto in search for a better language, Couturat and similar restless souls reinforced the internal cohesion of the Esperanto movement: for when there is only one way to be an orthodox, one can be a reformist in a thousand different ways, as the Idists realized too late.[45]

Idists were not the last contestants in the battle of artificial languages. Rather, their fight against Esperanto unleashed a pent-up linguistic inventiveness that they had always tried to contain. If they thought that Ido could dislodge Esperanto, then there were others equally convinced that they could do better and thus dislodge both Eperanto *and* Ido. These included the ex-

Volapükist and ex-Esperantist Edgar de Wahl; the Danish linguist and president of the Ido Academy Otto Jespersen; the linguists associated with the International Auxiliary Language Association—a new organization generously sponsored by the philanthropist Alice Vanderbilt Morris—and the British linguist and philosopher C. K. Odgen, the only artificial language inventor able to catch the attention and financial assistance of a government. It is time now to turn to them.

CHAPTER 17

"Linguistic Cannibalism"

We have already met Edgar de Wahl (1867–1948), an enthusiast of artificial languages who had felt paralyzed by the success of Volapük. Probably de Wahl was the most restive mind in the already variegated and querulous tribe of artificial language supporters. A mathematician of Baltic German origins, de Wahl studied in Saint Petersburg when Volapük was in full swing. There, he made contact with Waldemar Rosenberger, the leader of the Saint Petersburg Volapük club, and became a Volapükist. He later abandoned Volapük to join the ranks of the first Esperantists. A reformist, he left Esperanto, unhappy with the result of the 1894 referendum. He then decided to concentrate his energies on helping Rosenberger reform his Idiom Neutral, and cooperated with Couturat's Commission for the Adoption of an International Language. But, also disappointed with the Commission, he began working on his own language. In 1922 he published a primer of his language, called Occidental, and launched its journal: *Kosmoglott* (or *Cosmoglotta*, since 1927). The timing was not accidental: in 1922 the League of Nations had decided to establish a commission to study the introduction of an artificial language in school curricula, and de Wahl did not want to miss the chance to compete in such a forum against Esperanto and Ido.

Occidental was probably the most naturalistic language project in the market. Broadly based on Latin, it was constructed to replicate Romance languages as closely as possible. There were also political reasons to support this choice, which also explains the language's name. As its inventor put it, the increased number of nations and national languages in postwar Europe made more imperative than ever a common European language, able to uphold what he called the European soul (*europäische Seele*). And this implied the restriction of English. As he explained it, if we want to remain Europeans, we have to protect our culture from the "unlimited narrowness of the practical and materialistic American spirit."[1] But American culture was not the only threat that concerned de Wahl. More menacing was Bolshevism, a handy scapegoat that de Wahl liberally used, not entirely without reason, to assail both Esperantists and Idists. De Wahl could point to the Comintern's 1920 decision to establish a commission to examine the potential utility of an artificial language for the advancement of communism.[2] Although this commission only vaguely approved of the idea of either Ido or Esperanto, de Wahl tried to profit from this episode by framing the contest between his language and its rivals in the larger contest "between civilization and barbarism." As he expressed it in 1922: "It seems to me that the victory of this or that [or] another language system depends on whether Bolshevism triumphs and (once it has destroyed our old culture) constructs a new Esperanto culture with the help of the new nations (and with a Middle Age interim of some hundred years), or the great European nations are able to maintain their cultural dominance, with the end result that Esperanto (a not sufficiently international language), will perish like Volapük did."[3]

All his life a passionate reformist, de Wahl naturally tried to find recruits among likeminded reformists in the Ido camp. He had some success. In 1925, the Idist clubs of Prague and Brno (Moravia) joined Occidental. But de Wahl was most successful after the split in 1926 between conservative and reformist Idists. He scored a sensational victory in 1927, when the former member of the Central Committee of the Idist Uniono, the Frenchman Louis de Guesnet, converted to Occidental. Similarly, in December 1928, some of the Idists who had organized the Ido congress earlier that year transferred their loyalties to de Wahl and established the international Occidentalist organization: the Occidental-Union.[4] And some years later, a thunderstorm broke out, although only a very small portion of the world population noticed it, when the Idist Alphonse Matejka, former editor-in-chief of *Progreso*, and secretary of the Idist Uniono, switched to de Wahl's army.

These conversions aside, de Wahl was never able to collect more than a handful of followers. His political views deterred him from campaigning among the working class and in Soviet Russia.[5] But more important, perhaps, was the intervention of a very wealthy woman in the battle of artificial languages, which practically destroyed the tiny Occidentalist movement.

The granddaughter of the railroad mogul William Henry Vanderbilt, Alice Vanderbilt Morris (1874–1947) was a member of one of the wealthiest American families. She was also a very determined woman. Contrary to her family's wishes, and sparking a sensational scandal in New York's high society, she married a Harvard student who did not belong to the small clique of the extravagantly rich. David Morris was not exactly poor, however. According to the *New York Times*, his fortune amounted to one million dollars, which he had accrued from a stable of racing horses. Horse racing was a family interest that David inherited from his father, the "Lottery King" John A. Morris, owner of the Louisiana State Lottery Company. Eventually, the Vanderbilts came to terms with the marriage and accepted Morris, who substantially increased his personal fortune and became the American ambassador to Belgium in the mid-1930s. Their marriage worked out very well, and David never hesitated to use his influence and personal fortune to help Alice pursue her interests.

Most important among these interests was the artificial language question. In 1921 Alice met the Esperantist chemist Frederick Cottrel, founder of the still extant Research Corporation and a former student of Wilhelm Ostwald. Alice became very interested in Esperanto and made the issue of an international language her life's mission. After some social gatherings and informational meetings in Morris's mansion in New York City, with dozens of invited academics and influential business people, a resolution was made to create an institution to conduct research on an international language.

This institution, the International Auxiliary Language Association (IALA), was finally established in 1924. IALA had two standing bodies: the Board of Directors and the General Advisory Committee. Whereas the board, mainly composed of scholars, was entrusted with conducting scientific research in cooperation with colleges and universities, the General Advisory Committee was manned by philanthropists and influential people. But towering above them all was the personality and the initiative of Alice Vanderbilt.[6]

Following the advice of Cottrell, who as a scientist preferred to launch research into the question rather than endorse any of the existing artificial languages, IALA's goal was to "promote widespread study, discussion and publicity of all questions involved in the establishment of an auxiliary language."[7] Thus, and at least at its inception, IALA did not aim at the creation of a new language. It portrayed itself as a detached player and, rather than pass judgment on any of the existing languages, it confined itself, at least during its first years, to being a clearinghouse for ideas and research. To conduct research and confer IALA with scientific legitimacy, Vanderbilt needed to overcome the traditional reluctance of linguists toward artificial languages—still conceived of as a sort of *Homunkulus* or Frankenstein's tongue—and obtain their cooperation.

The founding of the Linguistic Society of America (LSA) in the same year as IALA's facilitated Vanderbilt's goals. LSA members wanted to detach the study of language from the humanities in order to transform the field of linguistics into a scientific discipline. Since this goal fit with IALA's initial interests—research on comparative linguistics, the possibility of a universal grammar, and the linguistic prerequisites of a successful artificial language—it was able to establish a working relationship with American linguists, especially after Vanderbilt, also a founding member of the LSA, promised to provide generous research funds.

Research funds and grants began pouring in to East Coast colleges and universities, and both young and well-established linguists agreed to cooperate with IALA's research division. One of them was the then relatively unknown American linguist Edward Sapir. He began working for IALA in 1925, and from 1930 to 1931 he was IALA's director of research. In 1931 he obtained a position at Yale University and curtailed his cooperation with Alice Vanderbilt, although he remained associated with IALA until his death. Sapir was one of the fathers of what was later known as the Sapir-Whorf hypothesis, a direct descendant of the Herderian philosophy of language that propounded linguistic relativism and the ultimate incommensurability of languages. That Sapir became engaged in the artificial language movement may look surprising. But Sapir's interest in the topic was sincere. He complained that the traditional hostility toward artificial languages was "bound up with all kinds of romantic notions . . . of the eighteenth and beginning of the nineteenth centuries [that a language] was . . . something like a tree that grew up without human care and could not be interfered with without spoiling the growth." He added, "I have been very much under the influence of this bad metaphor, myself [and] I am trying hard to now to get rid of it."[8]

Also, given that the main obstacle to international communication was "the great diversity of languages," Sapir asserted that it was "almost unavoidable that the civilized world will adopt one language of intercommunication." We do not know if Sapir saw any contradiction between the hypothesis of the intimate connection between a language and the worldview of its native speakers, and the suggestion that a language can flourish in the absence of a community of native speakers. We do know, however, that his students have traditionally tried to gloss over and downplay his association with IALA.[9] Like

Sapir, the former Idist Otto Jespersen was also enticed by Vanderbilt's "intelligence, personal charm, and wealth" and was recruited to cooperate with IALA. In any case, IALA's appeal to linguists was uneven. Whereas linguists coming from multilingual Europe were more inclined to cooperate with IALA, American linguists remained skeptical.

IALA's original goal was to work out a consensus among artificial language supporters. This implied obtaining the cooperation of linguists to conduct research on comparative semantics and tempering the mutual animosity between Idists and Esperantists, in the hope of aligning their interests with those of IALA. Thus, in 1925, and to break new ground, Vanderbilt invited the two camps to Geneva. Edgar de Wahl, who had just released his Occidental, and Otto Jespersen were also invited.

Vanderbilt primarily hoped to persuade Idists and Esperantists to call a truce. Married to a diplomat, she knew very well how to stage the discussion. For about a week, she lavishly hosted the contenders in her impressive hotel Beau Rivage and arranged separate dinners. Some proposals were exchanged, but the meeting was a fiasco. Relations between Idists and Esperantists were still too bitter.

An unexpected consequence of these conversations, though, was Jespersen's decision to collect his cogitations and create his own language: Novial. This new contender was born in 1928, accompanied, as was by now customary, with its own journal, *Novialiste*, and its own academy, the Lingue-Jurie del Novialistes, founded in 1937.[10] Notwithstanding the creation of Novial— which by 1939 had only twelve registered speakers[11]—Jespersen continued to cooperate with IALA.

After the Beau Rivage fiasco, IALA decided to try a new persuasive tack. In 1930, it organized a two-week conference in Geneva. With Jespersen presiding, the conference brought together interested linguists and academics, representatives of Esperanto, Esperanto II (a reformed Esperanto created by the mathematician René de Saussure, brother of the linguist Ferdinand), Ido, Novial, Occidental, and Latino sine flexione. Expenses for travel and for accommodations in a first-class hotel for all attendees came from Vanderbilt's pocket.[12] But this time, rather than seeking a compromise between rival projects, Vanderbilt intended to co-opt European linguists into IALA's agenda. And to this extent, she was successful: the Second International Conference of Linguistics, held the following year in Geneva, gave IALA's research activities on artificial languages a reserved vote of assent.[13] Vanderbilt's next move was to establish a Committee for Agreement that should work out the long-desired compromise among competing rival languages. She had a back-up plan, however. Wanting a compromise, IALA would concentrate on "the formulation of a definitive constructed language."[14] In 1936, representatives of the rival languages convened regularly, together with interested linguists and academics. But, again, compromise proved impossible. Vanderbilt gave up and went ahead with her plan to create a new artificial language. Thus, rather than simplifying the scenario, IALA added anxiety and confusion by its decision to join the battle and introduce a new player—a battle that, as everybody understood, promised to be quite unbalanced, given Vanderbilt's wealth and largesse. But to the relief of Esperantists and Idists, IALA's language, Interlingua, only came to be after World War II, shortly after Vanderbilt died.[15]

With the IALA research department working on a new language, the Idists badly hit by their split in the mid-1920s, and Occidentalists and Novialists preying on the Idists and each other, it was not uncommon to read in the journals of the artificial language movement appeals to put an end to this *cannibalisme interlinguistic*, as the Novialist Per Albergh expressed it, and to reach a consensus to prevent Esperanto or, worse, English from winning the day. As an Occidentalist put it presciently, if this "mortal combat" continued, "the English language is going to triumph."[16]

But if many were rightly concerned about the growing importance of English, few anticipated that it was going to enter the battle as another artificial language as well, in the form of a simplified "Basic English." In 1930 the British Charles K. Ogden (1889–1957) published his *Basic English: A General Introduction with Rules and Grammar*. Ogden had already obtained some notoriety with his book *The Meaning of Meaning* (1923), which he co-authored with Ivor A. Richards. But unlike Richards, who would later become a renowned Harvard literary critic, Ogden preferred to make a living at the margins of academia, working as an editor for the Kegan Paul publishing group. While a Cambridge student, he had been the editor-in-chief of the *Cambridge Magazine*, which he transformed into an influential journal in political and academic circles. He was also president of the Heretics Society, an informal club that invited leading intellectuals, such as Chesterton, Russell, or Frank Ramsey, to discuss their ideas.[17]

As he conceived it, Basic English had only 850 words, which, combined in paraphrases and circumlocutions, would satisfy all practical communication purposes. Although he was not a pacifist, Ogden was convinced that the dissemination of English would put a definitive end to the threat of war and that a simplified version would be more suitable to realize this possibility.

To promote his new language, he founded the Orthological Institute in 1927, "orthology" meaning a new discipline wherein philosophy, linguistics, and psychology converged. But beyond those already involved in the artificial language movement, Ogden's Basic English did not attract much attention. He was able to publish some textbooks and collect the support of luminaries such as George Bernard Shaw, Julian Huxley, and H. G. Wells (Russell had had enough of language inventors), but that was all, and the outbreak of World War II only made his dream look more fanciful. Thus, it came as a surprise when in a public speech at Harvard University, the British prime minister Winston Churchill devoted a sizeable part of his discourse to Ogden's Basic English. This was in September 1943, when the Allies were more confident about their eventual victory. As Churchill said:

> I do not see why we [British and Americans] should not try to spread our common language even more widely throughout the world. . . . Here you have a plan [Basic English]. . . . Might it not be also an advantage to many races and an aid to the building-up of our new structure for preserving peace? . . . Such plans offer far better prizes than taking away other's peoples provinces or land, or grinding them down in exploitation. The empires of the future are the empires of the mind.[18]

Those more closely associated with Churchill were not surprised. Some months before his Harvard speech, he had established a cabinet committee to evaluate Basic English as an international auxiliary language. By December 1943, the committee, composed of the secretaries of state of the colonies and India, the minister of information, the undersecretary of state for foreign affairs, and other officials, released its conclusion. It strongly supported the development and use of Basic English by the British Council, the colonial office, diplomats, official representatives, and even the BBC. It also recommended that Ogden's Orthological Institute be provided with generous funding. To operationalize this scheme an interdepartmental committee, led by the Foreign Office, was established in 1944, but in the following year, and as a consequence of Churchill's defeat in the July elections, the whole plan was gradually phased out. Even so, Ogden's institute, renamed the Basic English Foundation, obtained a £18,600 grant in 1947 from the Ministry of Education (around $870,000 at current values). But by the early 1950s public officials had lost interest and the state coffers were sealed for Churchill's linguistic ambitions.[19]

It is important to note, however, that even before Basic English captured Churchill's imagination, the British government was already moving in the same direction. In 1938, and anticipating the international Esperanto congress scheduled to take place in London, the Foreign Office sent a warning note that "it is undesirable to support organizations which have as their object the encouragement of artificial languages, when we are seeking to secure the adoption of English as the second language in all foreign countries."[20] That the British government decided to pursue this goal by means of either real English or a simplified version did not matter much to artificial language supporters.

As Sapir put it, be it Full or Basic, the real thing or a Trojan horse, the promotion of English or any other ethnic language could only kindle resentment.[21] Similarly, for the Stanford professor and IALA associate Albert L. Guérard, Basic English was another example of the all-too-common "linguistic imperialism" of the time, explained in this case by "the magnificent insularity which is the pride of the Anglo-Saxon mind."[22] No less critical, but more biased, was the ex-Idist and Occidentalist Alphonse Matejka. Probably with earlier discussions in Germany about the creation of a simplified German for use in the German colonies still in his mind, he thought that Basic English would serve the same purpose and "reduce us to the linguistic level of black Africans."[23]

Notwithstanding the travails of IALA, Jespersen's and de Wahl's decisions to take the plunge and launch new languages, and Ogden's Basic English, the fact was that Esperanto had long before won the battle. It reached its heyday in the 1920s, when, weary of World War I and its consequences, many saw in Esperanto a suitable instrument to promote international cooperation among people of different languages. In 1926, attendance at the international Esperanto congress was the highest ever, with almost 5,000 participants, and the Universala Esperanto Asocio reached its membership peak in 1935 with 16,000 affiliated Esperantists. Similarly, in the early 1920s, Esperanto was taught as an elective or compulsory subject in some primary and secondary schools in France, Belgium, the United Kingdom, the United States, the Netherlands, Spain, Hungary, Czechoslovakia, and some German states such as Hesse, Saxony, and Brunswick, among other places. It was also taught on the premises of the Chambers of Commerce of Paris and London. The 1920 World

Congress of International Associations recommended its use, as well as other associations such as the Red Cross, the YMCA, the International Catholic League, the International Bibliographic Institute, the International Women's Suffrage Alliance, and the International Peace Bureau. Even the League of Nations, as we see below, seriously considered Esperanto as an auxiliary language.[24]

Although Esperanto prevailed among the crowded and fractious field of artificial languages, it failed to become the international auxiliary language that many expected. The movement reached its peak in the mid-1920s, but only ten years later Esperanto's prospects were rather bleak. It had defeated rival artificial languages but lost the war against natural languages—in particular, English—to become the world's lingua franca.

How this did happen? What factors combined against the final adoption of Esperanto as the international language?

Conclusion

Figure 3 illustrates the number of Volapük, Esperanto, and Ido journals from 1880 to 1928. This is probably the best measure of each language movement's strength. As the figure shows, by the time Ido entered the scene, Volapük had already exited, defeated by Esperanto and its own internal divisions. For its part, Esperanto had a very difficult time during its first decade of existence, only taking off at the turn of the century. When Zamenhof published his *Unua Libro*, Volapük was still thriving and about to reach its peak. The Volapük movement was certainly experiencing some difficulties, but its inability to overcome them would only become visible a couple of years later.

Even before the Ido movement's decline looked irreversible, the Esperantists were claiming victory, a victory that, according to contemporary Esperantist sources, was practically foreordained. Compared to Ido and its offspring, Esperantists had long been asserting to whoever was inclined to listen that their language was superior: the easiest to learn, the most beautiful, the closest to natural languages, and so on. Hence their final triumph.

But was this true? Did Esperanto crowd out its rivals because it was a better language? Similarly, is it possible to claim, for example, that Novial is worse than Occidental, or that Esperanto is better than Idiom Neutral?

In late nineteenth- and early twentieth-century linguistic theory, the idea that languages could be ranked by their level of complexity and perfection had much currency. It was claimed that primitive cultures spoke primitive languages, and advanced societies had more logical, precise, and beautiful languages. Current linguistics, however, has rejected this idea and maintains that all natural languages, be they languages of hunting and gathering societies or of advanced, post-industrial societies, are equally complex. For modern linguistics, ranking languages by their degree of complexity, or claiming that language A is simpler, easier to learn, or better suited for human communication than language B, does not make sense. There are no better or worse

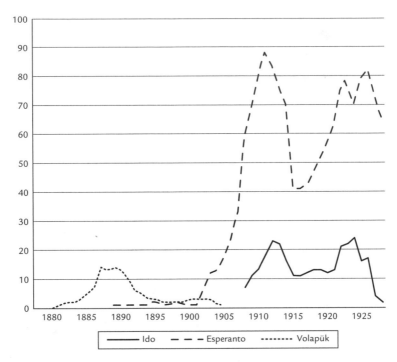

Figure 3. Number of Volapük, Esperanto, and Ido journals, 1880–1928.
Source: Petr E. Stojan, *Bibliografio de Internacia Lingvo* (New York:
Georg Olms, 1973 [1929]), 305–54, 483, and 502–5.

languages: all of them are equally complex, as well as equally efficient when
it comes to serving the communication needs of their speakers.[1]

A similar claim can be made about artificial languages. Since they mir-
ror the essential characteristics of natural languages, it is equally difficult
to rank them by complexity or learnability. Rather than their complexity or
learnability, the proof of the pudding of artificial languages is their feasibility, their actual "languagehood," which can only be positively tested by
their natural evolution.[2] In existence for over 100 years, Esperanto has
passed this test. Very much like other languages, it has evolved, absorbing
the irregularities, ambiguities, and modifications that its speakers have been
infiltrating into Zamenhof's original Esperanto for decades. But the argument that Esperanto has passed the languagehood test because it was better
than its rivals is unpersuasive. A more plausible argument is precisely the
opposite: Esperanto was able to maintain over time a relatively large com-

munity of speakers so that it could evolve and eventually pass the language-hood test.

Zamenhof himself candidly conceded as much. In 1889 he claimed that because of its deficiencies, especially its vocabulary and unpleasant sounds, Volapük was doomed to fail. In the 1911 Congress of Esperantists, however, when Volapük was already dead, he volunteered a more balanced view. Volapük, he claimed, did not die "because of its strange sounds or any other similar reason, since everybody can get used to anything; and what might sound strange today, it will look completely natural and beautiful to-morrow." Volapük died because, constantly quarrelling, the Volapükists did not give it a chance to evolve. Had Volapükists behaved differently and agreed on the final shape of their language, it could have naturally evolved, and "we all would be probably speaking Volapük now."[3] Russian Esperantist Lev Zhirkov made a similar point in 1931. According to him, Esperanto did not triumph because of its superior qualities on paper. "After the emergence of Esperanto," he argued, "other, much better planned languages, more con-sistent and detailed in their linguistic qualities, made their appearance."[4] Esperanto defeated its rivals because it was already a *living* language, be-cause it had a community of speakers who, whether pacifists, language afi-cionados, or stamp collectors, were using the language to communicate with kindred spirits, either through necessity or choice, unburdened by the quar-rels unfolding at the margins of the community.[5]

This takes us to one of the main arguments of path dependence litera-ture. Rarely are the potential applications and presumed benefits of compet-ing technologies known in advance, and the same is true with artificial languages. We know retrospectively that Esperanto was good enough to be-come a serious contender or even the eventual winner, but contemporaries could not know for sure, particularly when supporters of rival languages were making exactly the same claims. Everybody was guessing, both regarding the relative superiority of this or that language and the eventual outcome of the battle.[6] In other words, extra-linguistic considerations rather than linguistic qualities better explain Esperanto's success.

A similar argument applies to English and to former lingua franca*s*. English has attained that status not because of its syntax and morphology, but as the result of a historical contingency: the economic and political power of English-speaking peoples. But in the case of Esperanto, the historical contingency was different. Their supporters, as well as those of Ido or Volapük, operated in a power vacuum. They volunteered to create a public good, a lingua franca, without much support from governments and the general public. They had to stand by themselves, increase their numbers as best they could, and strive for the recognition of an outside and not very sympathetic world.

The battle of artificial languages was similar to other standardization contests, such as the battle between QWERTY and alternative keyboards, or the contest between VHS and Betamax. A standardization battle of this kind ends when the accumulated decisions of adopters ultimately tip the balance to one technology, but not necessarily the best or most suitable one, and crowd out competing alternatives. Some particularly intuitive contemporaries perceived the battle of artificial languages in exactly these terms. For example, this was the case of the linguist Hugo Schuchardt: "Even when [the artificial languages] are really fighting to win the place, it does not mean that the survivor will be the best. On the one hand, because, very much like the stenographic systems, they do not differ substantially. . . . On the other hand, because their diffusion is not primarily determined by their own qualities, but by those of their supporters, their insight, and social influence."[7]

Neither Schleyer nor Zamenhof nor Couturat were aware that they were fighting in a scenario of positive feedback mechanisms. They simply used different organizational strategies. On the surface, the three language movements look very much alike. Established around the same time, shaped by a similar economic and technological context, their organizational contour did not differ much. They all provided themselves with an academy, official journals, address books of speakers and supporters, and annual international meetings. But there were substantial differences in their organizational strategies, which can be explained by the mental models and well-established predilections of their leaders. Schleyer's original plan incorporated the authoritarian and highly formalized organizational blueprint of the Catholic Church; Zamenhof had taken from his experience in the proto-Zionist movement his conviction about the relevance of participation and commitment for the survival of a social movement; Couturat took from his academic milieu the idea of enforcing a division of labor between scientists and lay people in the Ido movement.

These three different organizational approaches confronted the same basic problem—to obtain agreement about the final shape of the language—and produced divergent results. Unwilling to share power, Schleyer applied a top-down, authoritarian strategy. Proprietary about his linguistic creation and convinced that nobody was as linguistically competent as himself, he tried hard to have the final word on *his* language. When, led by Kerckhoffs, the reformists were about to deprive him of his veto power, he dismissed all attempts to find a common ground and let the movement split. Rather than sharing power, he preferred to be the unquestionable leader of one of its factions, weaker in terms of membership, but on a firmer foundation in both political and linguistic cohesion.

This strategy proved suicidal. It took many years for reformists to devise a new language (Idiom Neutral). In the meantime their movement disappeared, since there was no point in propagating, learning, and teaching a language that did not yet exist. More important, there was a rival language in the market (Esperanto) that made loyalty to Volapük less attractive.

Zamenhof's bottom-up strategy had the opposite effect. When he faced reformist challenges, he addressed them directly and called for a referendum. The language was not his, he claimed: it belonged to its community of speakers, and they must decide. This was a risky move, which almost killed the movement. But it did not. Its stronghold in the Pale of Settlement kept it alive, and then a new wave of Esperantists in France gave it new life. Having reached an agreement about the shape of the language, ratified once again at the Boulogne Congress with the endorsement of the *Fundamento*, the Esperanto community began to diversify. As is the case with natural language speakers, fewer Esperantists worried about the presumed deficiencies of their language than about the advancement of their particular agendas. An eclectic array of special interest groups emerged in the Esperanto community (e.g., socialists, positivists, pacifists, Catholics, Herderians). A lack of consensus about the movement's international organization only reinforced its internal diversity, which mirrored the varied cultural, social, and political trends of the period. To borrow from Elisabeth Clemmens's terminology,[8] the Esperantists developed a wide range of "organizational repertoires" that helped deploy the language in different institutional fields and make it more visible to larger sectors of society. This bottom-up strategy, which resulted in a common agreement about the basics of the language and the diversification of the movement along different lines, most mimicked the development of natural languages, and let Esperantists successfully meet the Ido challenge. Rather than undoing what they had already done, a majority of Esperantists chose to build on their own accomplishments and turn a blind eye to the Idists.

For his part, Couturat, the initiator of Ido, opted for a technocratic and elitist strategy. Confident that the outside world would distinguish between the better and the satisfactory, and always choosing the former over the latter, Couturat focused on attracting the intellectual elite to his side rather than building a grassroots movement. Since, for the improvement of the language, linguistic engineering was preferable to speakers' intuitions and feedback, he drew a clear line between the Academy, composed by scientists and linguists, and common speakers who would be required to abide by their decisions. Only a small coterie of wise people had voice in the process. After a first wave of defections, Couturat reacted by decreeing a transitory stabilization period. This was a smart move, since putting a temporary end to the constant improvement of the language let the movement diversify. Communist, Catholic, and even vegetarian Idist organizations materialized, but only ephemerally: when the stabilization period came to an end, the quarrel between conservatives and reformists, who claimed to better represent the original drive of the language, recurred. The movement practically collapsed, fracturing into several even tinier language movements.

Operating against the backdrop of a standardization battle where positive feedback mechanisms were critical, Zamenhof's democratic strategy was the most expedient. Also critical for the final success of Esperanto, however, were the messages and purposes associated with each of the languages.

While Kerckhoffs emphasized the utility of Volapük for international commerce, and others concentrated on scientific communication, Schleyer was content to broadly depict his language as a new Latin. Couturat pursued a similar hands-off policy. He wanted the language movement to be free of "vacuous and chimeric ideas."[9] As rational and circumspect as they were, pronouncements like this deprived these two language movements of a hard core of faithful speakers willing to sustain the movement in critical times. We have seen that all three movements split at one point in their history. But whereas a new Latin, or a language tailored for international commerce or scientific communication, can hardly motivate speakers to sustain an artificial language through the crises, the association of such language with a set of ideals that vaguely refer to a future society based on peace, justice, and mutual respect, can. Thus, when the reformists left Esperanto after the 1894 referendum, Zamenhof put his cards on the table and reinforced the political message that he and many others in the Pale of Settlement associated with his language. The movement was then able to survive until it could gather new momentum in Western Europe at the turn of the century.

But, while important, the *interna ideo* did not create a homogenous Esperantist community. Zamenhof never tried to impose his political agenda in the movement, which became quite heterogeneous. In fact, as we have seen by exploring the secondary characters and membership of the three language movements, all of them had the potential to diversify. But it was only the Esperantists who could realize this potential, since only they had been able to agree on the basics of their language and, thus, to make it useful to promote different and sometimes conflicting agendas, which resulted in a vibrant constellation of distinct social movements.

Esperanto triumphed, in sum, not because of its linguistic qualities. In the same way that there was nothing preordained in the triumph of QWERTY or VHS over their rivals, there was nothing preordained in the final triumph of Esperanto. A combination of organizational factors and ideology can better explain the final outcome of the battle of artificial languages.

*   *   *

Contrary to Esperantist dreams and expectations, their language was not adopted as the international language. How can we account for this? One possible explanation has to do with the rivalries between the artificial language movements and their incapacity to reach a consensus when the issue of an artificial language, in the abstract, was seriously considered and had a chance of success. Consider, for example, the International Research Council's discussion about the possible introduction of an artificial language. In its 1919 meeting, it agreed to publish an international journal of abstracts of chemistry. Since the open policy of the Council was to ostracize German scientists and language (which by and large was the dominant language in chemistry), they had to agree upon the language that could successfully substitute for German.[10] In 1920, the British Association for the Advancement of Science took matters in hand and narrowed the issue to three possible solutions: Latin, a national language (preferably English), or an artificial language. To make an informed decision, the British Association gathered information from the Catholic Church, Latin scholars, the English Language Union, English-speaking scholars, the British Ido and Esperanto associations, and scientists from different fields. In September 1921, the British Association made the results of its deliberations public. Latin was discarded. Although many technical and scientific terms, especially in botany, zoology, and anatomy, were directly derived from Latin, the British Association rejected it because of its difficulties as an inflectional language, and the tremendous work to coin modern terminology that this solution would create. Although it was the "probable world language of the future," English was also discarded.[11] The formal adoption of English would not require coining new words, and, compared with Latin, the British Association considered it easier to learn, or at least more expedient to acquire. The spelling difficulty with English was a minor problem that could be solved by a spelling reform. Despite all these advantages, the British association rejected it for essentially political reasons: "The great international languages of the past, Greek, Latin, Arabic, French (in the East), and English at the present day have all borne the marks of imperial prestige which prevented them from being welcomed by alien races. To spread a national language by international effort would be, in effect, to extend the power of that nation or race, however impartial might be the intentions of the promoters."[12]

An artificial language was the default solution. Artificial languages still aroused some misgivings, but the British Association regarded these misgivings as a product of linguistic chauvinism and questionable linguistic theories. According to the British Association, both Ido and Esperanto had proven to be practical solutions for international communication. There was one problem, which still had to be solved. Since there was room for only one language, Idists and Esperantists had to reach an agreement and put an end to the schism: "Unity is essential, and it would be lamentable if a project to unite the nations were to be shipwrecked by disunion within the ranks."[13] But neither the Esperantist nor the Idist took notice. When the report was publicly discussed, both sides initiated such an embarrassing quarrel that the issue was finally dropped.[14]

Aside from the usual quarrels among rivals, technological factors might also help explain why Esperanto failed to be adopted as a lingua franca. If advances in transport and communications technologies had made the problem of international communication more salient, later technological advances ameliorated this same problem. This was particularly the case in international meetings, where printed communication could not substitute for face-to-face interactions. Before simultaneous translation systems, a common arrangement in international meetings was to seat participants according to their language, let the speaker pronounce a few sentences, and have the interpreters stand up to simultaneously translate them into the languages of the audience, until the end of the speech. This was a clumsy process, and a living illustration of the problem of Babel. The 1926 invention of the Filene-Finlay Speech Translator, first used by the International Labour Office and much popularized some years later at the Nuremberg Trials, was of great help in large international conferences. Only important international organizations could afford this technology, but these organizations or the governments that supported them eventually framed the international communication problem and its solution.

Perhaps even more important than rivalries and technological advancements to explain Esperanto's failure was the popular idea among the European elites that Esperanto was a threat to the international standing of nation-states (particularly for the most powerful ones) and national cohesion, a concern shared by both democratic and non-democratic countries. As mentioned, the British Foreign Office was not up to supporting Esperanto "when we are seeking to secure the adoption of English as the second language in all foreign countries."[15]

Linguistic imperialism was more openly supported in France, as a reaction to the perceived decline of French. As early as the turn of the century, businessman Paul Chappellier had explained that Esperanto threatened the French nation and language, both internally and internationally. Internally, Esperanto could reinforce patois and regional identities, undermining French national consciousness and cohesion. Internationally, a widespread acceptance of Esperanto as a second language could only make the French language retreat to within her "natural" borders, very much like a snail hides in its shell (*comme le limaçon dans sa coquille*).[16] To deal with the problem of international communication, and to halt the spread of Esperanto, Chappellier suggested a linguistic alliance between France, the United Kingdom, and the United States by which French would be compulsory in American and British schools and English in French schools. He hoped that the Germans would put aside their national sentiments and accept the economic advantages of his plan, although, in truth, he was not at all concerned about the Germans. As he plainly asserted, the plan would "lessen the concurrence of German and will annihilate that of English, since both French and English, instead of rivals, will become partners."[17] Inevitably, the Chappellier Plan, as it was later called, caught the attention of conservative circles. As the public came closer to a new world war, the plan attracted more publicity. For example, Albert Dauzat, in *La défense de la langue française*, enthusiastically endorsed the plan as a bulwark against the no less menacing threat: Esperanto.[18]

Linguistic imperialisms converged to work against Esperanto. For the Esperantists, the League of Nations was the most important forum to advance their cause in the international arena, but it was equally important for the French and English governments, which had succeeded in making their national languages the League's only official ones. A public discussion began in December 1920, when, following the undertakings of the Esperanto lobby in Geneva, the representatives of Brazil, Chile, Colombia, Czechoslovakia, Haiti, Italy, Japan, India, Persia, Poland, Rumania, and South Africa petitioned the General Assembly of the League to endorse Esperanto instruction in the schools of member states as an auxiliary, second language. The petition was not accepted, by the rationale that it was immature and lacked relevant data. Undaunted, the Esperantists brought more pressure, and in September 1921, eleven representatives of the Committee on the Agenda of the League voted to request that the secretary general call for research on the status and prospects of Esperanto. Only the French representative on the Committee, Gabriel Hanotaux, voted against.

The possibility that the Esperantists might prevail was real, or at least this is what Hanotaux and his government thought. Thus, while research on the qualities and prospects of Esperanto was being conducted, the French Minister of Public Instruction Léon Bérard issued a directive to forbid the teaching of Esperanto in public schools. But Bérard's directive was not only addressed to French public opinion. Widely reproduced in the international press, it was intended to alert all nations to a common danger: the danger of the dissolution of the sacred link between language and nation. And he showed no mercy:

> I feel today that I have to call to your attention the dangers that,
> to my mind, the teaching of Esperanto represents in our present
> circumstances. . . . These dangers seem to have increased in recent
> times. . . . The purpose of their propaganda [of the Esperantists] is
> not so much to simplify the linguistic relations among peoples, as to
> emasculate in the minds of both children and adults the principles
> that sustain national cultures. . . . According to the manifestation of
> an Esperantist, the goal is to detach language from nation. Esperanto
> has become the active instrument of a systematic internationalism,
> enemy of national languages and the original thoughts expressed in
> their development.[19]

In 1922, the League of Nations had completed the research. The report, *Esperanto as an International Auxiliary Language,* was very positive. Although approved by the General Assembly, it recommended further discussion on the Esperantists' main petition to introduce Esperanto in the school curricula. But eventually the French delegate was able to kill the debate by transferring the discussion to the Committee on Intellectual Cooperation, which, instead of Esperanto, recommended the study of national languages.[20]

There are two ways that a language can become a lingua franca: it can be formally adopted following a decision of an international body, or it can become the de facto lingua franca following the strength and extension of its community of speakers. The defeat of the Esperantist lobby in the League of Nations blocked the first path, and this made the second one imperative, that the community of speakers expand. The political climate of the first postwar years was in fact very congenial for Esperanto's expansion. Following the victory of the Allied powers in 1918, parliamentary democracy and liberal constitutions seemed to be the default model of government when the states that had emerged after the collapse of the Central and Eastern European empires embraced it. But what seemed to be the final triumph of democracy in European soil was only a mirage, and the Wilsonian dream of a new European order based on national self-determination and democracy proved unrealistic. The international and domestic tensions triggered by national minorities (it was estimated that around 25 million people were living within the "wrong" state borders), combined with the international economic depression, drastically changed the political landscape. Beginning with Miklós Horthy's Regency in 1920 Hungary, democracies were toppling like dominoes and replaced with nationalist, right-wing regimes. Italian democracy was next to collapse in 1922, and by the mid-1930s all Central and Eastern European countries, with the exception of Czechoslovakia, were under the rule of one kind or another of anti-democratic and nationalist regime. Only France and the northern fringe of Europe had been able to contain this anti-democratic wave.[21] Esperantists of Central and Eastern Europe, harassed by the conservative press and government officials as untrustworthy members of the new national states when not indicted as friends of the Jews or the spearhead of Bolshevism, found it more difficult to recruit new members.[22] In Western Europe the movement suffered its hardest blow in Germany, with the dismantling of the labor Esperanto movement and, shortly after, of the neutral Esperantist movement.

In sum, the big nations' fears of falling behind in the international competition for linguistic hegemony combined with the authoritarian and ethnonationalist character of many European nation-states became insuperable obstacles to the Esperantists, conveniently labeled as either well-intentioned but ultimately eccentric cranks, or enemies of the nationalist (or revolutionary, in the case of the USSR) aspirations of the new autocrats.

In the era of nationalism, Zamenhof conceived of Esperanto as an instrument to solve the Jewish question and, by extension, the ethnic and religious hatred that was poisoning European societies. If the problem was nationalism, the solution was not more nationalism, but less, and a non-national language could help. But the opposite solution triumphed. Deeply imbued with a nationalist ideology, Zamenhof's contemporary, the Lithuanian-born Eliezer Ben-Yehuda (1858–1922), was also very aware of the political dimension of language. As with Zamenhof, he was a language builder —and certainly the most successful among his contemporaries. Driven by a quasi-religious passion, he moved to Palestine before the 1881 pogroms to give the Jewish nationalists what they most needed: a national language. From a stock of 8,000 words in the Bible and around 20,000 in rabbinical commentaries, he codified, planned and, to borrow Romaine's expression "reinvented" a new language, Modern Hebrew, which in 1922, along with English and Arabic, became official in British Palestine.[23]

Ben-Yehuda succeeded because there was a real need for a lingua franca, given the different languages that diaspora Jews spoke when they moved to Palestine. Second, as a reinvented language, Modern Hebrew was neutral. Since it was not anybody's mother language, everybody was on the same footing. Third, and perhaps more important, it was a language constructed or reinvented on the basis of a sacred language. Ben-Yehuda therefore simultaneously proved Zamenhof right and wrong. As Modern Hebrew demonstrated, Zamenhof's dream of making an artificially constructed language the language of millions of people proved possible. But at the same time, he proved Zamenhof wrong: in the era of nationalism and national rivalries, an artificial language could not succeed if it was not adopted by a nation to become part and parcel of a nation-building project.

*   *   *

When the battle of artificial languages began, three main languages, German, English, and French, competed against each other to become *the* international language. Today, English holds that position. According to some estimates, around one-fourth of the world's population has at least a basic knowledge of English. More important, English is spoken in all corners of the world. This combination of a huge number of speakers and geographical distribution is unprecedented in the history of language. Compared with other lingua francas such as Latin, Arabic, Persian, or French, all geographically and socially bounded, English has spread over the five continents and through many echelons of society. It has become the first global language. And although it might also be the last one—with computer translation technology allowing everyone to use their own language and be understood by everybody else, as Nicolas Ostler suggests—for the time being no other language can challenge English's dominance.[24]

Given this new scenario, what are the odds for an artificial language such as Esperanto to be adopted internationally? Can we picture an international body embracing Esperanto as its only language, or as just another official language? With twenty-eight countries and twenty-four official languages following the entry of Croatia in July 2013, the European Union can help us explore this issue. Few question that the EU is entrapped in a linguistic dilemma that opposes a democratic principle (the valuing of multilingualism and the equal treatment of all official languages) with an efficiency principle (having less multilingualism and simplifying the EU's linguistic regime).[25]

This tension has economic and political effects. For example, for ten years EU members were not able to agree on a unified patent system, given Spain and Italy's objections to the idea that European patents could only be in English, French, or German. Only in December 2012 did the remaining twenty-five EU members pass a unified patent system, which, due to the complaints of Spain and Italy, had to be sanctioned by the European Court of Justice.[26] Also, the one billion-plus euros that the European Union annually spends in translation and interpretation services could perhaps be better allocated to other programs.[27] Unable to fully implement multilingualism and grant all European languages the same status, the EU has ended up discovering that some languages are more equal than others. Most of the internal documents and negotiations are written and conducted in the three main languages: English, French, and German. In the second tier of the hierarchy are Spanish, Italian, and sometimes Polish, due to the sheer number of their speakers. The remaining official languages lag far behind, and English dwarfs them all. Not being official at the state level, regional languages such as Sami, Breton, and Catalan do not even enter the picture. This hierarchical order affects the working routines of European officials as well as their communications with the citizens they serve. For example, a laudable practice recently introduced by the European Commission is to post draft proposals on its website and let individual citizens, professionals, academics, and organizations participate in an open discussion about them. The documents for discussion, however, are not translated in all official languages. In fact, quite often they are only available in English, and occasionally also in French and German, with the end result that the ability to participate in the European demos is somewhat filtered by language and, indirectly, wealth.[28]

Given these problems and the fact that English is the preferred second language among the young, some have suggested that it should become the official language of Europe.[29] But an English-only approach is not going to succeed. Even when the relatively small countries are not radically opposed to this suggestion (given that they cannot expect their languages to have a prominent function internationally), it is difficult to picture the other two main languages gallantly giving up their prerogatives and acquiescing to a linguistic scenario where English would emerge as the uncontested hegemon. Rather, the official policies of both the French and German governments aim at preventing this possibility. Hence, the French Boudon Law passed in 1994, which enforced the use of French in conferences, commercial advertisements, radio and TV broadcasts, and publicly subsidized educational institutions. More effective has been the French initiative to promote multilingualism, currently the official policy of the EU, which recommends that Europeans learn two foreign languages (or three, if their mother language is not official at the state level). Having to choose a second foreign language, French officials anticipate, more Europeans would pick up French.[30] On its side, after the reunification of the country in 1990 and the entry of Austria in 1994, Germany has become more adamant in the protection of its language, in contrast to its laissez-faire approach of the past. This new attitude, reinforced by its position as the largest contributor to the European coffers, has proven successful, and German has obtained the status of a working language previously reserved for French and English. This more pro-active German stance is accompanied by growing reservations about the expansion and popularity of English, both internationally and inside its own borders, which some perceive as a hindrance to the international standing and visibility of the country. In fact, in 2000 the French and German foreign ministers signed a mutual support agreement to prevent the retreat of their languages vis-à-vis English in the European institutions.[31]

Fairness also recommends against the adoption of English or any other native language as a lingua franca. If a lingua franca is a public good, fairness dictates an even distribution of the burdens required to provide for such a good, a requirement difficult to meet if the lingua franca is a national language. To begin with, whereas those who speak a different language are forced to invest time and money to communicate internationally, the native speakers of the lingua franca have the option to invest those resources in other activities. Certainly they might resolve to learn languages, but that would be their choice, not an imperative.

This basic inequality translates into economic transfers from the non-speakers to native speakers. As the chair of the British Council reported in his preface to David Graddol's research: "The English language teaching sector directly earns nearly £1.3 billion for the UK in invisible exports and our other education-related exports earn up to £10 billion a year more."[32] Aside from economic transfers, this linguistic inequality also importantly affects the balance of power. Whereas native speakers can use their own language, those who have learned English as their second language are not able to express themselves as fluently, accurately, and convincingly as they do in their native language. This unbalance might not be of importance in many communicative settings, but at negotiating tables it can undermine the non-native speakers' positions. This is why Danes proposed, when negotiating their entry in the European Union, that meetings be conducted in English, French, and German, provided that their native speakers did not use them. Some think that the English-only solution can be accepted only if native English speakers make substantial compensations to the non-native.[33]

The adoption of a neutral non-national language such as Esperanto would *prima facie* solve all these problems at the stroke of a pen by placing all member states and citizens on an equal footing. It is not surprising, then, that Esperanto occasionally has been suggested as the best solution, and that European Esperantists have mobilized to advance it.[34] In fact, a one-day conference convened in September 1992 by the president of the European Parliament and sponsored by a think tank linked to the Bavarian Christian Democrats discussed the potential benefits of an artificial language for the European Union. Also, under the initiative of the German Esperantists, a new, transnational party, Eŭropo-Demokratio-Esperanto (EDE), was launched before the 1994 elections to the European parliament. The EDE's German candidate was the old Esperantist and Nobel Prize winner in economics Reinhard Selten. But these initiatives have yielded no results.

Two large obstacles stand in the way of the Esperantists, still viewed as unrepentant utopians, unable to see that politics is not only about fairness, but also about power.

First, the current international language regime is different from the triglossic linguistic regime of late nineteenth- and early twentieth-century Europe. Although not de jure, English has become the de facto official language of the European Union and people are aware of it. They also know that English maximizes their communication potential and work opportunities. For this reason, and no matter the intensity of the campaign that the EU would need to launch to implement the Esperanto solution, if it decided to go for it, it would be unlikely that Europeans would shift from English to Esperanto when, outside the EU, English still holds the hegemonic position.

Second, and no less important, are philosophical considerations. The EU has never seriously considered the adoption of an artificial language. The closest we have come to an official statement were comments released in February 2008 by the European Commissioner for Multilingualism, Leonard Orban, in his official blog. Responding to the requests of Esperantists, Orban claimed that, lacking a culture, Esperanto is not a real language. Orban, however, was not referring to the lack of a literary corpus. As he elaborated in 2011, no longer acting as European Commissioner, Esperanto does not stand a chance because it does not have "a people and a culture" behind it, which takes us back to the old mystical thinking that links language and ethnicity.[35] This old, taken-for-granted myth is perhaps the most important obstacle to the consideration of an artificial language. For the problem is not artificiality itself. There is much artifice and linguistic engineering in the construction of national languages (Modern Hebrew is an extreme case), as well as in the current efforts to "revitalize" non-national languages.[36] But while this artifice is glossed over and perceived as a legitimate endeavor when there is an identifiable ethnic group behind it, it is considered grotesque in the absence of such a group. As long as this mystical link between language and ethnicity forged by the Romantics two hundred years ago is in full force, the artificial language solution will not succeed.

NOTES

Introduction

1. Bernard Crick, *George Orwell: A Life* (London: Penguin, 1992), 189–90.

2. On Esperanto in the Spanish Civil War, see José Antonio del Barrio and Ulrich Lins, "La dangera lingvo en la hispana civitana milito," paper presented at the Congreso sobre la Guerra Civil Española, Madrid, November 2006; and Antonio Marco, *Laboristaj kronikoj* (Baudé: SAT, 1996), 53–62.

3. George Orwell, "Appendix: The Principles of Newspeak," in *Nineteen Eighty-Four* (New York: Plume, 2003 [1949]), 309. See also David W. Sisk, *Transformations of Language in Modern Dystopias* (Westport, Conn.: Greenwood Press, 1997), 38–55.

4. See, for example, Philippe van Parijs, *Linguistic Justice for Europe and for the World* (Oxford: Oxford University Press, 2011).

5. For a survey of artificial languages in Wikipedia, see Ziko van Dijk, "Wikipedia and Lesser-Resourced Languages," *Language Problems and Language Planning* 33, no. 3 (2009): 234–50. According to the *Ethnologue*—the standard reference of living languages, maintained by the linguist profession—Esperanto is the second language of 2,000,000 people. More conservative Esperantists, however, estimate the number of fluent speakers at only 100,000. See Marcus Sikosek, *Esperanto sen mitoj*, 2nd ed. (Antwerp: Flandra Esperanto Ligo, 2003), 55.

6. On the evolution of the language, see Sabine Fiedler, "Standardization and Self-Regulation in an International Speech Community: The Case of Esperanto," *International Journal of the Sociology of Language* 177 (2006): 67–90; from the same author "Phraseology in Planned Language," in *Phraseology: An International Handbook of Contemporary Research,* ed. Harald Burger (Berlin: Walter de Gruyter, 2007), 779–88; Detlev Blanke, *Internationale Plansprachen. Eine Einführung* (Berlin: Akademie Verlag. 1985), 105–7; István Szerdahelyi, "Entwicklung des Zeichnensystems einer internationalen Sprache: Esperanto," in *Language Reform: History and Future*, ed. István Fodor and Claude Hagège (Hamburg: Buske Verlag, 1984), 1:277–308.

7. For these standardization battles, see Paul A. David, "Clio and the Economics of QWERTY," *American Economic Review* 75, no. 2 (1985): 332–37; from the same author, "Heroes, Herds and Hysteresis in Technological History: Thomas Edison and 'The

Battle of the Systems' Reconsidered," *Industrial and Corporate Change* 1, no. 1 (1991): 129–76; Michael A. Cusumano, Yiorgos Mylonadis, and Richard S. Rosenbloom, "Strategic Maneuvering and Mass-Market Dynamics: The Triumph of VHS over Beta," *Business History Review* 66, Special Issue no. 1 (1992): 51–94; and Robin Cowan, "Nuclear Power Reactors: A Study in Technological Lock-In," *Journal of Economic History* 50, no. 3 (1990): 541–67. For the application of path dependence theory to historical sociology, see Jack A. Goldstone, "Initial Conditions, General Laws, Path Dependence, and Explanation in Historical Sociology," *American Journal of Sociology* 104, no. 3 (1998): 829–45.

8. Brian Arthur, *Increasing Returns and Path Dependence in the Economy* (Ann Arbor: University of Michigan Press), 25.

9. See, e.g., John Edwards, *Language and Identity* (Cambridge: Cambridge University Press, 2009).

10. See, for example, Elisabeth S. Clemmens and Debra C. Minkoff, "Beyond the Iron Law: Rethinking the Place of Organizations in Social Movement Research," in *The Blackwell Companion to Social Movements*, ed. David A. Snow, Sarah A. Soule, and Hanspeter Kriesi (Malden: Blackwell, 2004), 156–70; Debra C. Minkoff and John D. McCarthy, "Reinvigorating the Study of Organizational Processes in Social Movements," *Mobilization* 10, no. 2 (2005): 289–308. On leadership, see Joseph Campbell, "Where Do We Stand? Common Mechanisms in Organizations and Social Movements Research," in *Social Movements and Organization Theory*, ed. Gerald F. Davis et al. (Cambridge: Cambridge University Press, 2005), 41–68; Marshall Ganz, "Resources and Resourcefulness: Strategic Capacity in the Unionization of California Agriculture," *American Journal of Sociology* 105, no. 4 (2000): 1003–62; and Aldon Morris and Suzanne Staggenborg, "Leadership in Social Movements," in *The Blackwell Companion to Social Movements*, ed. David A. Snow, Sarah A. Soule, and Hanspeter Kriesi (Malden, Mass.: Blackwell, 2004), 171–96.

11. On the impact of past experiences and cultural settings on the leaders' decisions, see Arthur T. Denzau and Douglass C. North, "Shared Mental Models: Ideologies and Institutions," *Kyklos* 47, no. 1 (1994): 3–31; Bart Nooteboom, *Learning and Innovations in Organizations and Economies* (Oxford: Oxford University Press, 2000), 35–51; Lee G. Bolman and Terrence E. Deal, *Reframing Organizations: Artistry, Choice, and Leadership* (San Francisco: John Wiley and Sons, 2008), 3–44; and Arthur L. Stinchcombe, "Social Structure and Organizations," in *Handbook of Organizations*, ed. James G. March (New York: Rand McNally, 1965), 142–93. On how leaders extrapolate former experiences to new organizational settings, see Warren Boeker, "Strategic Change: The Effects of Founding and History," *Academic Management Journal* 32, no. 3 (1989): 489–515; and Victoria Johnson, "What Is Organizational Imprinting? Cultural Entrepreneurship in the Founding of the Paris Opera," *American Journal of Sociology* 113, no. 1 (2007): 97–127.

Chapter 1

1. For the concept of "critical junctures," see Giovanne Capoccia and R. Daniel Kelemen, "The Study of Critical Junctures: Theory, Narrative, and Counterfactuals in Historical Institutionalism," *World Politics* 59, no. 3 (2007): 341–69.

2. Sue Wright, "French as a Lingua Franca," *Annual Review of Applied Linguistics* 26 (2006): 35–60; Nicholas Ostler, *Empires of the Word: A Language History of the World* (New York: HarperCollins, 2005), 403–21.

3. Sue Wright, *Language Policy and Language Planning: From Nationalism to Globalization* (New York: Palgrave, 2004), 20–25.

4. Qtd. in Marc Fumaroli, "The Genius of French Language," in *The Realms of Memory*, ed. Pierre Nora (New York: Columbia University Press, 1998), 3:591–92.

5. Peter Burke, *Languages and Communities in Early Modern Europe* (Cambridge: Cambridge University Press, 2004), 67.

6. Ibid., 54.

7. Ann Blair, "La persistance du latin comme langue de science à la fin de la Renaissance," in *Sciences and Langues in Europe*, eds. Roger Chartier and Petro Corsi (Paris: Office for Official Publications of the European Communities, 2000), 19–40; Robin Rider, "Measure of Ideas, Rule of Language: Mathematics and Language in the 18th Century," in *The Quantifying Spirit in the Eighteenth Century*, ed. Tore Frangsmyr, J. L. Heilbron, and Robin E. Rider (Berkeley: University of California Press, 1990), 113–41.

8. James Knowlson, *Universal Language Schemes in England and France, 1600–1800* (Toronto: University of Toronto Press, 1975), 29.

9. Harcourt Brown, "History and the Learned Journal," *Journal of the History of Ideas* 33, no. 3 (1972): 365–78.

10. Ralph W. V. Elliot, "Isaac Newton's 'Of a Universal Language,'" *Modern Language Review* 52 (1957): 1–18.

11. For Dalgarno's and Leibniz's artificial languages, see David Cram and Jaap Maat, *George Dalgarno on Universal Language* (Oxford: Oxford University Press, 2001); Olga Pombo, *Leibniz and the Problem of a Universal Language* (Münster: Nodus, 1987). For a general overview of the seventeenth-century universal languages, see Jonathan Cohen, "On the Project of a Universal Character," *Mind* 63 (1954): 49–63; Andrew Large, *The Artificial Language Movement* (Oxford: Basil Blackwell, 1985), 19–42; Jaap Maat, *Philosophical Languages in the Seventeenth Century: Dalgarno, Wilkins, Leibniz* (Dordrecht: Kluwer, 2004); and Umberto Eco, *The Search for the Perfect Language* (Cambridge, Mass.: Blackwell, 1995), 209–92.

12. Qtd. in Knowlson, *Universal Language Schemes*, 191. For the new conception of language, see Burke, *Languages and Communities*, 160–72.

13. Knowlson, *Universal Language Schemes*, 183–209; Eco, *The Search*, 290–92.

14. Burke, *Languages and Communities*, 163–72.

15. Johann Gottfried Herder, *Philosophical Writings*, trans. and ed. Michael N. Forster (Cambridge: Cambridge University Press, 2002), 50. For Herder's philosophy of language, see Edward Sapir, "Herder's *Ursprung der Sprache*," *Modern Philology* 5, no. 1 (1907): 109–42.

16. Wilhelm von Humboldt, *On Language, On the Diversity of Human Language Construction and Its Influence on the Mental Development of the Human Species*, ed. Michael Losonsky (Cambridge: Cambridge University Press, 1999), 46.

17. Maurice Olender, *The Languages of Paradise* (Cambridge, Mass.: Harvard University Press, 1992).

18. Thomas Bonfiglio, *Mother Tongues and Nations: The Invention of the Native Speaker* (New York: Walter de Gruyter, 2010), 142–84.

19. Johann Gottlieb Fichte, *Addresses to the German Nation*, trans. and ed. Gregory Moore (Cambridge: Cambridge University Press, 2008), 161. For an analysis of Fichte's ethnolinguistic nationalism, see David Martyn, "Borrowed Fatherland: Nationalism and Language Purism in Fichte's *Addresses to the German Nation*," *Germanic Review* 72, no. 3 (2001): 303–15. For a more critical perspective, see Arash Abizadeh, "Was Fichte an Ethnic Nationalist? On Cultural Nationalism and Its Double," *History of Political Thought* 26, no. 2 (2005): 334–59.

20. See Michael D. Bordo, Alan M. Taylor, and Jeffrey G. Williamson, eds., *Globalization in Historical Perspective* (Chicago: University of Chicago Press, 2003).

21. Guillaume Daudin, Matthias Morys, and Kevin H. O'Rourke, "Globalization, 1870–1914," in *The Cambridge Economic History of Modern Europe. Vol. 2: 1870 to the Present,* ed. Stephen N. Broadberry and Kevin H. O'Rourke (Cambridge: Cambridge University Press, 2010), 5–29.

22. Kevin H. O'Rourke and Jeffrey G. Williamson, *Globalization and History* (Cambridge, Mass.: MIT Press, 1999), 119.

23. Union of International Associations, *Les 1978 Organisations Internationales fondées depuis le Congrès de Vienne* (Brussels: UIA, 1957), 5–11.

24. Herbert N. Shenton, *Cosmopolitan Conversation* (New York: Columbia University Press, 1933), 27; Akira Iriye, *Global Community* (Berkeley: University of California Press), 9–36.

25. David Crystal, *English as a Global Language*, 2nd ed. (Cambridge: Cambridge University Press, 2003), 12.

26. See the aggregate data in biology, chemistry, physics, medicine, and mathematics publications in Ulrich Ammon, "Deutsch als Wissenschaftssprache: die Entwicklung im 20. Jahrhundert und die Zukunftsperspektive," in *Sprache und Sprachen in den Wissenschaften: Geschichte und Gegenwart,* ed. Herbert E. Wiegand (Berlin / New York: de Gruyter), 207. A different estimate, which considers astronomy, chemistry, mathematics, physics, and zoology, shows that German was the most important language in the natural sciences already in the last decade of the nineteenth century: Brigitte Schroeder-Gudehus, "Une langue internationale pour la science?" in *L'avenir du français dans les publications et les communications scientifiques et techniques* (Mon-

treal: Conseil de la Langue Française, 1983), http://www.cslf.gouv.qc.ca/bibliotheque -virtuelle.

27. Herbert Spencer, *An Autobiography* (New York: Appleton, 1904), 1:247; Friedrich W. Nietzsche, *Human, All Too Human*, trans. Marion Faber with Stephen Lehman (Lincoln: University of Nebraska Press, 1984 [1878]), 64.

28. For the political use of language in the era of nationalism, see Daniel Baggioni, *Langues et nations en Europe* (Paris: Payot, 1997), 210-87; Eric Hobsbawm, *Nations and Nationalism Since 1780* (Cambridge: Cambridge University Press, 1990); from the same author, "Language, Culture, and National Identity," *Social Research* 63, no. 4 (1996): 165-95; Ernest Gellner, *Nations and Nationalism* (Oxford: Basil Blackwell, 1983); Benedict Anderson, *Imagined Communities*, rev. ed. (London: Verso, 2006); and Tomasz Kamusella, *The Politics of Language and Nationalism in Modern Central Europe* (New York: Palgrave Macmillan, 2009). For a case-by-case description of the invention of new national languages, see Istvan Fodor and Claude Hagège, eds., *Language Reform: History and Future*, 3 vols. (Hamburg: Buske Verlag, 1983).

Chapter 2

1. Qtd. in Reinhard Hauptenthal, *Über die Startbedingungen zweier Plansprachen* (Saarbrücken: Iltis, 2005), 13.

2. For Schleyer's life, see Johann Martin Schleyer, "Meine Biographie (1880)," in *Prälat- Schleyer-Jahrbuch*, ed. Reinhard Hapenthal (Saarbrücken: Iltis, 2007), 121-46; Sigmund Spielmann, ed., *Volapük-Almanach für 1888* (Leipzig: Mayer, 1887), 11-15; Albert Sleumer, *Johan Martin Schleyer (18. Juli 1831-16. August 1912). Ein Lebensbild* (Saarbrücken: Iltis, 1981 [1914]); Reinhard Hauptenthal, *125 Jahre Volapük. Leben und Werk Johann Martin Schleyer (1831-1912)* (Saarbrücken: Iltis, 2005); from the same author, *La pastro de Litzelstetten. Decenio (1875-1885) en la vivo de Johann Martin Schleyer (1831-1912)* (Saarbrücken: Iltis, 2005).

3. By the time Schleyer created his international phonetic alphabet, some linguists were already working to produce a standardized graphic representation of sounds, which in 1886 gave way to the establishment of the International Phonetic Association. See Michael K. C. MacMahon, "The International Phonetic Association: The First 100 Years," *Journal of the International Phonetic Association* 16, no. 1 (1986): 30-38.

4. Schleyer was not the first one to jump from the idea of creating a new alphabet to crafting a new language able to clothe that alphabet. Dalgarnos's universal language, as well as Herbert Spencer's scheme of an artificial language, follows the same pattern; see Cram and Maat, *George Dalgarno*, 9, and Spencer, *An Autobiography*, 1:247 and 617-21.

5. This example and the description of the language come from Klaus A. Linderfelt, *Volapük: An Easy Method of Acquiring the Universal Language* (Milwaukee: Gaspar and Zahn, 1888).

6. Johann Martin Schleyer, *Hauptgedanken meiner öffentlichen Vortrage über die von mir ersonnene Allsprache Volapük* (Konstanz: A. Moriell, 1885); Sleumer, *Johan Martin Schleyer*, 20.

7. On the strength of Volapük in 1888, see Rupert Kniele, *Der erste Jahrzehnt der Weltsprache Volapük* (Saarbrücken: Iltis, 1989); and Johann Schmidt, *Geschichte der universalsprache Volapük*, ed. Reinhard Haupenthal (Saarbrücken: Iltis, 1986 [1964]), 8–13.

Chapter 3

1. For the aesthetic mission of *Sionsharfe*, see Alfred Eble, "Die *Sionsharfe*, eine katholische Zeitschrift für christliche Poesie," in Haupenthal, *Prälat Schleyer Jahrbuch 2008*, 29–54.

2. A reprint of the official diploma is included in Johann Martin Schleyer, *Volapük. Die Weltsprache. Entwurf einer Universalsprache für alle Gebildete der ganzen Welt*, ed. Reinhard Haupenthal (Hildesheim: Olms, 1982 [1880]).

3. Cornelia Mannewitz, "Deutsche St. Petersburger Beiträge zur Idee der Welthilfssprache," in *Sankt Petersburg — 'der akkurate Deutsche': Deutsche und Deutsches in der anderen russischen Hauptstadt. Beiträge zum Internationalen Symposium in Potsdam, 23.–28. September 2003*, ed. Norbert Franz and Ljuba Kirjuchina (Peter Lang: Frankfurt am Main, 2006), 365–76.

4. Schleyer, *Volapük. Die Weltsprache*, iii.

5. Qtd. in Carlos Sanhueza, "El objetivo del instituto pedagógico no es el de formar geógrafos. Hans Steffen y la transferencia del saber geográfico alemán a Chile, 1893–1907," *Historia* 45, no. 1 (2012): 188n71.

6. Alfred Kirchhoff, "Wie ich Volapükist wurde," *Rund um die Welt* (April 1890): 1–6.

7. A short biography of Rudolf Menke at http://www.biographie-portal.eu/, a research site launched by the Bavarian State Library and other academic organizations of Austria and Switzerland.

8. See Johannes Bierey, "Alfred Kirchhoff," in *Mitteldeutsche Lebensbilder, Erster Band. Lebensbilder des 19. Jahrhunderts* (Magdeburg: Verlag der Historischen Kommission, 1926), 357–75.

9. Kirchhoff, "Wie ich Volapükist," 4.

10. Among others, he also translated into Volapük works of Jacob and Wilhelm Grimm and Hans Christian Andersen. For his defense of Volapük as a literary language, see *Rund um die Welt* (December 1890): 273–76; (January 1891): 289–92, and (March 1891): 369–80. For a biography of Siegfried Lederer, see Reinhard Haupenthal, *Prof. Dr. Siegfried Lederer (1861–1911) und die VolapüK-Zeitschrift "Rund um die Welt"* (Saarbrücken: Iltis, 2001).

11. See Konrad Meisterhans, "Volapük und der Weltfrieden," *Rund um die Welt* (February 1891): 340; Simon Buisman, "Volapük und der Weltfrieden," *Rund um die*

Welt (March 1891): 353–56. Peace activists did not share this enthusiasm for Schleyer's language, however. For example, in its report about Volapük, the journal *Le Désarmament européen et l'arbitrage* (August 8, 1885): 121–22, edited by the pro-socialist Jean-Baptiste Godin, did not recommend its readers to learn it, given that the future of the language was still in the air. Similarly, even when the peace movement was by this time pondering about the utility of an artificial language—given the discontent of some activists with the decision to use French as the official language at the annual Peace Conferences—Volapük was not considered. Thus, rather than Schleyer's language, the delegates of the Fourth Peace Conference (Bern, 1892) decided to study the possibility of "putting forward and extend an international language (neo-Hellenic) (*néohellenique*)," still to be invented. See Bureau International de la Paix, *Bulletin Officiel du IVme Congrès universel de la paix* (Berne: Haller, 1892), 200.

12. Joseph Bernhaupt, *J. M. Schelyer's Weltsprache "Volapuk"* (Überlingen: Aug. Feyel, 1884), 4. See also Carl Zetter, *Eine Volapüktour* (Staatsfurt: Trippo, 1898), 9; L. P. Jensen, "Volapük und die Geschäftswelt," *Rund um die Welt* (December 1890): 257–60; and Ludwig Zamponi, "Volaküp und Fremdenverkehr," *Rund um die Welt* (May 1890): 33–36.

13. See Charles E. Sprague, *The Philosophy of Accounts*, 5th ed. (New York: Ronald Press Con, 1922), v.

14. Charles E. Sprague, *Hand-Book of Volapük*, 5th ed. (London: Trübner and Co., 1888), vii.

15. The American Spelling Reform Association was set up in 1876 by academics and teachers' organizations. It had the support of the Philological Society of England and the American Philological Association. Like its counterpart in France, the Société de réforme orthographique, the American spelling reform movement had a political agenda. It considered that an easier spelling system could help break down educational barriers, foster social mobility, and, consequently, political participation. See Francis A. March, "The Spelling Reform," Bureau of Education, *Circular of Information no. 8* (Washington, D.C.: Government Printing Office, 1893).

16. The biographical data on Charles E. Sprague comes from the Accounting Hall of Fame of the Fisher College of Business at Ohio State University, and the official site of the New York State Society of Certified Public Accountants, which Sprague founded in 1897.

17. See Jean-Claude Caraco, "Auguste Kerckhoffs (1835–1903) kaj lia rolo en la Volapük-movado," in *Menade bal püki bal. Festlibro por la 50ª naskitago de Reinhard Haupenthal*, ed. Reinhard Haupenthal (Saarbrücken: Iltis, 1998), 391–404.

18. See *Rund um die Welt* (December 1889): 1.

19. For the place of Kerckhoffs in the history of cryptography, see David Kahn, *The Code-Breakers: The Comprehensive History of Secret Communication from Ancient Times to the Internet* (New York: Scribner, 1996), 230–40. Regarding Solresol, in 1886 Kerckhoffs published an *Examen critique de la Langue Musicale Universelle*, which I have not been able to find. Solrerol was based on the combination of the seven musical notes.

Thus, "doremi" was day, "dorefa" week, "doresol" month, "dorela" year, and "doresi" century. For a description of Solresol and a biography of his inventor, Jean-François Sudre, see Andrew Large, *The Artificial Language Movement*), 60–63; and Paul Collins, "Solresol, the Universal Musical Language," *McSweeney's* 5 (2000): 50–66.

20. Qtd. in Jean-Claude Lescure, *Un imaginaire transnational? Volapük et Espéranto vers 1880–1939*, unpublished habilitation thesis (Paris: Institute d'Etudes Politiques de Paris, 1999), 96.

21. Ibid., 100–101.

22. Auguste Kerckhoffs, *Langue commercial international. Cours complet de Volapük*, 8th ed. (Paris: Le Soudier, 1887).

23. Auguste Kerckhoffs, *International Commercial Language*, adapted by Karl Dornbusch (Chicago: S. R. Winchell and Co., 1888).

24. Lescure, *Un imaginaire*, 85–86.

25. For a small biography of Kniele, see Reinhard Haupenthal, "Personennotiz zu Rupert Kniele (1844–1911)," *Prälat Schleyer Jahrbuch 2008*: 109–16.

26. See Reinhard Haupenthal, *Der erste Volapük-Kongress. Friedrichshafen, August 1884* (Saarbrücken: Iltis, 1984). The lyrics and music of the Volapük anthem were authored by the theology student Franz Zorell and Schleyer, respectively. An English translation of the first six verses of the hymn would read like this: "Peace, brotherhood to maintain / a sense for harmony is our banner / Acclaim this work / "One language" cry with me / "for the entire globe / to this strives our association." Zorell's original version can be found in Haupenthal, *Der erste Volapük-Kongress*, 63.

27. Rupert Kniele, *Der erste Jahrzehnt*, 25.

28. Ibid., my emphasis.

Chapter 4

1. Qtd. in Lescure, *Un imaginaire*, 48–49. Sarcey—last line, first stanza—was the much-feared literary critic Francisque Sarcey, also member of the Association française pour la propagation du Volapük. See Louis Couturat and Léopold Leau, *Histoire de la langue universelle*, ed. Reinhard Haupenthal (Hildesheim: Georg Olms, 2001), 142.

2. Qtd. in Lescure, *Un imaginaire*, 45–46.

3. Ibid., 66.

4. Ibid., 67.

5. Ibid., 120.

6. *Rund um die Welt* (October 1888): 196.

7. On the standardization of German after 1871 and the linguistic policies of the new country, see Tomasz Kamusella, *The Politics of Language and Nationalism in Modern Central Europe* (New York: Palgrave Macmillan, 2009), 84–85; and Marjorie Lamberti, *State, Society and the Elementary School in Imperial Germany* (Oxford: Oxford University Press, 1989), 109–53.

8. Michael Burleigh, *Earthly Powers* (New York: Harper, 2005), 323.

9. Alfred Kirchhoff, "Ist Volapük antinational?" *Rund um die Welt* (August-September 1890): 148.

10. Thaddäus Devidé, "Dr. Römer's Schmähschrift *Volapük und Deutsche Professoren*," *Rund um die Welt* (October 1888): 193–96.

11. Alexander M. Bell, "Volapük," *Science* 27 (January 1888): 39–40.

12. Alexander M. Bell, *World-English: The Universal Language* (New York: N. D. C. Hodges, 1888), 16. In the text above, I have tried to reproduce in Unicode the invented characters used by the author.

13. A. Schinz, "La question d'une langue international artificielle," *Revue Philosophique de la France et de l'Étranger* 60 (July-December 1905): 24–44; Dan Savatovsky, "Les linguistes et la langue internationale (1880–1920)," *Histoire, Épistémologie, Langage* 11 (1989): 37–65.

14. August Schleicher, *Darwinism Tested by the Science of Language*, trans. Alex V. W. Bikkers (London: John Candem, 1869), 20–21. For a review of Schleicher and the "language as organism" metaphor, see Lia Formigari, *A History of Language Philosophies* (Amsterdam: John Benjamins, 2004), 144–46.

15. Ernst Müller, *Der Phantom der Weltsprache. Worte der Aufklärung und Ernüchterung über das Volapük und den Weltsprach-Gedanken im Allgemeinen* (Berlin: Ulrich, 1888); H. Ziemer, "E. Müller. Das Phantom der Weltsprache," *Berliner Philologische Wochenschrift* 47 (1888): 1458–59; Gustav Meyer, "Weltsprache und Weltsprachen," in *Plansprachen. Beiträge zur Interlinguistik*, ed. Reinhard Haupenthal (Darmstadt: Wissenschaftliche Buchgesellschaft, 1976), 28–45.

16. See Raoul de la Grasserie, *De la possibilité et des conditions d' une langue internationale* (Paris: Maisonneuve, 1892); from the same author, *Nouvelle langue internationale. Langue internationale pacifiste, ou apoléma, basée sur les radicaux techniques déjà internationaux* (Paris: E. Leroux, 1907).

17. Hugo Schuchardt, *Weltsprache und Weltsprachen, an Gustav Meyer* (Strassburg: Karl J. Trübner, 1894), 31.

18. See Hugo Schuchardt Hugo, *Auf Anlass des Volapüks* (Berlin: Robert Oppenheim, 1888); from the same author, "Bericht über die auf Schaffung einer künstlichen Hilfssprache gerichtete Bewegung," in *Plansprachen. Beiträge zur Interlinguistik*, ed. Reinhard Haupenthal (Darmstadt: Wissenschaftliche Buchgesellschaft, 1991 [1904]), 46–58. For his biographical reflections on the linguistic wars in the Austro-Hungarian empire, see "Bekenntnisse und Erkenntnisse," *Wissen und Leben* 13 (1919): 179–98.

19. Emphasis in the original. For the *Homunkulus* metaphor, see, e.g., Karl Brugmann and August Leskien, *Zur Kritik der künstlichen Weltsprachen* (Strasbourg: Karl J. Trübner, 1907); and Herman Diels, *Internationale Aufgaben der Universität* (Berlin: Gustav Schade, 1906). De Courtenay's quotation is from Jan Baudouin de Courtenay, "Zur Kritik der künstlichen Weltsprachen," in *Plansprachen. Beiträge zur Interlinguistik*, ed. Reinhard Haupenthal (Darmstadt: Wissenschaftliche Buchgesellschaft, 1976), 69, emphasis in the original.

20. Ibid., 67.

21. Piet Desmet and Pierre Swiggers, "Le problem des langues et des nationalités chez Michel Bréal: reflects epistolaires," in *Bréal et le sens de la semantique*, ed. Gabriel Bergounioux (Orléans: Presses Universitaires d'Orléans, 2000), 38.

22. For a description of these languages, see Couturat and Leau, *Histoire de la langue*, 168–80, 272–303, 373–80, and 401–7.

23. American Philosophical Society, "Report of the Committee Appointed Oct. 21, 1887, to Examine into the Scientific Value of the Volapük," *Nature* 38 (1888): 351–55. Flexional languages use word endings to mark grammatical functions, while non-flexional languages prefer stricter word order rules and prepositions for the same purpose. Following the theory of language of Friedrich Schlegel (1772–1829), it was still common in the nineteenth century to think that inflectional languages were positioned at a higher level of language evolution; see Bonfiglio, *Mother Tongues*, 143–45. Current linguistic theory, though, does not support this claim; see, e.g., Juan Carlos Moreno, *La dignidad e igualdad de las lenguas* (Madrid: Alianza Editorial, 2000), 90–97.

24. See Alexander Ellis, "On the Conditions of a Universal Language," *Transactions of the Philological Society* (1888): 59–98. More precisely, the American Association for the Advancement of Science and the Massachusetts Institute of Technology, as well as other American universities, backed the American Philosophical Society's proposal, but the response from the other side of the Atlantic was less encouraging. See American Philosophical Society, "Ergänzungs-Bericht des Comitè zur Formulierung einer international Sprache erstatet von demselben . . . am 7. Dezember 1888," in Leopold Einstein, *Weltsprachliche Zeit- und Streitfragen* (Nuremberg: Stein, 1889), 21–26.

25. Ellis, "On the Conditions," 97.

Chapter 5

1. Lescure, *Un imaginaire*, 99.

2. Couturat and Leau, *Histoire de la langue*, 142–46.

3. Qtd. in Lescure, *Un imaginaire*, 43.

4. Alfred Kirchhoff, "Die Ziele der Weiter-Entwicklung des Volapük," in *Volapük-Almanach für 1888*, ed. Sigmund Spielmann (Leipzig: Mayer, 1887), 44.

5. *Rund um die Welt* (April 1888): 42–44.

6. Julius Lott, *Ist Volapük die beste und einfachste Lösung des Weltsprache-Problems?* (Vienna, 1888); from the same author, *Un lingua internazional* (Vienna: Frankenstein and Wagner, 1890); Adolphe Nicolas, *Rapport sur un projet de langue scientifique international* (Clermont: Daix freères, 1889).

7. Schmidt, *Geschichte*, 16–17; Heinrich Löw, "Christian Karl Gross. Ein Gedenkblatt," *Rund um die Welt* (September-October 1891): 193–96; Marcus Sikosek, "Doku-

mente zum Weltsprachverein Nürnberg," *Esperantologio / Esperanto Studies* 3 (2005): 45–54.

8. See Rupert Kniele, *Herr Leopold Einstein und la linguo internacia* (Überlingen: A. Feyer, 1890). Concerns about the apparent antisemitism of Schleyer and his closest associates were present in the movement given that in his German-Volapük dictionary Schleyer introduced the verb "yudanön," meaning "acting like a Jew." Kerckhoffs severely criticized this word, which according to him "should be expelled from the language"; see Leopold Einstein, *Weltsprachliche Zeit- und Streitfragen* (Nuremberg: A. Stein, 1889), 14. If aside from the ominous coinage of "yudanön" there are no other antisemitic remarks in Schleyer's work, plain anti-Roma sentiments are unquestionable. Thus, in his 1912 brochure *Ein Idealvolk* that portrays his utopian vision of society, Schleyer remarked that "Roma people should be either subdue and converted, or otherwise sent back to their land"; see Johann Martin Schleyer, *Ein Idealvolk*, 2nd ed. (Constanz: Weltsprache Verlag), 24.

9. Ellis, "On the Conditions," 66; see also Vera Barandovská-Frank, "Über die *Academia pro Interlingua,*" in *Plansprachen und ihre Gemeinschaften*, ed. Detlev Blanke (Berlin: Gesellschaft für Interlinguistik e. V., 2002), 6.

10. Charles E. Sprague, "The Volapük Congress at Paris," *Volapük: A Monthly Journal of the World Language* (1889): 40.

11. Kniele, *Der erste Jahrzehnt*, 69; Schmidt, *Geschichte*, 13–16.

12. Sprague, "The Volapük Congress," 40–61; Waldemar Rosenberger, "Brief History of the International Academy of the Universal Language," in Michael A. F. Holmes, *Dictionary of the Neutral Language* (Rochester: John P. Smith, 1903), 277–300; and *Rund um die Welt* (August- September 1889): 145–50.

13. For Sprague's recollection of his conversation with Schleyer before the Paris Congress, see North American Association for the Propagation of Volapük, *First Annual Convention of Volapükists: Boston, Aug 21, 22, 23, 1890* (Boston, 1890).

14. Rosenberger, "Brief History," 282.

15. *Volapük: A Monthly Journal of the World Language* (Boston, 1889): 53.

16. *Rund um die Welt* (February-March 1892): 359–64.

17. *Rund um die Welt* (December 1890): 283–84.

18. Kniele, *Der erste Jahrzehnt*, 71–73.

19. Reinhard Haupenthal, "Nachwort zum Neudruck (1989)," in Kniele, *Der erste Jahrzehnt*, 139–40.

20. In the early 1930s the language witnessed a short revival under the leadership of Arie de Jong, a Dutch physician. By that time, however, Esperanto had already taken the field and the reformed Volapük of de Jong did not prosper. See Brian R. Bishop, "La 'ĉifaloj' de Volapük," in *Menade bal püki bal. Festlibro por la 50ᵃ naskiĝ-tago de Reinhard Haupenthal*, ed. Reinhard Haupenthal (Saarbrüken: Iltis, 1998), 375–90; and Schmidt, *Geschichte*, 41–45.

Chapter 6

1. Edgar de Wahl, "Wege und Irrwege zur Weltsprache," in *Occidental. Die Weltsprache*, ed. Engelbert Pigal (Stuttgart: Frankische Verlagshandlung, 1950 [1930]), 21.

2. Ludwig L. Zamenhof, *Originala verkaro*, ed. Johannes Dietterle (Leipzig: Ferdinand Hirt and Sohn, 1929), 404.

3. Natasha Staller, "Babel: Hermetic Languages, Universal Languages, and Anti-Languages in fin de siècle Parisian Culture," *Art Bulletin* 76, no. 2 (1994): 331–54.

4. Haupenthal, *Der erste Volapük-Kongress*, 70.

5. *Rund um die Welt* (December 1890): 283–84.

6. Haupenthal, *Prälat Johann Martin Schleyer*, 28.

7. Edward E. Y. Hales, *Pio Nono: A Study in European Politics and Religion in the Nineteenth Century* (London: Eyre and Spottiswoode, 1954), 255–313; Frank J. Coppa, *Pope Pius IX: Crusader in a Secular Age* (Boston: Twayne Publishers, 1979), 140–68.

8. Coppa, *Pope Pius IX*, 189.

9. Michael Gross, *The War Against Catholicism* (Ann Arbor: University of Michigan Press, 2004), 246–58.

10. Lothar Gall, "Die partei- und sozialgeschichtliche Problematik des badischen Kulturkampfes," *Zeitschrift für die Geschichte des Oberrheins* 113 (1965): 153; Konrad Gröber, "Der Altkatholizismus in Messkirch. Die Geschichte seiner Entwiklung und Bekämpfung," *Freiburger Diozesan-Archiv* 40 (1912): 135–98.

11. Thomas Mergel, "Ultramontanism, Liberalism, Moderation: Political Mentalities and Political Behavior of the German Catholic *Bürgertum*, 1848–1914," *Central European History* 29, no. 2 (1996): 151–74.

12. Gröber, "Der Altkatholizismus"; Gross, *The War Against Catholicism*, 253–54. For the reaction of Rome against Old Catholics, see J. B. Mullinger, *The New Reformation: A Narrative of the Old Catholic Movement from 1870 to the Present Time* (London: Longmans, 1875), 93–136; and A. M. E. Scarth, *The Story of the Old Catholic and Kindred Movements* (London: Simpkin, 1883), 31–40.

13. Mullinger, *The New Reformation*, 232.

14. Haupenthal, *Der erste Volapük-Kongress*, 105.

15. Johann Martin Schleyer, *100 Gründe warum ich katolische bleibe* (Aachen: Gustav Schmidt, 1901), 3–4.

Chapter 7

1. Nikolao Stepanov, "Esperantistaj viktimoj de stalinismo," *Sennaciulo* 9 (1990): 76–78.

2. Ulrich Lins, *Die gefärhliche Sprache* (Gerlingen: Bleicher, 1988), 117.

3. Qtd. in Christopher Hutton, *Linguistics and the Third Reich: Mother-Tongue Fascism, Race, and the Science of Language* (London: Routledge, 1999), 302.

4. Qtd. in Aleksander Korzhenkov, *The Life of Zamenhof*, trans. Ian Richmond and ed. Humphrey Tonkin (New York: Mondial, 2010), 5.

5. Tomasz Wisniewski, *Jewish Białystok* (Ipswich: Ipswich Press, 1998), 120.

6. Ya'akov Samid, *The Immortal Spirit: The Bialystok Hebrew Gymnasium, Poland, 1919–1939* (Haifa: Traffic Publications, 1995), 12–13.

7. Israel Bartal, *The Jews of Eastern Europe, 1772–1881* (Philadelphia: University of Pennsylvania Press, 2002), 90–101; Eli Lederhendler, "Modernity Without Emancipation or Assimilation? The Case of Russian Jewry," in *Assimilation and Community: The Jews in Nineteenth Century Europe*, ed. Jonathan Frankel and Steven J. Zipperstein (Cambridge: Cambridge University Press, 1992), 324–43; and Marvin Fox, "Law and Ethics in Modern Jewish Philosophy: The Case of Moses Mendelssohn," *Proceedings of the American Academy for Jewish Research* 43 (1976): 1–13.

8. See Stephen Berk, *Years of Crisis, Years of Hope: Russian Jewry and the Pogroms of 1881–1882* (Westport, Conn.: Greenwood Press, 1985), 13–15; Bartal, *The Jews*, 88; Aleksander Korjenkov [Korzhenkov], *Homarano. La vivo, verkoj kaj ideoj de d-ro L. L. Zamenhof*, 2nd ed. (Kaunas: Litova Esperanto Asocio, 2011), 40; and Naftali Zvi Maimon, *La kaŝita vivo de Zamenhof* (Tokyo: Japana Esperanto Instituto, 1978), 27–36.

9. In 1876, three years before Zamenhof began his studies at the University of Moscow, there were only 247 Jewish students in Russian universities. In the mid-1880s, amounting to 15 percent of the student body, the Jews were overrepresented in Russian higher education; see Benjamin Nathans, *Beyond the Pale: The Jewish Encounter with Late Imperial Russia* (Berkeley: University of California Press, 2002), 218 and 229.

10. Berk, *Years of Crisis*, 37–55; I. Michael Aronson, "The Anti-Jewish Pogroms in Russia in 1881," in *Pogroms: Anti-Jewish Violence in Modern Russian History*, ed. John D. Klier and Shlomo Lambroza (Cambridge: Cambridge University Press, 1992), 44–61; and John D. Klier, *Russians, Jews, and the Pogroms of 1881–1882* (Cambridge: Cambridge University Press, 2011).

11. Jonathan Frankel, *Prophecy and Politics: Socialism, Nationalism, and the Russian Jews, 1862–1917* (Cambridge: Cambridge University Press, 1981), 86.

12. See Joel S. Geffen, "Whither: To Palestine or to America in the Pages of the Russian Hebrew Press Ha-Melitz and Ha-Yom (1880–1890)," *American Jewish Historical Quarterly* 59 (1969): 179–200; Frankel, *Prophecy and Politics*, 88; and Berk, *Years of Crisis*, 108–10. Zamenhof's articles of 1881 and 1882 in *Razsvet* are reproduced in Adolf Holzhaus, *Doktoro kaj lingvo Esperanto* (Helsinki: Fondumo Esperanto, 1969), 87–120. For an Esperanto translation, see Ludwig L. Zamenhof, *Mi estas homo. Originalaj verkoj de d-ro L. L. Zamenhof*, ed. Aleksander Korjenkov (Kaliningrad: Sezonoj, 2006), 5–26.

13. Korjenkov, *Homarano*, 65–71; Maimon, *La kaŝita vivo*, 85–102.

14. Frankel, *Prophecy and Politics*, 141–47; Alexander Orbach, "The Development of the Russian Jewish Community, 1881–1903," in Klier and Lambroza, *Pogroms: Anti-Jewish Violence in Modern Russian History*, 146–48.

15. Frankel, *Prophecy and Politics*, 84.

16. The acronym "BILU" is formed by the initial letters of the Hebrew expression "House of Jacob, come, let us go!" BILU was a society of pioneers who wanted to establish agricultural settlements in Palestine.

17. Yosef Salmon, "Ideology and Reality in the Bilu *Aliyah*," *Harvard Ukranian Studies* 2 (1978): 455.

18. See his letter to the BILU member S. Zuckerman in Zamenhof, *Mi estas homo*, 27–31.

19. Berk, *Years of Crisis*, 120.

20. Ehud Luz, *Parallels Meet: Religion and Nationalism in Early Zionist Movement (1882–1904)*, trans. Lenn J. Schramm (Philadelphia: Jewish Publication Society, 1988), 37.

21. On the intimate relationship between language and nationalism in Central and Eastern Europe, see Kamusella, *The Politics*. For a review of the legacies of linguistic nationalisms in Eastern Europe, see Cathie Carmichael, "Coming to Terms with the Past: Language and Nationalism in Russia and Its Neighbours," in *Language and Nationalism in Europe*, ed. Stephen Balbour and Cathie Carmichael (Oxford: Oxford University Press 2000), 221–39.

22. Alfred Holzhaus, *Doktoro kaj lingvo Esperanto* (Helsinki: Fondumo Esperanto, 1969), 19–34.

23. Ludwig L. Zamenhof, *Mi estas homo. Originalaj verkoj de d-ro L. L. Zamenhof*, ed. Aleksander Korĵenkov (Kaliningrad: Sezonoj, 2006), 102.

24. On Herder's preference for "nationally bounded states," see Allan Patten, "The Most Natural State: Herder and Nationalism," *History of Political Thought* 31, no. 4 (2010): 658–89.

25. Karl Popper, *Unended Quest: An Intellectual Autobiography* (Glasglow: Fontana /Collins, 1974), 105.

26. Malachi H. Hacohen, "Dilemmas of Cosmopolitanism: Karl Popper, Jewish Identity and Central European Culture," *Journal of Modern History* 71 (March 1999): 105–49.

27. For an analysis of Zamenhof's philosophical ideas, see Roberto Garvía, "Religion and Artificial Languages at the Turn of the 20th Century: Ostwald and Zamenhof," *Language Problems and Language Planning* 37, no. 1 (2013): 47–70.

Chapter 8

1. Ludovikito (pseud. Ito Kanzi), *Historieto de Esperanto* (Tokio: Libroteko Tokio, 1998), 1–12.

2. Adam Zakrzewski, *Historio de Esperanto, 1887–1912* (Warsaw: Gebethner and Wolff, 1913), 8–9.

3. Kamusella, "Language as an Instrument," 247.

4. Ludwig L. Zamenhof, *Internationale Sprache. Vorrede und vollständiges Lehrbuch. For germanoj* (Warsaw: Gebethner and Wolff, 1887), 31.

5. Ibid., 2.

6. Ibid., 8 and 29.

7. Ibid., 4.

8. On this concept, see Paul A. David, "Clio and the Economics of QWERTY," 336.

9. Ludwig L. Zamenhof, *Dua Libro de l'lingvo internacia* (Warsaw: Kelter, 1888), 12.

10. Ludwig L. Zamenhof, *Aldono al la Dua Libro de l'lingvo internacia* (Warsaw: Kelter, 1929 [1888]), 33.

11. Ibid., 35.

12. Zamenhof, *Dua libro*, 10–11. Emphasis in the original.

13. Ibid., 34.

14. Ibid., 40.

Chapter 9

1. Leopold Einstein, *La lingvo internacia als beste Lösung des internationalen Weltspracheproblems* (Nuremberg: A. Stein, 1888), 6.

2. Einstein, *Weltsprachliche*, 3. The "mystical obfuscation" comes from Einstein, *La lingvo*, 5.

3. Einstein, *Weltsprachliche*, 14–15.

4. Zamenhof, *Originala*, 70.

5. The combined list of the 1,709 Volapükists has been collected from Auguste Kerckhoffs, *Yelabuk pedipedals* (Paris, 1887); Spielman, *Volapük-Almanach*, 20–27; and the pages of *Rund um die Welt*. The first *Adresaro* was published by Zamenhof in 1889, right after the *Dua Libro*.

6. There was certainly a Volapük movement in St. Petersburg, but, as mentioned, it was mostly made of German immigrants; see Mannewitz, "Deutsche St. Petersburger."

7. See Zamenhof's letter to Mainov of May 11, 1889, in Zamenhof, *Originala*, 478–81. See also Adolf Holzhaus, *Doktoro kaj lingvo Esperanto* (Helsinki: Fondumo Esperanto, 1969), 210–22; and Korjenkov, *Homarano*, 98–101.

8. *La Esperantisto* (December 1890), 17–18.

9. Letter to Guminskij of August 1890, included in Zamenhof, *Originala*, 492. Sikosek is also inclined to think that Schmidt had tried to twist Zamenhof's hand. See Marcus Sikosek, *Die neutrale Sprache. Eine politische Gesichichte des Esperanto-Weltbundes* (Skonpres: Bydgoszcz, 2006), 41.

10. *La Esperantisto* (November 1890), 54.

11. For the negotiations and correspondence between Zamenhof and the leader of the Nuremberg club in these months, see Annakris Szimkat, "Kion Zamenhof skribis al Christian Schmidt," in *Li kaj Ni: Festlibro por la 80a naskiĝtago de Gaston Waringhien*, ed. Reinhard Haupenthal (Antwerp / La Laguna: Stafeto, 1984), 337–48.

12. Letter to Guminskij of August 29, 1894, in Zamenhof, *Originala*, 496.

13. See his article "Folieto de Posrednik," in *La Esperantisto* (February 1895): 26–27. The Tolstoyans were followers of the last, most spiritual Leo Tolstoy, who in 1884 became a supporter of Esperanto. They were pacifists, who also rejected church and secular authorities. See *La Esperantisto* (July 1894): 99–100; and Lev Tolstói, *Correspondencia*, ed. Salma Ancira (Barcelona: Acantilado, 2005), 516–17. The Posrednik (Intermediary) publishing group was set up to serve as the intermediary between Russian intellectuals and peasants: *La Esperantisto* (February 1895): 27–28.

14. Letter to Mainov of July 31, 1889, in Zamenhof, *Originala*, 482. See also Gaston Waringhien, "Historia skizo de la Esperanto movado," in *Lingvo kaj vivo*, ed. Gaston Waringhien, 2nd ed. (Rotterdam: Universala Esperanto Asocio, 1989), 398.

15. Geoffrey Sutton, *Concise Encyclopedia of the Original Literature of Esperanto* (New York: Mondial, 2008), 35, 38 and 41. On Leo Belmont (real name Leopold Blumental), see Zofia Banet-Fornalowa, *La pereintoj in memorian* (Czeladź: Eldonejo Hejme, 2003), 15–49.

16. Korjenkov, *Homarano*, 136–38 and 175–76.

Chapter 10

1. For brief biographies of the leading French Esperantists of this period, see Gaston Waringhien, "Prologo," in Ludwig L. Zamenhof, *Leteroj de Zamenhof*, comp. and ed. Gaston Waringhien (Paris: SAT, 1948), 1–9; and Lescure, *Un imaginaire*, 151–67.

2. *L'Espérantiste* (January 1898): 5.

3. See Louis de Beaufront, "Ce que nous voulons," *L'Espérantiste* (January 1898): 1–3. On the political polarization in France resulting from the Dreyfus Affair, see Jean-Marie Mayeur and Madeleine Rebérioux, *The Third Republic from Its Origins to the Great War, 1871–1914* (Cambridge: Cambridge University Press, 1987), 179–208.

4. Zeev Sternhell, "The Political Culture of Nationalism," in *Nationhood and Nationalism in France: From Boulanguism to the Great War 1889–1918*, ed. Robert Tombs (London: Harper Collins, 1991), 22–38.

5. Ludwig L. Zamenhof, *Mi estas homo. Originalaj verkoj de d-ro L. L. Zamenhof*, ed. Aleksander Korjenkov (Kaliningrad: Sezonoj, 2006), 36.

6. On top of Gaston Moch and René Lemaire, there were other Esperantists very active in the international pacifist movement. In Chapter 13, I explore the connections between these two movements.

7. The original article of Zamenhof, "Esenco kaj estonteco de la ideo de Lingvo Internacia," is reproduced in Zamenhof, *Originala*, 276–312.

8. On the dealings of Zamenhof and the French leadership with Hachette, see Zamenhof, *Leteroj de Zamenhof*, 17–88; and Ito Kanzi, "La firmo Hachette kaj la Kolekto Aprobita," in *Menade bal püki bal: Festlibro por la 50ᵃ naskitago de Reinhard Haupenthal*, ed. Reinhard Haupenthal (Saarbrücken: Iltis, 1998), 145–60.

9. Schmidt, *Geschichte*, 30.

10. Johann Martin Schleyer, *Über die Pfuscher-Sprache des Pseudo-Esperanto* (Konstanz, 1907), 7.

11. Alberto Liptay, *Gemeinsprache der Kulturvölker* (Brockhaus: Leipzig, 1891), 150–64.

12. See Rosenberger, "Brief History," 277–300; and Tazio Carlevaro, "Mondlingvaj akademioj," in *Li kaj Ni: Festlibro por la 80a naskiĝtago de Gaston Waringhien*, ed. Reinhard Haupenthal (Antwerp / La Laguna: Stafeto, 1985).

13. Sikosek, "Dokumente," 52.

14. Albert L. Guérard, *A Short History of the International Language Movement* (London: Fisher Unwin, 1922), 140.

15. See Lescure, *Un imaginaire*, 162–63. On sports societies and the popularization of tourism in France, see Pierre Arnaud, "Dividing and Uniting: Sports Societies and Nationalism, 1870–1914," in Tombs, *Nationhood and Nationalism in France*, 182–94; and Eugen Weber, *France, fin de siècle* (Cambridge, Mass.: Harvard University Press, 1986), 186–212.

16. For the bylaws of the Tutmonda Esperantista Ligo proposed by Zamenhof, as well as the ensuing debates and counterproposals, see *Lingvo Internacia* (July 1905): 295–327; and Korĵenkov, *Homarano*, 189–95.

17. Geraldo Mattos, "Esenco kaj estonteco de la Fundamento de Esperanto," *Esperantologio / Esperanto Studies* 1 (1999): 21–37.

Chapter 11

1. Ludwig L. Zamenhof, *Mi estas homo*, 110.

2. Zamenhof, *Leteroj*, 175.

3. Garvía, "Religion and Artificial," 54–64.

4. Qtd. in Korĵenkov, *Homarano*, 171.

5. Zamenhof, *Originala*, 360–65.

6. *British Esperantist* (September-October 1905): 145.

7. Javal's letter in Zamenhof, *Leteroj*, 120. Emphasis in the original. Probably the only article Javal referred to was the report on "Dr. Zamenhof and the Boulogne Congress of Esperantists" published by the *Jewish Chronicle* (July 21, 1905): 8–9.

8. Emphasis in the original. I am using here the translation printed in *British Esperantist* (September-October 1905): 138–39. The original Esperanto version is available in Zamenhof, *Originala*, 237–38.

9. *Daily Mail* (August 7, 1905): 5; and *La Vanguardia* (August 7, 1905): 8.

10. Qtd, in Paul A. Schilpp, *The Philosophy of Rudolf Carnap* (Cambridge: Cambridge University Press, 1963), 69.

11. Ibid., 69.

12. Qtd. in Korĵenkov, *Homarano*, 218.

13. Qtd. in ibid., 218. Emphasis in the original

14. Zamenhof, *Originala*, 373-74.

15. This was the society of the "Homaranists," as Zamenhof called it. The Homaranists uphold the universality of ethics represented by the Golden Rule and reject the idea that nations "own" territories. The society of the Homaranists would be permanently on guard against those who refuse to accept the moral autonomy of human beings and try to take them back to the tribe, national or religious. See Ludwig L. Zamenhof, "Homaranismo," in Zamenhof, *Mi estas homo*, 139-46.

16. Ibid., 371.

17. Louis de Beaufront, "Esperanto in France," *North American Review* (March 1907): 520-24.

18. See Lajos Kökény, Vilmos Bleier, Kálmán Kalocsay, and Ivan Ŝirjaev, eds., *Enciklopedio de Esperanto* (Budapest: Literatura Mondo, 1933), 177-84.

Chapter 12

1. Reuben A. Tanquist, "A Study of the Social Psychology of the Diffusion of Esperanto with Special Reference to the English Speaking Peoples," M.A. thesis, University of Minnesota, 1927.

2. Reproduced in *Esperanto* (July-August 1928): 133-56.

3. See Pamela M. Graves, *Labour Women: Women in British Working-Class Politics* (Cambridge: Cambridge University Press, 1994), 22-28; and Atina Grossmann, "German Communism and New Women: Dilemmas and Contradictions," in *Women and Socialism: Socialism and Women,* ed. Helmut Gruber and Pamela Graves (Providence: Berghahn Books, 1998), 139.

4. The corresponding national data on age and education have been obtained from the *Statistical Abstract of the United States, 1928*, 10-11 and 104; the *Statistisches Jahrbuch für das Deutsche Reich* (1930), 14-15 and 408-9; Paul Bolton, *Education: Historical Statistics* (Library House of Commons, 2007), 21; and the *Statistisches Handbuch für die Republik Österreich, 1926*.

5. On the extension of Esperanto in primary and secondary schools, see the report of the General Secretariat of the League of Nations, *Esperanto as an International Auxiliary Language* (Paris: PUF, 1922). The international demand of Esperanto teachers explains the establishment in the late 1920s of the Cseh Institute (officially the Internacia Esperanto Instituto), with headquarters in Arnhem, whose main goal was to train and certify Esperanto teachers and produce teaching materials. On the institute and its founder, see Eric Borsboom, *Vivo de Andreo Cseh* (The Hague: Internacia Esperanto Instituto, 2003).

6. Kökény et al, *Enciklopedio*, 54-56. It is important to notice that this was an organization *of* the blind, but not *for* the blind. At the beginning of the twentieth century a new elite of blind people was contesting the patronizing representation of their

interests by benefactors, welfare professionals and physicians. In this sense, Esperanto was also important for the empowerment of blind people, since it allowed them to side-step non-blind intermediaries and directly exchange information about living conditions and programs for the blind in different countries. On Javal's campaign for Esperanto among the blind, see his book *On Becoming Blind*, trans. Carroll Everett Edson (New York: Macmillan, 1905), 143–46; and his intervention at the *Congrès International pour l'Amélioration du sort des Aveugles tenu à Bruxelles, du 6 au 10 août 1902* (Manage: Imprimiere de l'École professionelle de l'Institut de la Sainte Famille, 1902), 79–80.

7. Data on membership in Forster, *The Esperanto*, 25. The Universala Esperanto Asocio (UEA) was created in 1908. It got momentum after World War I, when the creation of the League of Nations convinced may Esperantists of the need to be represented with a single voice in the international arena. Differences regarding the division of labor between the UEA and national Esperanto associations drastically affected the former, which not until the second half of the twentieth century was able to operate in an effective manner. For a history of UEA in this period, see Sikosek, *Die neutrale,* 57–160.

8. Joseph Gusfield, "Social Movements and Social Change: Perspectives of Linearity and Fluidity," in *Research in Social Movements: Conflict and Change*, ed. Louis Kriesberg (Greenwich: JAI Press, 1981), 317–39.

Chapter 13

1. The positivist philosophy of Ernst Mach (1838–1916), sometimes called "neutral Monism," rejected the Kantian dualism between pure and practical reason and left no room for metaphysics, not grounded in empirical data. Mach's materialism tried to supersede the divide between natural and social sciences. In 1906, and influenced by Mach, the biologist Ernest Haeckel (1834–1919) set up the German Monistic League. Monists campaigned for the substitution of scientific for religion education, against the Christian churches, particularly Catholicism, and for social reforms aiming at the improvement of the living conditions of the working class. They also supported the peace movement. However, some Monists, like Haeckel himself, advocated eugenics and Social Darwinism. On the Monist movement in Germany, see Horst Groschopp, *Dissidenten. Freidenkerei und Kultur in Deutschland* (Berlin: Dietz, 1997), 243–99; Niles R. Holt, "Ernst Haeckel's Monistic Religion," *Journal of the History of Ideas* 32, no. 2 (1971): 265–80; and from the same author, "Monists and Nazis: A Question of Scientific Responsibility," *Hastings Center Report* 5, no. 2 (1975): 37–43.

2. Qtd. in Philipp Blom, *The Vertigo Years: Europe, 1900–1914* (New York: Basic Books, 2007), 193.

3. Wilhelm Ostwald, "Scientific Management for Scientists. 'The Bridge.' The Trust Idea Applied to Intellectual Production," *Scientific American* 108 (1913): 5–6.

4. Wilhelm Ostwald, *Der Energetische Imperativ* (Leipzig: Akademische Verlagsgesellschaft, 1912), 253–63. See also Niles R. Holt, "Wilhelm Ostwald's 'The Bridge,'" *British Journal for the History of Science* 10, no. 2 (1977): 146–50.

5. Ostwald, *Der Energetische*, 199–216.

6. Hervé Hasquin, Suzanne Lecocq, and Daniel Lefebre et al., *Henri La Fontaine—Prix Nobel de la paix—Tracé(s) d'une vie* (Mons: Mundaneum, 2002), 71–110.

7. On the Dewey system and its commonalities with Taylorism, see Marion Casey, "Efficiency, Taylorism and Libraries in Progressive America," *Journal of Library History* 16 (Spring 1981): 265–79.

8. Paul Otlet, "The Union of International Organizations: A World Center," in *International Organization and the Dissemination of Knowledge: Selected Essays of Paul Otlet*, trans. and ed. W. Boyd Rayward (Amsterdam: Elsevier, 1990 [1914]), 112 and 115.

9. On the project of the World City, see Valérie Piette, "Le project de creation d'une Cité Mondiale ou l'utopie pacifiste faite de bruques," in *Cent ans de l'Office international de bibliographie: 1895–1995. Les Premisses du Mundaneum* (Mons: Editions Mundaneum, 1995), 271–301. On the connection between scientific management and modernist architecture, see Mauro Guillén, *The Taylorized Beauty of the Mechanical: Scientific Management and the Rise of Modernist Architecture* (Princeton, N.J.: Princeton University Press, 2006).

10. In fact, one of its regular contributors was the Austrian engineer Eugen Wüster, who after World War II became responsible of the ISO section entrusted with the standardization of scientific terminology.

11. Sandi E. Cooper, "Pacifism in France, 1889–1914: International Peace as a Human Right," *French Historical Studies* 17, no. 2 (1991): 359–86.

12. Paul-Henri Bourrelier, "Gaston Moch, polytechnicien combatant de la paix," *Réalités industrielles* (August 2008): 48–62.

13. Moch was not the first pacifist to propose the introduction of an artificial language in the movement. The Fourth Universal Peace Congress, which took place in 1892, had already raised this topic. See Bureau International de la Paix, *Bulletin Officiel du IVme Congrès*, 200. For his defense of Esperanto against Volapük, see Gaston Moch, "La question de la langue internationale, et sa solution par l'Esperánto," *Revue internationale de sociologie* 4 (1897): 249–95.

14. Bertha von Suttner, *Memoiren* (Stuttgart and Leipzig: Deutsche Verlags-Anstalt, 1909), 272–80. See also Irwin Abrams, "Bertha von Suttner and the Nobel Peace Prize," *Journal of Central European Affairs* 22 (October 1962): 286–307.

15. For Moch's conception of pacificism, see Gaston Moch, "Kio estas pacifisto kaj pacifismo?," *Espero Pacifista* (July 1905): 6–18.

16. See Alfred H. Fried, *Die Grundlagen des revolutionären Pacifismus* (Tübingen: J. C. B. Mohr, 1908), 35. See also Roland Schnell,"Nobelpriesträger Alfred Hermann Fried als Pazifist und Esperantist," *Interlinguistische Informationen. Mitteilungsblatt der Gesellschaft für Interlinguistik e.V.* 19 (2001): 105–17; and Solomon Wank, "The Austrian Peace Movement and the Habsburg Ruling Elite, 1906–1914," in *Peace Movements*

and Political Cultures, ed. Charles Chatfield and Peter van den Dungen (Knoxville: University of Tennessee Press, 1988), 44.

17. Charles Richet, *La selection humaine* (Paris: Félix Alcan, 1919 [1913]), 67.

18. Ibid., 166.

19. Charles Richet, *L'homme stupide* (Paris: Ernest Flammarion, 1919), 44.

20. Bernhard Kuechenhoff, "The Psychiatrist Auguste Forel and His Attitude to Eugenics," *History of Psychiatry* 19 (June 2008): 215–23.

21. Auguste Forel, *Les Etats-Unis de la Terre* (Lausanne: E. Peytrequin, 1915), 50–55.

22. Kuechenhoff, "The Psychiatrist," 221.

23. Eloise Brown, *"The Truest Form of Patriotism": Pacifist Feminism in Britain, 1870–1902* (Manchester: Manchester University Press, 2003), 82–83.

24. Hendrik A. de Hoog, *Nia historio. Kristana Esperanto Ligo de 1911–1961* (Amsterdam: Hardinxveld, 1964), 36–37 and 54.

25. Forster, *The Esperanto Movement*, 269–74.

26. *Espero Pacifista* (July 1905): 33.

27. See Sandi E. Cooper, "The Work of Women in Nineteenth Century Peace Movements," *Peace and Change* 9 (Winter 1983): 11–28; from the same author, "French Feminists and Pacifism, 1889–1914: The Evolution of New Visions," *Peace and Change* 36, no. 1 (2011): 5–33; and Jen Vellacott, "Women, Peace and Internationalism, 1914–1920: 'Finding New Words and Creating New Methods,'" in *Peace Movements and Political Cultures*, ed. Charles Chatfield and Peter van den Dungen, 106–24.

28. Shenton, *Cosmopolitan*, 401.

29. See Kökény et al., *Enciklopedio*, 134–35. Einstein's League refers to the New Fatherland League, set up in 1915 by the physician Georg Nicolai and physicist Albert Einstein. The League petitioned the German government to put an end to the war. It was proscribed that same year but reemerged in 1922.

30. *Espero Pacifista* (October-November 1905): 209.

Chapter 14

1. Blom, *Vertigo*, 212–15.

2. See John Gray, *The Immortalization Commission: Science and the Strange Quest to Cheat Death* (London: Allen Lane, 2011); and Janet Oppenheim, *The Other World: Spiritualism and Psychical Research in England, 1850–1914* (Cambridge: Cambridge University Press, 1985).

3. Alex Owen, *The Place of Enchantment: British Occultism and the Culture of the Modern* (Chicago: University of Chicago Press, 2004), 17–50.

4. Warren S. Smith, *The London Heretics, 1870–1914* (London: Constable, 1967), 41–68.

5. Blom, *Vertigo*, 211; and Juliet Nicolson, *The Great Silence, 1918–1929: Living in the Shadow of the Great War* (London: John Murray, 2009), 119–20.

6. Kökény et al., *Enciklopedio,* 538.

7. Ibid., 422–23.

8. Qtd. in *Vegetarian Messenger* (Manchester), December 1908, reproduced at http://www.ivu.org/congress/wvc08/other-reports.html.

9. Blom, *Vertigo,* 328–29.

10. Anne-Marie Thiesse, *La création des identités nationales. Europe xviiiᵉ–xixᵉ siècle* (Paris: Seuil, 2001), 242–52.

11. *Bohema Revuo Esperantista* (1909): 4–6.

12. Kökény et al, *Enciklopedio,* 495–96.

13. Carl C. Bry, *Verkappte Religionen* (Gotha: Klotz, 1925), 17.

14. Ulrich Matthias, *L'espéranto. Un nouveau latin pour l'Église et pour l'humanité* (Anvers: Flandra Esperanto-Ligo, 2005).

15. *Espero Katolika* 1 (1903): 2.

16. Nicolaas G. Hoen, "Historio de Internacia Katolika Unuiĝo Esperantista (1903–1983)," *Espero Katolika* 7–12 (1992): 114–63.

17. On the position of the German Catholic Church toward National Socialism, see Guenter Lewy, *The Catholic Church and Nazi Germany* (Boulder, Colo.: Da Capo Press, 2000).

18. Qtd. in Leonard Swidler, *Bloodwitness for Peace and Unity: The Life of Max Josef Metzger* (Denville, N.J.: Dimension Books, 1986), 54.

19. Ulrich Lins, "Max Joseph Metzger," *Kontakto* 2 (1971): 16–17.

20. Robert P. Ericksen, *Complicity in the Holocaust: Churches and Universities in Nazi Germany* (Cambridge: Cambridge University Press, 2012), 24–60.

21. de Hoog, *Nia historio,* 75.

Chapter 15

1. Edward Royle, *Radicals, Secularists and Republicans: Popular Free Thought in Britain 1866–1915* (Manchester: Manchester University Press, 1980), 77.

2. See *Le libre penseur de France* (June 1921): 2.

3. Malachi H. Hacohen, *Karl Popper: The Formative Years, 1902–1945* (Cambridge: Cambridge University Press, 2000), 66.

4. After World War I, the French teacher Marcel Boubou, also active in the labor Esperanto movement (and later killed in Auschwitz), launched *Novaj Tempoj* (1921–1926) with the aim of refounding the old association. This was accomplished in 1924 with the creation of the Tutmonda Asocio de Geinstruistoj Esperantistaj (TAGE, the Universal association of male and female Esperantist teachers). In 1930, TAGE's *Internacia Pedagogia Revuo* had 300 subscribers. But since TAGE's headquarters were in Germany and a sizeable number of its members were German and Austrian, the organization practically perished with the Nazis' rise to power. See Kökény et al, *Enciklopedio,* 243–45.

5. Detlev Blanke, "Esperanto und Atheismus," *Humanismus Aktuell* 19 (2006): 73–92.

6. Francisco Ferrer, *La escuela moderna* (Barcelona: Júcar, 1976 [1908]), 36.

7. Xavier Margais, *El moviment esperantista a Mallorca, 1898–1938* (Palma: Edicions Documenta Balear, 2002), 25.

8. Étienne Cabet, *Voyage en Icarie* (Paris, 1845), 369.

9. Qtd. in Kökény et al, *Enciklopedio*, 488

10. Platiel (pseud.), *Historio pri la skismo en la laborista esperanto-movado* (Beauville: SAT, 1994 [1934]), 2.

11. Ibid., 3.

12. See Eric Borsboom, *Vivo de Lanti* (Paris: SAT, 1976), 51–55. The anarchist-Esperantist international had its stronghold in Spain, where the old tension between anarchist and anti-Stalinist communists on the one side and pro-Moscow Esperantists on other reached its peak during the civil war (1936–1939). See Marco, *Laboristaj*, 58–87.

13. J. Arch Getty and Oleg V. Naumov, *The Road to Terror: Stalin and the Self-Destruction of the Bolshevists, 1932–1939* (New Haven, Conn.: Yale University Press, 2002), 481.

14. For the history of the labor Esperanto movement, see Jean-François Fayet, "Eine internationale Sprache für die Weltrevolution? Die Komintern und die Esperanto-Frage," *Jahrbuch für Historische Kommunismusforschung* (2008): 9–23; Lins, *Die gefärhliche*, 165–85; Sergej N. Kuznekov, "Drezen, lia verko, lia epoko," in Ernest Drezen, *Historio de la mondolingvo*, ed. Sergej N. Kuznecov (Moscow: Progreso, 1991); Sennacieca Asocio Tutmonda, *Historio de S.A.T, 1921–1952* (Paris: SAT, 1953); Borsboom, *Vivo de Lanti*; and Forster, *The Esperanto Movement*, 188–211.

15. See Patten, "The Most Natural State."

16. Velimir Piškorec, "Von Volapük zu Spelin. Zum Leben und Werk des kroatischen Plansprachlers Juraj (Georg) Bauer (1848–1900)," in *Die Rolle von Persönlichkeiten in der Geschichte der Planspranchen*, ed. Sabine Fiedler (Berlin: Gesellschaft für Interlinguistik e.V., 2010), 104.

17. Arnold Behrendt, "Ist Esperanto Deutschfeindlich?" *Rund um die Welt* 2 (1913): 32.

18. *Bohema Revuo Esperantista* (1909): 36.

19. Ivo Lapenna, Ulrich Lins, and Tazio Carlevaro, eds., *Esperanto en perspektivo. Faktoj kaj analizoj pri la Internacia Lingvo* (London: UEA, 1974), 467.

20. Sikosek, *Die neutrale Sprache*, 128.

21. Francesc Poblet, *Els inicis del moviment esperantista a Catalunya* (Barcelona: Associació Catalana d'Esperanto, 2004), 26.

22. Qtd. in Joaquim Gelabertó and Joan C. Gelabertó, "Frederic Pujulà i Vallès, escriptior i politic palamosí," *Revista de Girona* (November-December 2007): 55.

23. Lins, *Die gefährliche*, 101.

24. Ibid., 100–111.

Chapter 16

1. *L'Espérantiste* (August-September 1900): 103–8; Clara S. Roero, "I matematici e la lingua internazionale," *La matematica nella Società e nella Cultura. Bolletino della Unione Matematica Italiana* 8 (1999): 159–82.

2. The proceedings of the Congrès de philosophie were published in *Revue de métaphysique et de morale* (1900): 503–698; for the discussion about an international language, see 666–70.

3. Russell's response to Couturat is in Bertrand Russell, *Correspondance sur la philosophie, la logique et la politique avec Louis Couturat (1897–1913)*, ed. Anne-Françoise Schmid (Paris: Éditions Kimé, 2001), 209–11. For Russell it would have been difficult to ignore Couturat's petition for help, since the latter was planning to write a book that would popularize Russell's philosophy in France.

4. Forster, *The Esperanto*, 116.

5. For a biography of Peano, see Hubert C. Kennedy, *Peano: Life and Works of Giuseppe Peano* (Boston: Kluwer, 1980).

6. Boris Kotzin, *Geschichte und Theorie des Ido* (Dresden: Ader und Borel, 1916), 6.

7. See Forster, *The Esperanto*, 117 and 122; and Wilhelm Ostwald, *Lebenslinien. Eine Selbstbiographie*, ed. Karl Hansel (Leipzig: Sächsischen Akademie der Wissenschaften, 2003 [1927–1927]): 451–52.

8. Otto Jespersen, *An International Language* (London: Allen and Unwin, 1928), 43; Forster, *The Esperanto*, 142n42.

9. Letter to Ostwald of November 4, 1907, in Ludovikito (pseud. Ito Kanzi), *Por kaj kontraŭ reformoj!* (Tokio: Eldonejo Ludovikito 1980), 122–27.

10. Ibid., 131–35, 148–50, and 161–81.

11. Ibid., 165.

12. Qtd. in Forster, *The Esperanto*, 126; Boirac's emphasis.

13. Korĵenkov, *Homarano*, 249; Edmond Privat, *Historio de la lingvo Esperanto* (The Hague: Internacia Esperanto Instituto, 1982), 62.

14. Otto Jespersen, *A Linguist's Life*, trans. and ed. Arne Juul, Hans F. Nielsen, and Jørgen Erik Nielsen (Odense: Odense University Press, 1995), 153.

15. See ibid., 153–54. On the collaborative authorship of Ido, see Korĵenkov, *Homarano*, 234.

16. *Progreso* (March 1908): 3.

17. Richard Lorenz, "The 'Délégation pour l'adoption d'una langue auxiliaire international,'" in *International Language and Science*, ed. Louis Couturat (London: Constable and Cia, 1910), 19–20.

18. *Progreso* (October 1908): 425–31, and (December 1908): 581–87.

19. *Progreso* (April 1909): 99, and (September 1909): 415.

20. The 1914 reprint is available at http://interlanguages.net (accessed December 30, 2010).

21. See the letter of Ostwald to Jespersen of February 2, 1908, in Fritz Wollenberg, "Der Briefwechsel Wilhelm Ostwalds zu Interlinguistischen Problemen," in *Eine Sprache für die Wissenschaft. Beiträge und Materialien des Interlinguistik-Kolloquiums für Wilhelm Ostwald*, ed. Ulrich Becker and Fritz Wollenberg (Berlin: Gesellschaft für Interlinguistik e.V., 1998), 61.

22. Ostwald, *Lebenslinien*, 452–53.

23. *Progreso* (March 1909): 35; Joachim Mugdan, *Jan Baudouin de Courtenay (1845–1929). Leben und Werk* (München: Wilhelm Fink Verlag, 1984), 116.

24. Jespersen, *A Linguist's Life*, 156.

25. *International Language* (March 1911): 67–69; *Progreso* (September 1911): 380–81, and (January 1912): 676–77.

26. *Progreso* (February 1910): 748–49 and 767.

27. For Peano's and Couturat's ideas about the application of symbolic logic on the construction of an artificial language, see Ubaldo Sanzo, *L'artificio della lingua. Louis Couturat 1868-1914* (Milan: Franco Angeli, 1991), 104–8.

28. Academia pro Interlingua, *Historia de academia* (Cuneo: Unione tipografica editrice provincial, 1923), 1–3; Carlevaro, "Mondlingvaj akademioj," 384–85; Kennedy, *Peano*, 125–43.

29. For their last letters, see Erika Luciano and Clara S. Roero, eds., *Giuseppe Peano–Louis Couturat. Carteggio (1896-1914)* (Florence: Leo S. Olschki, 2005), 166–77.

30. Qtd. in Alasdair Urquhart, "The Couturat-Russell Correspondence," *Russell: The Journal of Bertrand Russell Studies* 22 (2002): 190.

31. André Lalande, "Philosophy in France," *Philosophical Review* 24 (1915): 249.

32. *Progreso* (November 1910): 526–27.

33. *Progreso* (March 1911): 7.

34. *Progreso* (April 1914): 196–97.

35. Guérard, *A Short History*, 149.

36. *Progreso* (April 1909): 68.

37. *Progreso* (July 1909): 259.

38. Forster, *The Esperanto*, 134.

39. *Progreso* (November 1911): 547–48.

40. Forster, *The Esperanto*, 134.

41. Qtd. in ibid., 133.

42. According to the *Yarlibro Idista 1922* (*Idist Yearbook 1922*).

43. See his article "Pri nia idealo" in *Progreso* (November 1911): 548–49. See also from Couturat, "Esperanto ed esperantismo," *Progreso* (September 1908): 264–76.

44. *Progreso* (July-September 1928). These specialized journals were, according to Stojan's data, the Catholic periodical *L'Idisto Katolika* (1909-1926), the teachers' journal *L'Edukero* (1921-1922), the anarchist publication *Libereso* (1922-1926), the communist periodical *Nia Standardo* (1922-1924), the working-class publication *Kombato* (1922-1926), and the vegetarian journal *Nova Vivo* (1923-1926). See Petr E. Stojan,

Bibliografio de Internacia Lingvo (New York: Georg Olms, 1973 [1929]), 503–4. For the evolution on membership in the Ido movement, see Detlev Blanke, "Wilhelm Ostwald, Ido und die Interlinguistik," in *Eine Sprache für die Wissenschaft. Beiträge und Materialien des Interlinguistik-Kolloquiums für Wilhelm Ostwald,* ed. Ulrich Becker and Fritz Wollenberg (Berlin: Gesellschaft für Interlinguistik e.V., 1998), 17–19; and for the current situation of the movement, see Günther Anton, "Einige Bemerkungen zu Ido and zur Ido-Bewegung heute," in *Plansprachen und ihre Gemeinschaften,* ed. Detlev Blanke (Berlin: Gesellschaft für Interlinguistik e. V., 2002), 22–26.

45. David K. Jordan, "Esperanto and Esperantism," *Language Problems and Language Planning* 11, no. 1 (1987): 104–25.

Chapter 17

1. de Wahl, "Wege und Irrwege," 17.

2. Fayet, "Eine internationale Sprache," 11–14.

3. Qtd. in Blanke, *Internationale Plansprachen,* 162.

4. *Cosmoglotta* (October 1928): 141; Louis M. de Guesnet, "25 annus de Cosmoglotta," *Cosmoglotta* (August 1947): 17–18.

5. Edgar de Wahl, "In personal affere," *Cosmoglotta* (March 1928): 46.

6. Julia S. Falk, *Women, Language, and Linguists* (London: Routeledge, 1999), 33–92.

7. Frank Esterhill, *Interlingua Institute: A History* (New York: Interlingua Institute, 2000), 3.

8. Qtd. in Julia S. Falk, "Words Without Grammar: Linguists and the International Auxiliary Language Movement in the United States," *Language and Communication* 15, no. 3 (1995): 247. See also Edward Sapir, "The Function of an International Language," in *International Communication,* ed. Herbert N. Shenton, Edward Sapir, and Otto Jespersen (London: Kegan Paul, 1931), 65–94; and James McElvenny, "Edward Sapir, Linguistic Relativity and International Language," paper presented at the Third International Free Linguistics Conference, Sydney, October 10–11, 2009.

9. Falk, *Women, Language,* 67.

10. See Jespersen, *A Linguist's Life,* 220–23; and his contribution to *Novialiste* (March 1938): 336–38.

11. *Novialiste* (May 1939): 476.

12. Jespersen, *An International Language,* 322–36.

13. Jespersen, *A Linguist's Life,* 227.

14. Falk, "Words Without," 251.

15. From 1924 to 1941, IALA spent around $310,000 in research and public relations, and approximately $2,500,000 in current market prizes; see Falk, *Women, Language,* 78. Aside from its use in some scientific journals for abstracting purposes, Interlingua did not have much impact. In the mid-1950s IALA was dissolved and succeeded by the Interlingua Institute, whose last executive director, Frank Esterhill, announced in

2000 that the language was dead: Frank Esterhill, "Interlingua—RIP," *Verbatim* 25 (2000): 20–21. Interlingua, though, is still alive. Wikipedia hosts an Interlingua encyclopedia (http://ia.wikipedia.org), and the Union Mundial pro Interlingua, founded in 1955, is still active (http://www.interlingua.com). For a basic description of the language, see Alexander Gode, *Interlingua–English Dictionary* (New York: Storm Publishers, 1951).

16. Julian Prorók, "5 annus de Occidental e li recent situation," *Cosmoglotta* (January 1927): 1.

17. W. Terrence Gordon, *C. K. Ogden: A Bio-Bibliographic Study* (London: Scarecrow Press, 1990), 1–55; P. Sargant Florence, "Cambridge 1909–1919 and Its Aftermath," in *C. K. Ogden: A Collective Memoir*, ed. P. Sargant Florence and J. R. L. Anderson (London: Elek Pemberton, 1977), 13–55.

18. Churchill's address is reproduced in the *New York Times*, September 7, 1943, 14.

19. K. E. Garay, "Empires of the Mind? C. K. Ogden, Winston Churchill, and Basic English," *Historical Papers / Communications Historiques* 23, no. 1 (1988): 280–91.

20. Akira Iriye, *Cultural Internationalism and World Order* (Baltimore: Johns Hopkins University Press, 1997), 118–19.

21. Sapir, "The Function," 71–74.

22. Albert L. Guérard, "Linguistic Imperialism," *New Republic*, September 20, 1943, 400.

23. Alphonse Matejka,"Ancor un vez: Basic English," *Cosmoglotta* (May 1943): 57.

24. See the report of General Secretariat of the League of Nations, *Esperanto*.

Conclusion

1. See Robert M. W. Dixon, *The Rise and Fall of Languages* (Cambridge: Cambridge University Press, 1997), 118; and Juan Carlos Moreno, *La dignidad*, 37–46.

2. Christo Moskovsky, "Reflections on Artificial Languages," in *Essays on Natural and Artificial Languages*, ed. Christo Moskovsky and Alan Libert (Frankfurt am Main: Peter Lang, 2009), 1–19; and Marc van Oostendorp, "Constructed Language and Linguistic Theory," http://www.vanoostendorp.nl/ (accessed February 2, 2010).

3. Zamenhof, *Originala*, 404.

4. Lev I. Zhirkov, *Kial venkis Esperanto?* (Leipzig: Ekrelo, 1931), 7–8.

5. Ibid., 17–18.

6. Detlev Blanke, "Causes of the Relative Success of Esperanto," *Language Problems and Language Planning* 33, no. 3 (2009): 253; Eco, *The Search*, 318.

7. Schuchardt, "Bericht," 56–57.

8. Elisabeth S. Clemmens, "Organizational Repertoires and Institutional Change: Women's Groups and the Transformation of U.S. Politics, 1890–1920," *American Journal of Sociology* 98, no. 4 (1993): 755–98.

9. *Progreso* (November 1911): 548.

10. On the boycott of the International Research Council to German science, see Schroeder-Gudehus, *Les scientifiques*, 131–60.

11. British Association for the Advancement of Science, "An International Auxiliary Language," in *Report of the Eighty-Ninth Meeting* (London: John Murray, 1922), 393.

12. Ibid., 399.

13. Ibid., 400.

14. Forster, *The Esperanto*, 275; *Amerika Esperantisto* (April 1921): 1–2.

15. Iriye, *Cultural Internationalism*, 118–19.

16. Paul Chappellier, *Notes sur la langue international* (Paris: L. Maretheux, 1901), 32.

17. Ibid., 47.

18. Albert Dauzat, *La défense de la langue française* (Paris: Armand Colin, 1912): 247. See also Baggioni, *Langues et nations*, 322–24. On the reactions of German-speaking intellectuals to this plan, see for example the comments of the rector of Humboldt University, Hermann Diels, *Internationale Aufgaben*, 35–38, and the Austrian linguist Hugo Schuchardt, "Le problem des langues," 29–47.

19. The full text of the directive is reproduced in Lescure, *Un imaginaire*, 700–702.

20. Forster, *The Esperanto*, 171–77; Shenton, *Cosmopolitan*, 375–87 and 437.

21. Mark Mazower, *Dark Continent: Europe's Twentieth Century* (New York: Vintage Books, 1998), 3–75.

22. For the difficulties in Poland in the late 1930s, see Banet-Fornalowa, *La pereintoj*.

23. Suzanne Romaine, "Revitalized Languages as Invented Languages," in *From Elvish to Klingon: Exploring Invented Languages*, ed. Michael Adams (Oxford: Oxford University Press, 2011), 185–225; Alain Dieckhoff, "Hebrew, the Language of National Daily Life," in *Language, Nation and State: Identity Politics in a Multilingual Age,* ed. Tony Judt and Denis Lacorne (New York: Palgrave Macmillan, 2004), 194; and Jack Fellman, *The Revival of a Classical Tongue: Eliezer Ben Yehuda and the Modern Hebrew language* (The Hague: Mouton, 1973).

24. Nicholas Ostler, *The Last Lingua Franca: English Until the Return of Babel* (New York: Walker and Co., 2010), 254–61. Also about the prospects of English as the global language, see David Graddol, *The Future of English? A Guide to Forecasting the Popularity of the English Language in the 21st Century* (London: British Council, 2007). On the current status of English, see David Crystal, *English as a Global Language*, 2nd ed. (Cambridge: Cambridge University Press, 2003); Wright, *Language Policy*, 254–61.

25. On the linguistic regime of the EU, see van Parijs, *Linguistic Justice*; Alan Patten, "Theoretical Foundations of European Language Debates," in *The Language Question in Europe and Diverse Societies: Political, Legal and Social Perspectives*, ed. Dario Castiglioni and Chris Longman (Portland: Hart Publishers, 2007), 15–36; Abram de Swaan, "The Language Predicament of the EU Since the Enlargements," *Sociolinguistica* 21 (2007): 1–21; Alexander Caviedes, "The Role of Language in Nation-Building Within the European Union," *Dialectical Anthropology* 27 (2003): 249–68; and Sue

Wright, *Community and Communication: The Role of Language in Nation State Building and European Integration* (Clevedon: Multilingual Matters, 2000).

26. *Economist*, December 15, 2012, 58.

27. Jan Fidrmuc and Victor Ginsburgh, "Languages in the European Union: The Quest for Equality and Its Cost," University of Michigan, William Davidson Institute Working Paper No. 715 (2004).

28. For the difference of opinion between the European Commission and the European Ombudsman on this topic, see http://europa.eu/rapid/press-release_EO-12-17_en.htm.

29. See, e.g., Theo van Els, "Multilingualism in the European Union," *International Journal of Applied Linguistics* 15, no. 3 (1995): 263–81.

30. Wright, "French."

31. Ulrich Ammon, "Language Conflicts in the European Union," *International Journal of Applied Linguistics* 16, no. 3 (2006): 319–38.

32. Graddol, *The Future.*

33. Philippe van Parijs, "Europe's Linguistic Challenge," in *The Language Question in Europe and Diverse Societies: Political, Legal and Social Perspectives*, ed. Dario Castiglioni and Chris Longman (Oxford: Hart Publishers, 2007), 217–53.

34. Paul P. Gubbins, "Sense and Pense: An Alternative Language Policy for Europe," in *Language, Culture and Communication in Contemporary Europe*, ed. Charlotte Hoffman (Philadelphia: Multilingual Matters, 1996), 124–29.

35. See http://www.debatingeurope.eu/2011/12/19/is-a-european-identity-possible/ (accessed May 6, 2013).

36. Romaine, "Revitalized," 185–225; see also Sue Wright, "What Is a Language? The Difficulties Inherent in Language Rights," in Castiglioni and Longman, *The Language Question in Europe*, 81–99.

BIBLIOGRAPHY

Abizadeh, Arash. "Was Fichte an Ethnic Nationalist? On Cultural Nationalism and Its Double." *History of Political Thought* 26, no. 2 (2005): 334–59.

Abrams, Irwin. "Bertha von Suttner and the Nobel Peace Prize." *Journal of Central European Affairs* 22 (October 1962): 286–307.

Academia pro Interlingua. *Historia de academia.* Cuneo: Unione tipografica editrice provincial, 1923.

American Philosophical Society. "Ergänzungs-Bericht des Comitè zur Formulierung einer international Sprache erstatet von demselben . . . am 7. Dezember 1888." In Leopold Einstein, *Weltsprachliche Zeit- und Streitfragen,* 21–26. Nuremberg: Stein, 1889.

American Philosophical Society. "Report of the Committee Appointed Oct. 21, 1887, to Examine into the Scientific Value of the Volapük." *Nature* 38 (1888): 351–55.

Ammon, Ulrich. "Deutsch als Wissenschaftssprache: die Entwicklung im 20. Jahrhundert und die Zukunftsperspektive." In *Sprache und Sprachen in den Wissenschaften: Geschichte und Gegenwart,* ed. Herbert E. Wiegand, 668–85. Berlin / New York: de Gruyter, 1999.

Ammon, Ulrich. "The European Union (EU—formerly European Community): Status Change of English During the Last Fifty Years." In *Post-Imperial English. Status Change in Former British and American Colonies, 1940–1990,* ed. Joshua Fishman, Andrew W. Conrad, and Alma Rubal-Lopez, 241–67. Berlin: Mouton de Gruyter, 1996.

Ammon, Ulrich. "Language Conflicts in the European Union." *International Journal of Applied Linguistics* 16, no. 3 (2006): 319–38.

Anderson, Benedict. *Imagined Communities.* Rev. ed. London: Verso, 2006.

Anton, Günther. "Einige Bemerkungen zu Ido und zur Ido-Bewegung heute." In *Plansprachen und ihre Gemeinschaften,* ed. Detlev Blanke, 22–26. Berlin: Gesellschaft für Interlinguistik e. V., 2002.

Arnaud, Pierre. "Dividing and Uniting: Sports Societies and Nationalism, 1870–1914." In *Nationhood and Nationalism in France: From Boulanguism to the Great War, 1889–1918,* ed. Robert Tombs, 182–94. London: HarperCollins, 1991

Aronson, I. Michael. "The Anti-Jewish Pogroms in Russia in 1881." In *Pogroms: Anti-Jewish Violence in Modern Russian History,* ed. John D. Klier and Shlomo Lambroza, 44–61. Cambridge: Cambridge University Press, 1992.

Arthur, Brian. *Increasing Returns and Path Dependence in the Economy.* Ann Arbor: University of Michigan Press, 1994.

Baggioni, Daniel. *Langues et nations en Europe.* Paris: Payot, 1997.

Banet-Fornalowa, Zofia. *La pereintoj in memorian.* Czeladź: Eldonejo Hejme, 2003.

Barandovská-Frank, Vera. "Über die *Academia pro Interlingua.*" In *Plansprachen und ihre Gemeinschaften,* ed. Detlev Blanke, 13–21. Berlin: Gesellschaft für Interlinguistik e. V., 2002.

Bartal, Israel. *The Jews of Eastern Europe, 1772–1881.* Philadelphia: University of Pennsylvania Press, 2002.

Behrendt, Arnold. "Ist Esperanto Deutschfeindlich?" *Rund um die Welt* 2 (1913): 25–32.

Bell, Alexander Melville. "Volapük." *Science* 27 (January 1888): 39–40.

Bell, Alexander Melville. *World-English: The Universal Language.* New York: N. D. C. Hodges, 1888.

Berk, Stephen M. *Years of Crisis, Years of Hope: Russian Jewry and the Pogroms of 1881–1882.* Westport, Conn.: Greenwood Press, 1985.

Bernhaupt, Joseph. *J. M. Schelyer's Weltsprache "Volapuk."* Überlingen: Aug. Feyel, 1884.

Bierey, Johannes. "Alfred Kirchhoff." In *Mitteldeutsche Lebensbilder. Erster Band. Lebensbilder des 19. Jahrhunderts,* 357–75. Magdeburg: Verlag der Historischen Kommission, 1926.

Bishop, Brian R. "La 'ĉifaloj' de Volapük." In *Menade bal püki bal. Festlibro por la 50ᵃ naskiĝ-tago de Reinhard Haupenthal,* ed. Reinhard Haupenthal, 375–90. Saarbrücken: Iltis, 1998.

Blair, Ann. "La persistance du latin comme langue de science à la fin de la Renaissance." In *Sciences et langues en Europe,* ed. Roger Chartier and Petro Corsi, 19–40. Paris: Office for Official Publications of the European Communities, 2000.

Blanke, Detlev. "Causes of the Relative Success of Esperanto." *Language Problems and Language Planning* 33, no. 3 (2009): 251–66.

Blanke, Detlev. "Esperanto und Atheismus." *Humanismus Aktuell* 19 (2006): 73–92.

Blanke, Detlev. *Internationale Plansprachen. Eine Einführung.* Berlin: Akademie Verlag, 1985.

Blanke, Detlev. "Wilhelm Ostwald, Ido und die Interlinguistik." In *Eine Sprache für die Wissenschaft. Beiträge und Materialien des Interlinguistik-Kolloquiums für Wilhelm Ostwald,* ed. Ulrich Becker and Fritz Wollenberg, 13–31. Berlin: Gesellschaft für Interlinguistik e.V., 1998.

Blom, Philipp. *The Vertigo Years: Europe, 1900–1914.* New York: Basic Books, 2007.

Boeker, Warren. "Strategic Change: The Effects of Founding and History." *Academic Management Journal* 32, no. 3 (1989): 489–515.

Bolman, Lee G., and Terrence E. Deal. *Reframing Organizations: Artistry, Choice, and Leadership.* San Francisco: John Wiley and Sons, 2008.

Paul Bolton, *Education: Historical Statistics.* Library House of Commons, 2007,

Bonfiglio, Thomas P. *Mother Tongues and Nations: The Invention of the Native Speaker.* New York: Walter de Gruyter, 2010.

Bordo, Michael D., Alan M. Taylor, and Jeffrey G. Williamson, eds. *Globalization in Historical Perspective*. Chicago: University of Chicago Press, 2003.

Borsboom, Eric. *Vivo de Andreo Cseh*. The Hague: Internacia Esperanto Instituto, 2003.

Borsboom, Eric. *Vivo de Lanti*. Paris: SAT, 1976.

Bourrelier, Paul-Henri. "Gaston Moch, polytechnicien combatant de la paix." *Réalités industrielles* (August 2008): 48–62.

British Association for the Advancement of Science. "An International Auxiliary Language." In *Report of the Eighty-ninth Meeting*, 390–401. London: John Murray, 1922.

Brown, Eloise. *"The Truest Form of Patriotism": Pacifist Feminism in Britain, 1870–1902*. Manchester: Manchester University Press, 2003.

Brown, Harcourt. "History and the Learned Journal." *Journal of the History of Ideas* 33, no. 3 (1972): 365–78.

Brugmann, Karl, and August Leskien. *Zur Kritik der künstlichen Weltsprachen*. Strasbourg: Karl J. Trübner, 1907.

Bry, Carl C. *Verkappte Religionen*. Gotha: Klotz, 1925.

Buisman, Simon. "Volapük und der Weltfrieden." *Rund um die Welt* (March 1981): 353–56.

Bureau International de la Paix. *Bulletin Officiel du IVme Congrès universel de la paix*. Bern: Haller, 1892.

Burke, Peter. *Languages and Communities in Early Modern Europe*. Cambridge: Cambridge University Press, 2004.

Burleigh, Michael. *Earthly Powers*. New York: Harper, 2005.

Cabet, Étienne. *Voyage en Icarie*. Paris, 1845.

Campbell, Joseph. "Where Do We Stand? Common Mechanisms in Organizations and Social Movements Research." In *Social Movements and Organization Theory*, ed. Gerald F. Davis, Doug McAdam, W. Richard Scott, and Mayer N. Zald, 41–68. Cambridge: Cambridge University Press, 2005.

Capoccia, Giovanni, and R. Daniel Kelemen. "The Study of Critical Junctures: Theory, Narrative, and Counterfactuals in Historical Institutionalism." *World Politics* 59, no. 3 (2007): 341–69.

Caraco, Jean-Claude. "Auguste Kerckhoffs (1835–1903) kaj lia rolo en la Volapük-movado." In *Menade bal püki bal. Festlibro por la 50ª naskitago de Reinhard Haupenthal*, ed. Reinhard Haupenthal, 391–404. Saarbrücken: Iltis, 1998.

Carlevaro, Tazio. "Mondlingvaj akademioj." In *Li kaj Ni: Festlibro por la 80a naskiĝtago de Gaston Waringhien*, ed. Reinhard Haupenthal, 381–91. Antwerp / La Laguna: Stafeto, 1985.

Carmichael, Cathie. "Coming to Terms with the Past: Language and Nationalism in Russia and Its Neighbours." In *Language and Nationalism in Europe*, ed. Stephen Balbour and Cathie Carmichael, 221–39. Oxford: Oxford University Press, 2000.

Casey, Marion. "Efficiency, Taylorism and Libraries in Progressive America." *Journal of Library History* 16 (Spring 1981): 265–79.

Caviedes, Alexander. "The Role of Language in Nation-Building within the European Union." *Dialectical Anthropology* 27 (2003): 249–68.

Chappellier, Paul. *Notes sur la langue international.* Paris: L. Maretheux, 1901.

Clemmens, Elisabeth S. "Organizational Repertoires and Institutional Change: Women's Groups and the Transformation of U.S. Politics, 1890–1920." *American Journal of Sociology* 98, no. 4 (1993): 755–98.

Clemmens, Elisabeth S., and Debra C. Minkoff. "Beyond the Iron Law: Rethinking the Place of Organizations in Social Movement Research." In *The Blackwell Companion to Social Movements*, ed. David A. Snow, Sarah A. Soule, and Hanspeter Kriesi, 156–70. Malden, Mass.: Blackwell, 2004.

Cohen, Jonathan. "On the Project of a Universal Character." *Mind* 63 (1954): 49–63.

Collins, Paul. "Solresol, the Universal Musical Language." *McSweeney's* 5 (2000): 50–66.

Congrès International pour l'Amélioration du sort des Aveugles tenu à Bruxelles, du 6 au 10 août 1902. Manage: Imprimiere de l'École professionelle de l'Institut de la Sainte Famille, 1902.

Cooper, Sandi E. "French Feminists and Pacifism, 1889–1914: The Evolution of New Visions." *Peace and Change* 36, no. 1 (2011): 5–33.

Cooper, Sandi E. "Pacifism in France, 1889–1914: International Peace as a Human Right." *French Historical Studies* 17, no. 2 (1991): 359–86.

Cooper, Sandi E. "The Work of Women in Nineteenth Century Peace Movements." *Peace and Change* 9 (Winter 1983): 11–28.

Coppa, Frank J. *Pope Pius IX: Crusader in a Secular Age.* Boston: Twayne Publishers, 1979.

Couturat, Louis. "Esperanto ed esperantismo." *Progreso* (September 1908): 264–76.

Couturat, Louis. "Pri nia idealo." *Progreso* (November 1911): 548–49.

Couturat, Louis, and Léopold Leau. *Histoire de la langue universelle.* Ed. Reinhard Haupenthal. Hildesheim: Georg Olms, 2001 (1903).

Cowan, Robin. "Nuclear Power Reactors: A Study in Technological Lock-in." *Journal of Economic History* 50, no. 3 (1990): 541–67.

Cram, David, and Jaap Maat. *George Dalgarno on Universal Language.* Oxford: Oxford University Press, 2001.

Crick, Bernard. *George Orwell: A Life.* London: Penguin, 1992.

Crystal, David. *English as a Global Language.* 2nd ed. Cambridge: Cambridge University Press, 2003.

Cusumano, Michael A., Yiorgos Mylonadis, and Richard S. Rosenbloom. "Strategic Maneuvering and Mass-Market Dynamics: The Triumph of VHS over Beta." *Business History Review* 66, Special Issue no. 1 (1992): 51–94.

Daudin, Guillaume, Matthias Morys, and Kevin H. O'Rourke. "Globalization, 1870–1914." In *The Cambridge Economic History of Modern Europe*, vol. 2: *1870 to the Present*, ed. Stephen N. Broadberry and Kevin H. O'Rourke, 5–29. Cambridge: Cambridge University Press, 2010.

Dauzat, Albert. *La défense de la langue française*. Paris: Armand Colin, 1912.

David, Paul A. "Clio and the Economics of QWERTY." *American Economic Review* 75, no. 2 (1985): 332–37.

David, Paul A. "Heroes, Herds and Hysteresis in Technological History: Thomas Edison and 'The Battle of the Systems' Reconsidered." *Industrial and Corporate Change* 1, no. 1 (1992): 129–76.

de Beaufront, Louis. "Ce que nous voulons." *L'Espérantiste* (January 1898): 1–3.

de Beaufront, Louis. "Esperanto in France." *North American Review* (March): 520–24.

de Courtenay, Jan Baudouin. *Zur Kritik der künstlichen Weltsprachen*. In *Plansprachen. Beiträge zur Interlinguistik*, ed. Reinhard Haupenthal, 59–110. Darmstadt: Wissenschaftliche Buchgesellschaft, 1976 (1907).

de Guesnet, Louis M. "25 annus de Cosmoglotta." *Cosmoglotta* (August 1947): 17–18.

de Hoog, Hendrik A. *Nia historio. Kristana Esperanto Ligo de 1911–1961*. Amsterdam: Hardinxveld, 1964.

de la Grasserie, Raoul. *De la possibilité et des conditions d'une langue internationale*. Paris: Maisonneuve, 1892.

de la Grasserie, Raoul. *Nouvelle langue internationale. Langue internationale pacifiste, ou apoléma, basée sur les radicaux techniques déjà internationaux*. Paris: E. Leroux, 1907.

del Barrio, José Antonio, and Ulrich Lins. "La danĝera lingvo en la hispana civitana milito." Paper presented at the Congreso sobre la Guerra Civil Española, Madrid, November 27–29, 2006.

Denzau, Arthur T., and Douglass C. North. "Shared Mental Models: Ideologies and Institutions." *Kyklos* 47, no. 1 (1994): 3–31.

Desmet, Piet, and Pierre Swiggers. "Le problem des langues et des nationalités chez Michel Bréal: reflects epistolaires." In *Bréal et le sens de la semantique*, ed. Gabriel Bergounioux, 29–47. Orléans: Presses Universitaires d'Orléans, 2000.

de Swaan, Abram. "The Language Predicament of the EU Since the Enlargements." *Sociolinguistica* 21 (2007): 1–21.

Devidé, Thaddäus. "Dr. Römer's Schmähschrift *Volapük und Deutsche Professoren*." *Rund um die Welt* (October 1888): 193–96.

de Wahl, Edgar. "In personal affere," *Cosmoglotta* (March 1928): 46.

de Wahl, Edgar. "Wege und Irrwege zur Weltsprache." In *Occidental. Die Weltsprache*, ed. Engelbert Pigal, 13–32. Stuttgart: Frankische Verlagshandlung, 1950 (1930).

Dieckhoff, Alain. "Hebrew, the Language of National Daily Life." In *Language, Nation and State: Identity Politics in a Multilingual Age*, ed. Tony Judt and Denis Lacorne, 187–99. New York: Palgrave Macmillan, 2004

Diels, Herman. *Internationale Aufgaben der Universität*. Berlin: Gustav Schade, 1906.

Dixon, Robert M. W. *The Rise and Fall of Languages*. Cambridge: Cambridge University Press, 1997.

Drezen, Ernest. *Historio de la mondolingvo*. Ed. Sergej N. Kuznecov. Moscow: Progreso, 1991 (1931).

Eble, Alfred. "Die *Sionsharfe*, eine katholische Zeitschrift für christliche Poesie." In *Prälat Schleyer Jahrbuch 2008*: 29–54.

Eco, Umberto. *The Search for the Perfect Language*. Cambridge: Blackwell, 1995.

Edwards, John. *Language and Identity*. Cambridge: Cambridge University Press, 2009.

Einstein, Leopold. *La lingvo internacia als beste Lösung des internationalen Weltspracheproblems*. Nuremberg: A. Stein, 1888.

Einstein, Leopold. *Weltsprachliche Zeit- und Streitfragen*. Nuremberg: A. Stein, 1889.

Elliot, Ralph W. V. "Isaac Newton's 'Of a Universal Language.'" *Modern Language Review* 52 (1957): 1–18.

Ellis, Alexander J. "On the Conditions of a Universal Language." *Transactions of the Philological Society* (1888): 59–98.

Ericksen, Robert P. *Complicity in the Holocaust: Churches and Universities in Nazi Germany*. Cambridge: Cambridge University Press, 2012.

Esterhill, Frank. *Interlingua Institute. A History*. New York: Interlingua Institute, 2000.

Esterhill, Frank. "Interlingua—RIP." *Verbatim* 25 (2000): 20–21.

Falk, Julia S. *Women, Language, and Linguists*. London: Routledge, 1999.

Falk, Julia S. "Words Without Grammar: Linguists and the International Auxiliary Language Movement in the United States." *Language and Communication* 15, no. 3 (1995): 241–59.

Fayet, Jean-François. "Eine internationale Sprache für die Weltrevolution? Die Komintern und die Esperanto-Frage." *Jahrbuch für Historische Kommunismusforschung* (2008): 9–23.

Fellman, Jack. *The Revival of a Classical Tongue: Eliezer Ben Yehuda and the Modern Hebrew Language*. The Hague: Mouton, 1973.

Ferrer Guardia, Francisco. *La escuela moderna*. Barcelona: Júcar, 1976 (1908).

Fichte, Johann Gottlieb. *Addresses to the German Nation*. Trans. and ed. Gregory Moore. Cambridge: Cambridge University Press, 2008 (1808).

Fidrmuc, Jan, and Victor Ginsburgh. *Languages in the European Union: The Quest for Equality and Its Cost*. University of Michigan, William Davidson Institute Working Paper no. 715, 2004

Fiedler, Sabine. "Phraseology in Planned Language." In *Phraseology: An International Handbook of Contemporary Research*, ed. Harald Burger, 779–88. Berlin: Walter de Gruyter, 2007.

Fiedler, Sabine. "Standardization and Self-Regulation in an International Speech Community: The Case of Esperanto." *International Journal of the Sociology of Language* 177 (2006): 67–90.

Florence, P. Sargant. "Cambridge 1909–1919 and Its Aftermath." In *C. K. Ogden: A Collective Memoir*, ed. P. Sargant Florence and J. R. L. Anderson, 13–55. London: Elek Pemberton, 1977.

Fodor, Istvan, and Claude Hagège, eds. *Language Reform: History and Future*. 3 vols. Hamburg: Buske Verlag, 1983.

Forel, Auguste. *Les Etats-Unis de la Terre*. Lausanne: E. Peytrequin, 1915.

Formigari, Lia. *A History of Language Philosophies*. Amsterdam: John Benjamin, 2004.

Forster, Peter G. *The Esperanto Movement*. The Hague: Mouton, 1982.

Fox, Marvin, "Law and Ethics in Modern Jewish Philosophy: The Case of Moses Mendelssohn." *Proceedings of the American Academy for Jewish Research* 43 (1976): 1–13.

Frankel, Jonathan. *Prophecy and Politics: Socialism, Nationalism, and the Russian Jews, 1862–1917.* Cambridge: Cambridge University Press, 1981.

Fried, Alfred H. *Die Grundlagen des revolutionären Pacifismus*. Tübingen: J. C. B. Mohr, 1908.

Fumaroli, Marc. 1998. "The Genius of French language." In *The Realms of Memory*, ed. Pierre Nora, vol. 3, 555–606. New York: Columbia University Press, 1998.

Gall, Lothar. "Die partei- und sozialgeschichtliche Problematik des badischen Kulturkampfes." *Zeitschrift für die Geschichte des Oberrheins* 113 (1965): 151–96.

Ganz, Marshall. "Resources and Resourcefulness: Strategic Capacity in the Unionization of California Agriculture." *American Journal of Sociology* 105, no. 4 (2000): 1003–62.

Garay, K. E. "Empires of the Mind? C. K. Ogden, Winston Churchill, and Basic English." *Historical Papers, Communications Historiques* 23, no. 1 (1988): 280–91.

Garvía, Roberto. "Religion and Artificial Languages at the Turn of the 20th Century: Ostwald and Zamenhof." *Language Problems and Language Planning* 37, no. 1 (2013): 47–70.

Geffen, Joel S. "Whither: To Palestine or to America in the Pages of the Russian Hebrew Press Ha-Melitz and Ha-Yom (1880–1890)." *American Jewish Historical Quarterly* 59 (1969): 179–200.

Gelabertó, Joaquim, and Joan C. Gelabertó. "Frederic Pujulà i Vallès, escriptior i politic palamosí." *Revista de Girona* (November-December 2007): 52–57.

Gellner, Ernest. *Nations and Nationalism*. Oxford: Basil Blackwell, 1983.

General Secretariat of the League of Nations. *Esperanto as an International Auxiliary Language*. Paris: PUF, 1922.

Getty, J. Arch, and Oleg V. Naumov. *The Road to Terror: Stalin and the Self-Destruction of the Bolshevists, 1932–1939.* New Haven, Conn.: Yale University Press, 2002.

Gode, Alexander. *Interlingua-English Dictionary*. New York: Storm Publishers, 1951.

Goldstone, Jack A. "Initial Conditions, General Laws, Path Dependence, and Explanation in Historical Sociology." *American Journal of Sociology* 104, no. 3 (1998): 829–45.

Gordon, W. Terrence. *C. K. Ogden: A Bio-Blibliographic Study*. London: Scarecrow Press, 1990.

Graddol, David. *The Future of English? A Guide to Forecasting the Popularity of the English Language in the 21st Century*. London: British Council, 1997.

Graves, Pamela M. *Labour Women: Women in British Working-Class Politics*. Cambridge: Cambridge University Press, 1994

Gray, John. *The Immortalization Commission: Science and the Strange Quest to Cheat Death*. London: Allen Lane, 2011.

Gröber, Konrad. "Der Altkatholizismus in Messkirch. Die Geschichte seiner Entwiklung und Bekämpfung." *Freiburger Diozesan-Archiv* 40 (1912): 135–98.

Groschopp, Horst. *Dissidenten. Freidenkerei und Kultur in Deutschland*. Berlin: Dietz, 1997

Gross, Michael. *The War Against Catholicism*. Ann Arbor: University of Michigan Press, 2004.

Grossmann, Atina. "German Communism and New Women: Dilemmas and Contradictions." In *Women and Socialism: Socialism and Women*, ed. Helmut Gruber and Pamela Graves, 136–68. Providence: Berghahn Books, 1998.

Gubbins, Paul P. 1996. "Sense and Pense: An Alternative Language Policy for Europe." In *Language, Culture, and Communication in Contemporary Europe*, ed. Charlotte Hoffman, 124–29. Philadelphia: Multilingual Matters, 1996.

Guérard, Albert L. *A Short History of the International Language Movement*. London: Fisher Unwin, 1922.

Guérard, Albert L. "Linguistic Imperialism." *New Republic* (September 20, 1943): 400.

Guillén, Mauro F. *The Taylorized Beauty of the Mechanical: Scientific Management and the Rise of Modernist Architecture*. Princeton, N.J.: Princeton University Press, 2006.

Gusfield, Joseph. "Social Movements and Social Change: Perspectives of Linearity and Fluidity." In *Research in Social Movements: Conflict and Change*, ed. Louis Kriesberg, 4: 317–39. Greenwich: JAI press, 1981.

Hacohen, Malachi H. "Dilemmas of Cosmopolitanism: Karl Popper, Jewish Identity and Central European Culture." *Journal of Modern History* 71 (March 1999): 105–49.

Hacohen, Malachi H. *Karl Popper. The Formative Years, 1902–1945*. Cambridge: Cambridge University Press, 2000.

Hales, Edward E. Y. *Pio Nono: A Study in European Politics and Religion in the Nineteenth Century*. London: Eyre and Spottiswoode, 1954.

Hasquin, Hervé, Suzanne Lecocq, and Daniel Lefebre. *Henri La Fontaine—Prix Nobel de la paix- Tracé(s) d'une vie*. Mons: Mundaneum, 2002.

Haupenthal, Reinhard. *125 Jahre Volapük. Leben und Werk Johann Martin Schleyer (1831–1912)*. Saarbrücken: Iltis, 2005.

Haupenthal, Reinhard. *Der erste Volapük-Kongress. Friedrichshafen, August 1884*. Saarbrücken: Iltis, 1984.

Haupenthal, Reinhard. *La pastro de Litzelstetten. Decenio (1875–1885) en la vivo de Johann Martin Schleyer (1831–1912)*. Saarbrücken: Iltis, 2005.

Haupenthal, Reinhard. "Nachwort zum Neudruck (1989)." In Rupert Kniele, *Der erste Jahrzehnt der Weltsprache Volapük*, ed. Reinahrd Haupenthal, 133–42. Saarbrücken: Iltis, 1989.

Haupenthal, Reinhard. "Personennotiz zu Rupert Kniele (1844–1911)." *Prälat Schleyer Jahrbuch 2008*: 109–16.

Haupenthal, Reinhard. *Prälat Johann Martin Schleyer (1831–1912)*. Saarbrücken: Iltis, 2007.

Haupenthal, Reinhard. *Prof. Dr. Siegfried Lederer (1861–1911) und die Volapük-Zeitschrift "Rund um die Welt."* Saarbrücken: Iltis, 2001.

Hauptenthal, Reinhard. *Über die Startbedingungen zweier Plansprachen.* Saarbrücken: Iltis, 2005.

Herder, Johann Gottfried. *Philosophical Writings.* Trans. and ed. Michael N. Forster. Cambridge: Cambridge University Press, 2002.

Hobsbawm, Eric. "Language, Culture, and National Identity." *Social Research* 63, no. 4 (1996): 165–95.

Hobsbawm, Eric. *Nations and Nationalism since 1780.* Cambridge: Cambridge University Press, 1990.

Hoen, Nicolaas G. "Historio de Internacia Katolika Unuiĝo Esperantista (1903–1983)." *Espero Katolika* 7–12 (1992): 114–63.

Holt, Niles R. "Ernst Haeckel's Monistic Religion." *Journal of the History of Ideas* 32, no. 2 (1971): 265–80.

Holt, Niles R. "Monists and Nazis: A Question of Scientific Responsibility." *Hastings Center Report* 5, no. 2 (1975): 37–43.

Holt, Niles R. "Wilhelm Ostwald's 'The Bridge.'" *British Journal for the History of Science* 10, no. 2 (1977): 146–50.

Holzhaus, Adolf. *Doktoro kaj lingvo Esperanto.* Helsinki: Fondumo Esperanto, 1969.

Humboldt, Wilhelm von. *On Language: On the Diversity of Human Language Construction and Its Influence on the Mental Development of the Human Species.* Ed. Michael Losonsky. Cambridge: Cambridge University Press, 1999.

Hutton, Christopher. *Linguistics and the Third Reich: Mother-Tongue Fascism, Race, and the Science of Language.* London: Routledge, 1999.

Iriye, Akira. *Cultural Internationalism and World Order.* Baltimore: Johns Hopkins University Press, 1997.

Iriye, Akira. *Global Community.* Berkeley: University of California Press, 2002.

Javal, Émile. *On Becoming Blind.* Trans. Carroll Everett Edson. New York: Macmillan, 1905.

Jensen, L. P. "Volapük und die Geschäftswelt." *Rund um die Welt* (December 1890): 257–60.

Jespersen, Otto. *An International Language.* London: Allen and Unwin, 1928.

Jespersen, Otto. *A Linguist's Life.* Trans. and ed. Arne Juul, Hans F. Nielsen, and Jørgen Erik Nielsen. Odense: Odense University Press, 1995.

Johnson, Victoria. "What Is Organizational Imprinting? Cultural Entrepreneurship in the Founding of the Paris Opera." *American Journal of Sociology* 113, no. 1 (2007): 97–127.

Jordan, David K. "Esperanto and Esperantism." *Language Problems and Language Planning* 11, no. 1 (1987): 104–25.

Kahn, David. *The Code-Breakers: The Comprehensive History of Secret Communication from Ancient Times to the Internet.* New York: Scribner, 1996.

Kamusella, Tomasz. "Language as an Instrument of Nationalism in Central Europe." *Nations and Nationalism* 7, no. 2 (2001): 235–51.

Kamusella, Tomasz. *The Politics of Language and Nationalism in Modern Central Europe.* New York: Palgrave Macmillan, 2009.

Kanzi, Ito. "La firmo Hachette kaj la Kolekto Aprobita." In *Menade bal püki bal: Festlibro por la 50ª naskitago de Reinhard Haupenthal,* ed. Reinhard Haupenthal, 145–60. Saarbrücken: Iltis, 1998.

Kennedy, Hubert C. *Peano: Life and Works of Giuseppe Peano.* Boston: Kluwer, 1980.

Kerckhoffs, Auguste. *International Commercial Language.* Adapted by Karl Dornbusch. Chicago: S. R. Winchell and Co., 1888.

Kerckhoffs, Auguste. *Langue commercial international. Cours complet de Volapük.* 8th ed. Paris: Le Soudier, 1887.

Kerckhoffs, Auguste. *Yelabuk pedipedals.* Paris, 1887.

Kirchhoff, Alfred. 1887. "Die Ziele der Weiter-Entwicklung des Volapük." In *Volapük-Almanach für 1888,* ed. Sigmund Spielmann, 43–46. Leipzig: Mayer, 1887.

Kirchhoff, Alfred. "Ist Volapük antinational?" *Rund um die Welt* (August-September 1890): 145–48.

Kirchhoff, Alfred. "Wie ich Volapükist wurde." *Rund um die Welt* (April 1890): 1–6.

Klier, John D. *Russians, Jews, and the Pogroms of 1881–1882.* Cambridge: Cambrige University Press, 2011.

Kniele, Rupert. *Der erste Jahrzehnt der Weltsprache Volapük.* Saarbrücken: Iltis, 1989 (1889).

Kniele, Rupert. *Herr Leopold Eisntein und la linguo internacia.* Überlingen: A. Feyer, 1890.

Knowlson, James. *Universal Language Schemes in England and France 1600–1800.* Toronto: University of Toronto Press, 1975.

Kökény Lajos, Vilmos Bleier, Kálmán Kalocsay, and Ivan Ŝirjaev, eds. *Enciklopedio de Esperanto.* 2 vols. Budapest: Literatura Mondo, 1933.

Korĵenkov [Korzhenkov], Aleksander. *Homarano. La vivo, verkoj kaj ideoj de d-ro L. L. Zamenhof.* 2nd ed. Kaunas: Litova Esperanto Asocio, 2011.

Korzhenkov, Aleksander. *The Life of Zamenhof.* Trans. Ian Richmond. Ed. Humphrey Tonkin. New York: Mondial, 2010.

Kotzin, Boris. *Geschichte und Theorie des Ido.* Dresden: Ader und Borel, 1916.

Kuechenhoff, Bernhard. "The Psychiatrist Auguste Forel and His Attitude to Eugenics." *History of Psychiatry* 19 (June 2008): 215–23.

Kuznecov, Sergej N. 1991. "Drezen, lia verko, lia epoko." In Ernest Drezen, *Historio de la mondolingvo,* ed. Sergej N. Kuznecov, 3–40. Moscow: Progreso, 1991.

Lalande, André. "Philosophy in France." *Philosophical Review* 24 (1915): 245–69.

Lamberti, Marjorie. *State, Society and the Elementary School in Imperial Germany.* Oxford: Oxford University Press, 1989.

Lapenna, Ivo, Ulrich Lins, and Tazio Carlevaro, eds. *Esperanto en perspektivo. Faktoj kaj analizoj pri la Internacia Lingvo.* London: UEA, 1974.

Large, Andrew. *The Artificial Language Movement.* Oxford: Basil Blackwell, 1985.

Lederhendler, Eli. "Modernity Without Emancipation or Assimilation? The Case of Russian Jewry." In *Assimilation and Community: The Jews in Nineteenth Century Europe*, ed. Jonathan Frankel and Steven J. Zipperstein, 324–43. Cambridge: Cambridge University Press, 1992.

Lescure, Jean-Claude. "Un imaginaire transnational? Volapük et Espéranto vers 1880–1939." Unpublished habilitation thesis, Institute d'Etudes Politiques de Paris, 1999.

Lewy, Guenter. *The Catholic Church and Nazi Germany.* Boulder, Colo.: Da Capo Press, 2000.

Linderfelt, Klaus A. *Volapük. An Easy Method of Acquiring the Universal Language.* Milwaukee: Gaspar and Zahn, 1888.

Lins, Ulrich. *Die gefährliche Sprache.* Gerlingen: Bleicher, 1988.

Lins, Ulrich. "Max Joseph Metzger." *Kontakto* 2 (1971): 16–17.

Liptay, Alberto. *Gemeinsprache der Kulturvölker.* Brockhaus: Leipzig, 1891.

Lorenz, Richard. "The 'Délégation pour l'adoption d'une langue auxiliaire international.'" In *International Language and Science*, ed. Louis Couturat, 11–26. London: Constable and Cia, 1910.

Lott, Julius. *Ist Volapük die beste und einfachste Lösung des Weltsprache-Problems?* Vienna, 1888.

Lott, Julius. *Un lingua internazional.* Vienna: Frankenstein and Wagner, 1890.

Löw, Heinrich. "Christian Karl Gross. Ein Gedenkblatt." *Rund um die Welt* (September 30–October 16, 1891): 193–96.

Luciano, Erika, and Clara S. Roero, eds. *Giuseppe Peano - Louis Couturat. Carteggio (1896–1914).* Florence: Leo S. Olschki, 2006.

Ludovikito (pseud. Ito Kanzi). *Por kaj kontraŭ reformoj!* Tokio: Eldonejo Ludovikito, 1980.

Ludovikito (pseud. Ito Kanzi). *Ludovikologia dokumentaro, IX. Adresaroj I, 1889–1902.* Tokio: Eldonejo Ludovikito, 1992.

Ludovikito (pseud. Ito Kanzi). *Historieto de Esperanto.* Tokio: Libroteko Tokio, 1998.

Luz, Ehud. *Parallels Meet: Religion and Nationalism in the Early Zionist Movement (1882–1904).* Trans. Lenn J. Schramm. Philadelphia: Jewish Publication Society, 1988.

Maat, Jaap. *Philosophical Languages in the Seventeenth Century: Dalgarno, Wilkins, Leibniz.* Dordrecht: Kluwer, 2004.

MacMahon, Michael K. C. "The International Phonetic Association: The First 100 Years." *Journal of the International Phonetic Association* 16, no. 1 (1986): 30–38.

Maimon, Naftali Zvi. *La kaŝita vivo de Zamenhof.* Tokyo: Japana Esperanto Instituto, 1978.

Mannewitz, Cornelia. "Deutsche St. Petersburger Beiträge zur Idee der Welthilfssprache." In *Sankt Petersburg—'der akkurate Deutsche': Deutsche und Deutsches in der an-*

deren russischen Hauptstadt. Beiträge zum Internationalen Symposium in Potsdam, 23.-28. September 2003, ed. Norbert Franz and Ljuba Kirjuchina, 365–76. Peter Lang: Frankfurt am Main, 2006.

March, Francis A. "The Spelling Reform." Bureau of Education: Circular of Information no. 8. Washington, D.C.: Government Printing Office, 1893.

Marco, Antonio. Laboristaj kronikoj. Baudé: SAT, 1996.

Margais, Xavier. El moviment esperantista a Mallorca, 1898–1938. Palma: Edicions Documenta Balear, 2002.

Martyn, David. "Borrowed Fatherland: Nationalism and Language Purism in Fichte's Addresses to the German nation." Germanic Review 72, no. 3 (2001): 303–15.

Matejka, Alphonse. "Ancor un vez: Basic English." Cosmoglotta (May 1943): 49–57.

Matthias, Ulrich. L'espéranto: Un nouveau latin pour l'Église et pour l'humanité. Anvers: Flandra Esperanto-Ligo, 2005.

Mattos, Geraldo. 1999. "Esenco kaj estonteco de la Fundamento de Esperanto." Esperantologio / Esperanto Studies 1 (1999): 21–37.

Mayeur, Jean-Marie, and Madeleine Rebérioux. The Third Republic from Its Origins to the Great War, 1871–1914. Cambridge: Cambridge University Press, 1987.

Mazower, Mark. Dark Continent: Europe's Twentieth Century. New York: Vintage Books, 1998.

McElvenny, James. "Edward Sapir, Linguistic Relativity and International Language." Paper presented at the Third International Free Linguistics Conference, Sydney, October 10–11, 2009.

Meisterhans, Konrad. "Volapük und der Weltfrieden." Rund um die Welt (February 1891): 337–40.

Mergel, Thomas. "Ultramontanism, Liberalism, Moderation: Political Mentalities and Political Behavior of the German Catholic Bürgertum, 1848–1914." Central European History 29, no. 2 (1996): 151–74.

Meyer, Gustav. "Weltsprache und Weltsprachen." In Plansprachen- Beiträge zur Interlinguistik, ed. Reinhard Haupenthal, 28–45. Darmstadt: Wissenschaftliche Buchgesellschaft, 1976 (1893).

Minkoff, Debra C., and John D. McCarthy. "Reinvigorating the Study of Organizational Processes in Social Movements." Mobilization 10, no. 2 (2005): 289–308.

Moch, Gaston. "Kio estas pacifisto kaj pacifismo?" Espero Pacifista (July 1905): 6–18.

Moch, Gaston. "La question de la langue internationale, et sa solution par l'Esperánto." Revue internationale de sociologie 4 (1897): 249–95.

Moch, Gaston. "Pri malarmo: Ĥimeroj kaj realaĵoj." Espero Pacifista (December 1906): 321–31.

Moreno, Juan Carlos. La dignidad e igualdad de las lenguas. Madrid: Alianza Editorial, 2000.

Morris, Aldon D., and Suzanne Staggenborg. "Leadership in Social Movements." In The Blackwell Companion to Social Movements, ed. David A. Snow, Sarah A. Soule, and Hanspeter Kriesi, 171–96. Malden, Mass.: Blackwell, 2004.

Moskovsky, Christo. "Reflections on Artificial Languages." In *Essays on Natural and Artificial Languages*, ed. Christo Moskovsky and Alan Libert, 1–19. Frankfurt am Main: Peter Lang, 2009.

Mugdan, Joachim. *Jan Baudouin de Courtenay (1845–1929). Leben und Werk*. Munich: Wilhelm Fink Verlag, 1984.

Müller, Ernst. *Der Phantom der Weltsprache: Worte der Aufklärung und Ernüchterung über das Volapük und den Weltsprach-Gedanken im Allgemeinen*. Berlin: Ulrich, 1888.

Mullinger, J. B. *The New Reformation. A Narrative of the Old Catholic Movement from 1870 to the Present Time*. London: Longmans, 1875.

Nathans, Benjamin. *Beyond the Pale: The Jewish Encounter with Late Imperial Russia*. Berkeley: University of California Press, 2002.

Nicolas, Adolphe. *Rapport sur un projet de langue scientifique international*. Clermont: Daix freères, 1889.

Nicolson, Juliet. *The Great Silence. 1918–1929. Living in the Shadow of the Great War*. London: John Murray, 2009.

Nietzsche, Friedrich W. *Human, All Too Human*. Trans. Marion Faber, with Stephen Lehman. Lincoln: University of Nebraska Press, 1984 (1878).

Nooteboom, Bart. *Learning and Innovations in Organizations and Economies*. Oxford: Oxford University Press, 2000.

North American Association for the Propagation of Volapük. *First Annual Convention of Volapükists. Boston, Aug 21, 22, 23, 1890*. Boston, Mass., 1890.

Olender, Maurice. *The Languages of Paradise*. Cambridge, Mass.: Harvard University Press, 1992.

O'Rourke, Kevin H., and Jeffrey G. Williamson. *Globalization and History*. Cambridge, Mass.: MIT Press, 1999.

Oostendorp, Marc van. "Constructed Language and Linguistic Theory." http://www.vanoostendorp.nl/. Accessed February 2010.

Oppenheim, Janet. *The Other World: Spiritualism and Psychical Research in England, 1850–1914*. Cambridge: Cambridge University Press, 1985.

Orbach, Alexander. "The Development of the Russian Jewish Community, 1881–1903." In *Pogroms: Anti-Jewish Violence in Modern Russian History*, ed. John D. Klier and Shlomo Lambroza, 137–63. Cambridge: Cambridge University Press, 1992.

Orwell, George. "Appendix: The Principles of Newspeak." *Nineteen Eighty-Four*. New York: Plume, 2003 (1949).

Ostler, Nicholas. *Empires of the Word: A Language History of the World*. New York: Harper Collins, 2005.

Ostler, Nicholas. *The Last Lingua Franca: English Until the Return of Babel*. New York: Walker and Co., 2010.

Ostwald, Wilhelm. *Der Energetische Imperativ*. Leipzig: Akademische Verlagsgesellschaft, 1912.

Ostwald, Wilhelm. *Lebenslinien. Eine Selbstbiographie.* Ed. Karl Hansel. Leipzig: Sächsischen Akademie der Wissenschaften, 2003 (1926–1927).

Ostwald, Wilhelm. "Scientific Management for Scientists. 'The Bridge.' The Trust Idea Applied to Intellectual Production." *Scientific American* 108 (1913): 5–6.

Otlet, Paul. "The Union of International Organizations: A World Center." In *International Organization and the Dissemination of Knowledge. Selected Essays of Paul Otlet.* Trans. and ed. W. Boyd Rayward, 112–19. Amsterdam: Elsevier, 1990 (1914).

Owen, Alex. *The Place of Enchantment: British Occultism and the Culture of the Modern.* Chicago: University of Chicago Press, 2004.

Patten, Alan. "The Most Natural State: Herder and Nationalism." *History of Political Thought* 31, no. 4 (2010): 658–89.

Patten, Alan. "Theoretical Foundations of European Language Debates." In *The Language Question in Europe and Diverse Societies: Political, Legal and Social Perspectives,* ed. Dario Castiglioni and Chris Longman, 15–36. Portland: Hart Publishers, 2007.

Piette, Valérie. "Le project de creation d'une Cité Mondiale ou l'utopie pacifiste faite de bruques." In *Cent ans de l'Office international de bibliographie: 1895–1995. Les Premisses du Mundaneum,* 271–301. Mons: Editions Mundaneum, 1995.

Piškorec, Velimir. "Von Volapük zu Spelin. Zum Leben und Werk des kroatischen Plansprachlers Juraj (Georg) Bauer (1848–1900)." In *Die Rolle von Persönlichkeiten in der Geschichte der Planspranchen,* ed. Sabine Fiedler, 99–131. Berlin: Gesellschaft für Interlinguistik e.V., 2010.

Platiel (pseud.). *Historio pri la skismo en la laborista esperanto-movado.* Beauville: SAT, 1994 (1934).

Poblet, Francesc. *Els inicis del moviment esperantista a Catalunya.* Barcelona: Associació Catalana d'Esperanto, 2004.

Pombo, Olga. *Leibniz and the Problem of a Universal Language.* Münster: Nodus, 1987.

Popper, Karl. *Unended Quest. An Intellectual Autobiography.* Glasglow: Fontana / Collins, 1974.

Privat, Edmond. *Historio de la lingvo Esperanto.* The Hague: Internacia Esperanto Instituto, 1982.

Prorók, Julian. "5 annus de Occidental e li recent situation." *Cosmoglotta* (January 1927): 1.

Richet, Charles. *La selection humaine.* Paris: Félix Alcan, 1919 (1913).

Richet, Charles. *L'homme stupide.* Paris: Ernest Flammarion, 1919.

Rider, Robin E. "Measure of Ideas, Rule of Language: Mathematics and Language in the 18th Century." In *The Quantifying Spirit in the Eighteenth Century,* ed. Tore Frangsmyr, J. L. Heilbron, and Robin E. Rider, 113–41. Berkeley: University of California Press, 1990.

Roero, Clara S. "I matematici e la lingua internazionale." *La matematica nella Società e nella Cultura. Bolletino della Unione Matematica Italiana* 8 (1999): 159–82.

Romaine, Suzanne. "Revitalized Languages as Invented Languages." In *From Elvish to Klingon: Exploring Invented Languages*, ed. Michael Adams, 185–225. Oxford: Oxford University Press, 2011.

Rosenberger, Waldemar. "Brief History of the International Academy of the Universal Language." In Michael A. F. Holmes, *Dictionary of the Neutral Language*, 277–300. Rochester: John P. Smith, 1903.

Royle, Edward. *Radicals, Secularists and Republicans: Popular Free Thought in Britain, 1866–1915*. Manchester: Manchester University Press, 1980.

Russell, Bertrand. *Correspondance sur la philosophie, la logique et la politique avec Louis Couturat (1897–1913)*. Ed. Anne-Françoise Schmid. Paris: Éditions Kimé, 2001.

Salmon, Yosef. "Ideology and Reality in the Bilu *Aliyah*." *Harvard Ukrainian Studies* 2 (1978): 430–66.

Samid, Ya'akov. *The Immortal Spirit: The Bialystok Hebrew Gymnasium, Poland, 1919–1939*. Haifa: Traffic Publications, 1995.

Sanhueza, Carlos. "El objetivo del instituto pedagógico no es el de formar geógrafos. Hans Steffen y la transferencia del saber geográfico alemán a Chile, 1893–1907." *Historia* 45, no. 1 (2012): 171–97.

Sanzo, Ubaldo. *L'artificio della lingua. Louis Couturat 1868–1914*. Milan: Franco Angeli, 1991.

Sapir, Edward. "The Function of an International Language." In *International Communication*, ed. Herbert N. Shenton, Edward Sapir, and Otto Jespersen, 65–94. London: Kegan Paul, 1931.

Sapir, Edward. "Herder's *Ursprung der Sprache*." *Modern Philology* 5 (1907): 109–42.

Savatovsky, Dan. "Les linguistes et la langue internationale (1880–1920)." *Histoire Épistémologie Langage* 11 (1989): 37–65.

Scarth, A.M.E. *The Story of the Old Catholic and Kindred Movements*. London: Simpkin, 1883.

Schilpp, Paul A. *The Philosophy of Rudolf Carnap*. London: Cambridge University Press, 1963.

Schinz, A. "La question d'une langue international artificielle." *Revue Philosophique de la France et de l'Étranger* 60 (July-December 1905): 24–44.

Schleicher, August. *Darwinism Tested by the Science of Language*. Trans. Alex V. W. Bikkers. London: John Candem, 1869.

Schleyer, Johann Martin. *100 Gründe warum ich katolische bleibe*. Aachen: Gustav Schmidt, 1901.

Schleyer, Johann Martin. *Ein Idealvolk*. 2nd ed. Constanz: Weltsprache Verlag, 1901.

Schleyer, Johann Martin. *Hauptgedanken meiner öffentlichen Vortrage über die von mir ersonnene Allsprache Volapük*. Konstanz: A. Moriell, 1885.

Schleyer, Johann Martin. "Meine Biographie (1880)." In *Prälat Johann Martin Schleyer (1831–1912)*, ed. Reinhard Haupenthal, 121–46. Saarbrücken: Iltis, 2008 (1880).

Schleyer, Johann Martin. *Über die Pfuscher-Sprache des Pseudo-Esperanto*. Konstanz, 1900.

Schleyer, Johann Martin. *Volapük. Die Weltsprache. Entwurf einer Universalsprache für alle Gebildete der ganzen Welt.* Ed. Reinhard Haupenthal. Hildesheim: Olms, 1982 (1880).

Schmidt, Johann. *Geschichte der universalsprache Volapük.* Ed. Reinhard Haupenthal. Saarbrücken: Iltis, 1986 (1964).

Schnell, Roland. "Nobelpriesträger Alfred Hermann Fried als Pazifist und Esperantist." *Interlinguistische Informationen. Mitteilungsblatt der Gesellschaft für Interlinguistik e.V* 19 (2011): 105–17.

Schroeder-Gudehus, Brigitte. *Les scientifiques et la paix. La communauté scientifique internationale au cours des années 20.* Montreal: Presses de l'Université de Montréal, 1978.

Schroeder-Gudehus, Brigitte. "Une langue internationale pour la science?" In *L'avenir du français dans les publications et les communications scientifiques et techniques.* 3 vols. Montreal: Conseil de la Langue Française, 1983. Available at http://www.cslf.gouv.qc.ca/bibliotheque-virtuelle.

Schuchardt, Hugo. *Auf Anlass des Volapüks.* Berlin: Robert Oppenheim, 1888.

Schuchardt, Hugo. "Bekenntnisse und Erkenntnisse." *Wissen und Leben* 13 (1919): 179–98.

Schuchardt, Hugo. "Bericht über die auf Schaffung einer künstlichen Hilfssprache gerichtete Bewegung." In *Plansprachen- Beiträge zur Interlinguistik*, ed. Reinhard Haupenthal, 46–58. Darmstadt: Wissenschaftliche Buchgesellschaft, 1991 (1904).

Schuchardt, Hugo. *Weltsprache und Weltsprachen, an Gustav Meyer.* Strassburg: Karl J. Trübner, 1894.

Sennacieca Asocio Tutmonda. *Historio de S.A.T, 1921–1952.* Paris: SAT, 1953.

Shenton, Herbert N. *Cosmopolitan Conversation.* New York: Columbia University Press, 1933.

Sikosek, Marcus. *Die neutrale Sprache. Eine politische Geschichte des Esperanto-Weltbundes.* Skonpres: Bydgoszcz, 2006.

Sikosek, Marcus. "Dokumente zum Weltsprachverein Nürnberg." *Esperantologio / Esperanto Studies* 3 (2005): 45–54.

Sikosek, Marcus. *Esperanto sen mitoj.* 2nd ed. Antwerp: Flandra Esperanto Ligo, 2003.

Sisk, David W. *Transformations of Language in Modern Dystopias.* Westport, Conn.: Greenwood Press, 1997.

Sleumer, Albert. *Johann Martin Schleyer (18. Juli 1831–16. August 1912). Ein Lebensbild.* Saarbrücken: Iltis, 1981 (1914).

Smith, Warren S. *The London Heretics, 1870–1914.* London: Constable, 1967.

Spencer, Herbert. *An Autobiography.* 2 vols. New York: Appleton and Cia, 1904.

Spielmann, Sigmund, ed. *Volapük-Almanach für 1888.* Leipzig: Mayer, 1887.

Sprague, Charles E. *Hand-Book of Volapük.* 5th ed. London: Trübner and Co., 1888.

Sprague, Charles E. *The Philosophy of Accounts.* 5th ed. New York: Ronald Press Con, 1922.

Sprague, Charles E. "The Volapük Congress at Paris." *Volapük: A Monthly Journal of the World Language* (1888): 40–46.

Staller, Natasha. "Babel: Hermetic Languages, Universal Languages, and Anti-Languages in fin de siècle Parisian Culture." *Art Bulletin* 76, no. 2 (1994): 331–54.

Stepanov, Nikolao. "Esperantistaj viktimoj de stalinismo." *Sennaciulo* 9 (1990): 76–78.

Sternhell, Zeev. "The Political Culture of Nationalism." In *Nationhood and Nationalism in France: From Boulanguism to the Great War, 1889–1918*, ed. Robert Tombs, 22–38. London: Harper Collins, 1991.

Stinchcombe, Arthur L. "Social Structure and Organizations." In *Handbook of Organizations*, ed. James G. March, 142–93. New York: Rand McNally, 1965.

Stojan, Petr E. *Bibliografio de Internacia Lingvo.* New York: Georg Olms, 1973 (1929).

Suttner, Bertha von. *Memoiren.* Stuttgart and Leipzig: Deutsche Verlags-Anstalt, 1909.

Sutton, Geoffrey. *Concise Encyclopedia of the Original Literature of Esperanto.* New York: Mondial, 2008.

Swidler, Leonard. *Bloodwitness for Peace and Unity: The Life of Max Josef Metzger.* Denville, N.J.: Dimension Books, 1986.

Szerdahelyi, István. "Entwicklung des Zeichnensystems einer internationalen Sprache: Esperanto." In *Language Reform: History and Future*, ed. István Fodor and Claude Hagège, 1:277–308. Hamburg: Buske Verlag, 1984.

Szimkat, Annakris. "Kion Zamenhof skribis al Christian Schmidt." In *Li kaj Ni: Festlibro por la 80a naskiĝtago de Gaston Waringhien*, ed. Reinhard Haupenthal, 337–48. Antwerp / La Laguna: Stafeto, 1984.

Tanquist, Reuben A. "A Study of the Social Psychology of the Diffusion of Esperanto with Special Reference to the English Speaking Peoples." M.A. thesis, University of Minnesota, 1927.

Thiesse, Anne-Marie. *La création des identités nationales. Europe xviiie-xixe siècle.* Paris: Seuil, 2001.

Tolstói, Lev. *Correspondencia.* Ed. Salma Ancira. Barcelona: Acantilado, 2005.

Union of International Associations. *Les 1978 Organisations Internationales fondées depuis le Congrès de Vienne.* Brussells, 1957.

Urquhart, Alasdair. "The Couturat–Russell Correspondence." *Russell: The Journal of Bertrand Russell Studies* 22 (2002): 188–93.

van Dijk, Ziko. "Wikipedia and Lesser-Resourced Languages." *Language Problems and Language Planning* 33, no. 3 (2009): 234–50.

van Els, Theo. "Multilingualism in the European Union." *International Journal of Applied Linguistics* 15, no. 3 (2005): 263–81.

van Parijs, Philippe. "Europe's Linguistic Challenge." In *The Language Question in Europe and Diverse Societies: Political, Legal and Social Perspectives*, ed. Dario Castiglioni and Chris Longman, 217–53. Oxford: Hart Publishers, 2007.

van Parijs, Philippe. *Linguistic Justice for Europe and for the World.* Oxford: Oxford University Press, 2011.

Vellacott, Jen. "Women, Peace and Internationalism, 1914–1920: 'Finding New Words and Creating New Methods.'" In *Peace Movements and Political Cultures*, ed. Charles Chatfield and Peter van den Dungen, 106–24. Knoxville: University of Tennessee Press, 1988.

Wank, Solomon. "The Austrian Peace Movement and the Habsburg Ruling Elite, 1906–1914." In *Peace Movements and Political Cultures*, ed. Charles Chatfield and Peter van den Dungen, 40–63. Knoxville: University of Tennessee Press, 1988.

Waringhien, Gaston. "Historia skizo de la Esperanto movado." In *Lingvo kaj vivo*, 2nd ed., ed. Gaston Waringhien, 397–423. Rotterdam: Universala Esperanto Asocio, 1989.

Waringhien, Gaston. "Prologo." In *Leteroj de Zamenhof*, comp. and ed. Gaston Waringhien, 1:1–9. Paris: SAT, 1948.

Weber, Eugen. *France, fin de siècle*. Cambridge, Mass.: Harvard University Press, 1986.

Wisniewski, Tomasz. *Jewish Białystok*. Ipswich: Ipswich Press, 1998.

Wollenberg, Fritz. "Der Briefwechsel Wilhelm Ostwalds zu Interlinguistischen Problemen." In *Eine Sprache für die Wissenschaft. Beiträge und Materialien des Interlinguistik-Kolloquiums für Wilhelm Ostwald*, ed. Ulrich Becker and Fritz Wollenberg, 32–107. Berlin: Gesellschaft für Interlinguistik e.V., 1998.

Wright, Sue. *Community and Communication: The Role of Language in Nation State Building and European Integration*. Clevedon: Multilingual Matters, 2000.

Wright, Sue. "French as a Lingua Franca." *Annual Review of Applied Linguistics* 26 (2006): 35–60.

Wright, Sue. *Language Policy and Language Planning: From Nationalism to Globalization*. New York: Palgrave, 2004.

Wright, Sue. "What Is a Language? The Difficulties Inherent in Language Rights." In *The Language Question in Europe and Diverse Societies: Political, Legal and Social Perspectives*, ed. Dario Castiglioni and Chris Longman, 81–99. Oxford: Hart Publishers, 2007.

Zakrzewski, Adam. *Historio de Esperanto, 1887–1912*. Warsaw: Gebethner and Wolff, 1913.

Zamenhof, Ludwig L. *Aldono al la Dua Libro de l'lingvo internacia*. Warsaw: Kelter, 1929 (1888).

Zamenhof, Ludwig L. *Dua Libro de l'lingvo internacia*. Warsaw: Kelter, 1888.

Zamenhof, Ludwig L. "Homaranismo." In *Mi estas homo*, ed. Aleksander Korĵenkov, 139–46. Kaliningrad: Sezonoj 2006 (1906).

Zamenhof, Ludwig L. *Internationale Sprache. Vorrede und vollständiges Lehrbuch. For germanoj*. Warsaw: Gebethner and Wolff, 1887.

Zamenhof, Ludwig L. *Leteroj de Zamenhof*. 2 vols. Comp. and ed. Gaston Waringhien. Paris: SAT, 1948.

Zamenhof, Ludwig L. *Mi estas homo. Originalaj verkoj de d-ro L. L. Zamenhof*. Ed. Aleksander Korĵenkov. Kaliningrad: Sezonoj, 2006.

Zamenhof, Ludwig L. *Originala verkaro.* Comp. and ed. Johannes Dietterle. Leipzig: Ferdinand Hirt and Sohn, 1929.

Zamponi, Ludwig. "Volaküp und Fremdenverkehr." *Rund um die Welt* (May 1890): 33–36.

Zetter, Carl. *Eine Volapüktour.* Staatsfurt: Trippo, 1898.

Zhirkov, Lev I. *Kial venkis Esperanto?* Leipzig: Ekrelo, 1931.

Ziemer, H. "E. Müller. Das Phantom der Weltsprache." *Berliner Philologische Wochenschrift* 47 (1888): 1458–59.

INDEX

ACKNOWLEDGMENTS

This book began as an article while I was benefiting from the friendly atmosphere of the Max-Planck Institute for the Study of Societies (Cologne). When the article kept growing, I was encouraged to transform it into a book. From the Max-Planck, I took the project to the Instituto Juan March and Universidad Carlos III of Madrid, and then to Georgetown University. I am ever grateful to the staffs of these institutions for their help in finding difficult sources, particularly to Paz Fernández and her library assistants at the Instituto Juan March.

I am also indebted to the students of my seminar on language and nationalism at Georgetown University. Their questions and insights into this topic gave me a better view of its many facets. Without the encouragement of Humphry Tonkin, this project would not have come to fruition. I am also very grateful to Ezra W. Zuckerman, Laurel Grassin-Drake, Julia DiBenigno, Sebatián Lavezzolo, and the anonymous reviewers from the University of Pennsylvania Press for their tremendous help in the early phase of this project. Celia Valiente and Peter Stamatov deserve especial mention here. I owe them much more than a couple cups of coffee. Peter Agree of the University of Pennsylvania Press took an interest in the manuscript when it was only a draft and was always very supportive. I am also much indebted to Jennifer Konieczny, Erica Ginsburg, Susan Thomas, Amanda Ruffner, and Eric Schramm for guiding the production of the book. Pamela Haag made a great contribution by organizing the book for the widest readership possible. I am also thankful to Walter de Gruyter for letting me reproduce Figure 1.

And finally, this book is dedicated to my wife, Genevieve, and our children, Paloma and Azucena, for their invaluable help and inspiration.